G rowing up, we are often taught never to question the value of a good education. From the moment they "graduate," young adolescents are measured by how enticing they will appear on the almighty "college application."

But if you stop to consider that the total student debt in the United States is estimated to be $1.3 trillion (*more than credit card and auto loan debt combined*), you may begin to wonder the true value of a college education.

In *Inspiring Champions in Advanced Manufacturing*, Terry Iverson challenges the assumption that sustainable careers may only be achieved through a college education. Through his own love and mastery of the fine art of manufacturing, Iverson contends that careers in manufacturing offer stability, security, and prosperity for our entire nation.

Iverson illustrates the power of manufacturing through in-depth research, personal stories, and over 40 interviews with some of the most remarkable authors, CEOs, sports figures, and influencers.

While half of the book speaks directly to parents, the other half helps inquisitive students know about the options available to them.

With practical application questions and video resources online, *Inspiring Champions in Advanced Manufacturing* teaches parents and students:

- Why cultural pressure steers parents and high school students toward college
- How college pathways leave even the brightest students in debt

- The untold potential of a career in manufacturing
- How the US has a skills shortage that rewards fulfillment with impressive salaries
- How technological advances have made manufacturing into a digital ecosystem
- Action plans for both parents and youth to get involved in manufacturing

Inspiring Champions in Advanced Manufacturing provides parents and students a roadmap for career success and a zero-debt foundation. Reading this book will help you envision the potential that awaits in a lucrative manufacturing career.

"There is a revolution going on in education. So much of what students learn today is not relevant or obsolete by the time they graduate. *Inspiring Champions in Advanced Manufacturing* hits at the heart of what America needs most: mentorship, manufacturing, and life skills that will sustain students long past college years."

Scott Hogle,
President of iHeartMedia Honolulu + Best Selling Author of
Persuade & Divine Intelligence

"Thinking about American manufacturing, many parents and teachers imagine what it used to be—not what it is today. And that's why this book powerfully meets this moment. *Inspiring Champions in Advanced Manufacturing* busts the myths and draws on inspiring stories by manufacturing leaders as it brings parents and teachers inside a high-tech, expanding sector that puts students—as young as high school and of all backgrounds—on a path to purpose-driven, high-paying careers. Readers will feel a call to action to get engaged in and contribute to this new era for American manufacturing."

Barbara Humpton,
President and CEO, Siemens USA

"*Inspiring Champions in Advanced Manufacturing* brings to the attention of a historically brainwashed culture that a traditional education may not be the correct career choice. The author really drives home this point by revealing to us the extraordinary benefits of a career in manufacturing. Mom and Dad are not always right!"

Sam Liebman,
Best Selling author of
Harvard Can't Teach What You Learn from the Streets

"We must rebuild our country's manufacturing industry and *Inspiring Champions* leads the way. Helping parents and their students multiply career choices is its focus. Having one book for students and one for parents facilitates a must needed stimulus for our manufacturing com."

Allan Colman,
Chief Revenue Accelerator, Professor of Marketing

"I greatly enjoyed Terry's interviews, personal stories, and valuable insights in exploring various pathways to achieve maximum potential for an impactful and rewarding career in manufacturing."

Rusty Komori,
Author of *Beyond The Lines and Beyond The Game*

"Inspiring Champions in Advanced Manufacturing" speaks to me on the potential that young people have in our industry. Mentoring is critically important, and the manufacturing sector needs to reach out to the minority communities to inspire young people about opportunities that they simply have no idea exist, as an alternative path to success.

David C. Williams,
Assistant Vice President AT&T and Best Selling Author of
Business Model

Parent Edition of Inspiring Champions in Advanced Manufacturing

TERRY M. IVERSON

Made for Success Publishing
P.O. Box 1775 Issaquah, WA 98027
www.MadeForSuccess.com

CHAMPION Now! ® is a registered trademark and will be referred to during this book as **CHAMPION Now!** Manufacturing Create$ ™ is a registered trademark and will be referred to during this book as Manufacturing Create$. CNC Rocks ™ is a registered trademark and will be referred to during this book as CNC Rocks.

Distributed by Blackstone Publishing

First Printing

Library of Congress Cataloging-in-Publication data

Iverson, Terry
   Inspiring Champions in Advanced Manufacturing: Discover the Path to a Debt-Free Career

   p. cm.

LCCN: 2022922708
ISBN: 978-1-64146-766-7 *(PBBK)*
ISBN: 978-1-64146-768-1 *(eBook)*
ISBN: 978-1-64146-767-4 *(AUDIO)*

Printed in the United States of America

For further information contact Made for Success Publishing
+1425-526-6480 or email service@madeforsuccess.net

CONTENTS

Family is everything. I was taught this by my parents.
Despite growing up in a broken family, both my parents
did their best, and I am a product of them both.
My father passed away at the age of 84 years old.
He was a guiding light in my life. The lifelong lessons
he taught me are too numerous to mention,
and many are in this book. All during my mom's
life and up until when she passed,
she taught me how to enjoy people
and life in general.

The Jerry R. Iverson Manufacturing Memorial Scholarship
was established in my father's honor. Both my Uncles
Ed and John Iverson led so many into manufacturing
greatness, and I thank them for helping me find
the champion within myself.

This book is for each of them.

ACKNOWLEDGMENTS
Parent Edition

Writing a book is both fun and painful. Writing two books at the same time and putting two books together is a formidable challenge. Of course, no big accomplishment is done by one person. Since this is the parent version of the book, I have decided to focus on the people that have supported me as an adult. Whether it be a family member, an employee, or someone else, a project this big requires a great deal of support and patience. I appreciate the sacrifices and contributions of those listed; without their efforts, I would not have been able to complete this book.

My wife, Kathy, has and continues to support me in every way possible. Her love, understanding, and patience each and every day are what allow me to succeed in ways I could never have achieved otherwise.

Our children and their spouses, Britton and Mariel Iverson; Lindsay and Jason Weglarz; and Cameron and Courtney Iverson. Each of them has been a source of pride and joy in so many ways that cannot be measured. They support me in numerous ways, and I am very grateful.

My father, Jerry R. Iverson, and my uncles, Edward A. Iverson and John C. Iverson. They have mentored me throughout my life and allowed me to enter the manufacturing industry with all the teachings and guidance I could ever hope for. My father-in-law, was one to admire and respect as well. During the limited time I was able to know Earl Thomas, I will be forever grateful to have found his daughter as my wife, and proud to have known him.

My siblings and their spouses, Kelly and Dave Pollock; Amy and Jim Aralis; Erik and Ela Iverson; and Todd and Amanda Hughes, all of whom have been supportive in so many ways, regardless of the miles that separate us at times.

My industry mentors, John Comparini, Ben Shore, and Kevin Sinnett. Without them, I would not have learned a fraction of what I know about our industry and the art of manufacturing.

My content and editorial advisor Michele Kelly, with whom I have thoroughly enjoyed the journey of writing this second book. I could not have finished either this book or the first one without her expertise.

Our Iverson & Company long-term employees, Jim Flauter, Maria Flores, Roger Hughes, Carolyn Kallevang, Stephen Luhrsen, Chris Miller, Dale Mular, Mike Ternstrom, and Jason Williams. Each one of them has contributed to our company's success, and without that, this book would not have been able to be a successful endeavor.

Last but not least our **CHAMPION Now!** Board: Grady Cope, Rodney Grover, Jerry Rex, Roy Sweatman, & Paul Wahnish, as well as Executive Director Britton Iverson and Intern Leyna Smith. There is no telling what heights this talented, passionate, and dedicated group can take the organization. It is an honor to have this group share my passion to make a difference for our youth in the US, and help our manufacturing sector elevate the workforce to boost a revitalized Made in America movement.

A NOTE FROM TERRY

From an early age, buying something made in America was important to me. Whether it was a car, a cell phone, or even clothes, I always felt that supporting someone in the United States who made the product should be a priority. To this day, every car that I have owned, both personally and for my machine tool distributorship, Iverson & Company, has been an American-made car. As you travel through the pages of my book, I invite you to share my passion—not just for manufacturing, but for guiding your child toward *their* passion. Aligning your inner fire with a career pays big dividends: a happier life, career advancement, a feeling of accomplishment, and even greater earning power.

To that end, there is a sleeping giant among us, an opportunity that lies ahead for your child, who is part of the future generation of leaders, thinkers, technologists, and makers. This opportunity is manufacturing. There is a great sense of accomplishment that comes from working with your hands, solving problems, and bringing new products to life, all the while earning good money. Giving your child the freedom to follow their passions and interests is incredibly important, as well as making sure they are investing money in a career that makes sense. The huge student debt crisis so many young people find themselves trapped in holds them back from living their best life.

There are many reasons manufacturing will take our country to greatness. However, this book is not meant to convince you or your child that manufacturing is *the* career for them. Instead, I hope you will consider it as one great option because, as we all know, parents are the most influential people in a child's life (even if we think they're not listening, they really are!). Thousands of young adults miss out on a fun, satisfying, and well-paying career for all the wrong reasons. If only parents would embrace the thought of investigating these careers for their children, the possibilities could be so exciting!

American culture has become blind to the importance of manufacturing, as evidenced by the COVID-19 pandemic. Many Americans were unaware of how vulnerable we are as a country to supply chain connections outside the U.S. We saw shortages well beyond the protective gear and medications needed throughout the pandemic.

My big lesson from those years is this: I had to market my profession. So many in our craft continue to do what I did—assume that my peers were not interested or would not find our trade interesting.

That's one reason you're holding this book right now. It will give you a quick overview about manufacturing as a career choice, something very few high school counselors or parents talk about.

Additionally, we will talk about the unique challenges you face as a parent. Parenting is the hardest task I have ever had to do. Thank God that Kathy and I treated this as a team sport—we were stronger together than either of us would have been independently. For the single parents out there, I applaud you for being resilient and I cannot stress enough the importance of good mentors both in your own life and the life of your child.

Here's a look at what's ahead:

- In Chapter 1, you'll get to see behind the curtain of manufacturing to learn what it is—and what it isn't.
- Chapter 2 will take it a step further so you can explore the many opportunities for young people and the trends toward buying American-made products.
- In Chapter 3, you will learn about internships and how they are one extraordinary path to manufacturing.
- Chapter 4 will talk about technology in manufacturing and another individual's path from working the streets to the speaker circuit on manufacturing.
- In Chapter 5, get ready to have your eyes opened as I give you a startling look at time, money, and your child's future career.
- You'll love Chapter 6, as it shows just how much control your child has over their future. Be open to joining in on the conversation.
- Dive into Chapter 7, and your child will be welcomed into a career in manufacturing with open arms and cash!
- Finally, in Chapter 8, we will start building the path to your child's success!

The skilled workforce needs problem-solvers and innovators! Salaries are going up as opportunities abound—that is, for those perceptive enough to recognize them. The biggest challenge is the negative perception of manufacturing in the U.S. Our culture looks down on it sometimes, while our European counterparts in Germany, Switzerland, and Italy hold careers in manufacturing in high regard.

I ask you to start a journey with me in this book. Whether you find the Champion in your child, a relative, or a friend, *I know your journey will be memorable, enlightening, and inspiring.*

This book will give you the tools, resources, and insight you need as a parent to inspire your children—the next generation—to potentially become Champions in manufacturing. My hope is to bring you on a journey from your current perceptions to what your child's career might be. Throughout the book, you will find QR codes to provide you with a digital experience on your cell phone. Plus, you'll hear from a myriad of others through in-depth interviews. Their voices, more than anything, paint the landscape of what a career in manufacturing might offer.

When you are done, you will open up opportunities by, well, opening up. Smack in the middle of this book are "conversation starters," or questions that you and your child or other young person in your life might discuss. Maybe they can discover the path to a debt-free career!

First, though, there are many exciting things I want to show you. Let's get going.

THE MAKER'S LIFE

*Makers make things. The Iverson family
certainly has fit the moniker of 'makers.'
There is an entire movement in the U.S.
called 'the maker movement,' and I am asking
you to consider it as a career option.
It all starts in Norway . . .*

This country has been shaped by a long history of crafts-men, artisans, and fishermen who have immigrated from countries near and far. In fact, my father's family originated in Norway. My great-grandfather came over on a ship and never got back on when it returned home. For decades, I had heard that he had "jumped ship" when he traveled over from Norway to the U.S. I took it to mean that he literally jumped off the ship, until, of course, I found out Dad meant it figuratively. Communication and storylines from families are incredibly important, and I have always felt a need to know our beginnings.

Like many immigrants coming to the United States, my grandfather started a family and hoped for a better life. The manufacturing sector has reaped the benefits of my grandfather's work and the labor of many talented and skilled tradesmen coming from lands far away. Our forefathers lived with a code of honesty that led to success and happiness.

Think about this: Where did the people who came before you live and work? What were their ambitions? What did they sacrifice to make a better life for you? This is part of your story, too.

Let me share the legacy that manufacturing has left for me, from parent to parent.

I believe in manufacturing. It has been good to my family, and it has been good to this great country. So many company owners and managers are struggling to find skilled workers to grow their businesses and replace Baby Boomer generation retirees.

My family has been in manufacturing for nearly a century due to the great careers it offers. My grandfather, Edward Iverson, worked for a small machine tool builder in Chicago back in 1925. Keep in mind that this was shortly before the Great Depression of 1929. When his father died at a young age, he had to quit school at 16 years old. He worked full-time to support his five siblings and mother.

He started at the shop by sweeping floors. I know this "humble beginnings" story may seem cliché, but it is true. His supervisor soon realized that he possessed talents, not only in math and science but also in drafting. Grandpa quickly became a vital part of the company and rose in importance in his department. When the company was bought out in 1931 and moved east to New York state, only three people were offered a position. He was, in fact, the only one to decline and, as a result, stayed back to represent the manufacturer.

I have thought many times about this bit of family history. Here my grandfather was, in the middle of the Great Depression in Chicago, and the company he worked for was purchased. He had to decide to move to New York or to stay. He made the tough decision to stay and not uproot the entire family. This bold move, and him being the major breadwinner at such a young age, were the first indicators I can remember of how important a sense of family is and how manufacturing is a difference-maker.

Grandpa was good at what he did and grew to know many industry leaders in the manufacturing sector. My father, Jerry, started working for my grandfather in machine tool sales in 1958. My father was very detail-oriented, analytical, and financially astute. My uncle John joined Iverson & Company a few years after. In 1957, my uncle Ed started his own subcontract machine shop called Chucking Machine Products, which initially machined parts for Bell & Howell. Uncle Ed's company, which specializes in high-precision aerospace, defense, and military subcontract machine work, has now been in business for more than 65 years. Uncle John bought a small shop called Customs Products, which became a 700+ person shop under his ownership and vision by the time he sold the company in the late 1990's. My father stayed with the company and perfected his craft of machine tool sales and rebuilding. He has been my greatest mentor to this day, and I thank him for teaching me so much about life and work. His greatest words of advice were: "Terry, you have everything if you have family and your health. Everything else is secondary."

GARY SKOOG: PARENTS, EDUCATE YOURSELF

But don't take my word about the importance of makers. Let's hear from Gary Skoog, a big supporter of the maker movement. Gary hails from the Makerspace and Innovation Center at Harper College, a community college just West of Chicago. He has worked with hundreds of parents and their children in his role as past president of the Golden Corridor Advanced Manufacturing Partnership (GCAMP). It has now become the Greater Chicago Advanced Manufacturing Partnership. He champions youth who are curious about the world around them, an important trait unique to makers.

After reading Gary's comments, you will likely ask yourself: Is my son or daughter a maker? These are Gary's words:

> Gary Skoog's thoughts:
> Really, the age for makerspace[1] is 8 to 80. An analogy might be a place you want to get some exercise. And you know you're not going to do it if you just put something down in the basement, or get some weights, or buy something to run on. So, you join a club, and you pay a membership fee. And then you can go in and use all the weights, and all the running equipment, and all the lifting equipment, and the shower, and all the facilities.

A makerspace is similar to that. You join as a member, and then you get discounts on classes, and you can come in and use the equipment. I mean, the equipment is things such as laser cutters and 3D printers. There's a special dye sublimation printer that does absolutely amazing detail printing. And you can print on T-shirts, or you can put it on pieces of metal and hang them up on the wall like pieces of art. We just got a much larger 3D printer, a Stratasys. We're even looking at maybe getting some service or certification in 3D printing and additive manufacturing, so that somebody could go use it in industry.

It's open to the community. We're obviously open to students, for classes for students that can actually get credit for. People can come in and take a course as continuing education for credit, or they can just do it for fun. So, why would a parent be interested in a makerspace for their kid? I think it's just because kids are curious. And I mean, obviously, down the road, you want them to get a good job, and be able to carry on life on their own, and start a family, and all that stuff. But right now, it's like, *What can I do to help stimulate Johnny or Susie in terms of learning new things and finding out what they like and what their skills are?*

[The Makerspace Movie] came out through Maker Faire (an annual convention for enthusiastic do-it-yourselfers). A lot of this started on the West Coast, and it's actually gone all over the world. That's what the movie was all about.

No doubt. We've got a robotics revolution coming.
It's already here!
Let's get our skill sets down
to accommodate that future.

I think it's exciting. And you can go on YouTube and put in words like: 'makerspaces,' 'children makerspaces,' 'youth makerspaces,' and 'robotics.'

Educate yourself as to what the options are and what the rest of the world out there is doing. This is a world-wide movement. You will be really surprised that this thing is really taking off around the world and a lot of people are getting involved. As a parent and as a kid in middle school on up, I really recommend that parents introduce their kids to Makerspaces.

MY JOURNEY INTO THE FAMILY BUSINESS

My father wanted me to go to college, but maybe not necessarily five different colleges! I disappointed him by getting married young and not finishing school. In the end, though, I made him very proud. Here's the story.

During the summers of the early '70s, around the start of my high school career, I started packing collets, cleaning machines, taking apart spindle motors, cleaning the shop, and mowing the lawn. We were in Chicago, where we had been for several decades. When we painted machines, the smell of fresh Sherwin Williams 7B paint permeated throughout the shop. To this day, when we paint machines, the smell brings back memories of when I was 14, starting in the family business.

I had a knack for academics, especially math, so I went to college. I was told it was what I was supposed to do if I wanted a great career. "College would open doors," they said. And they were right. I gave the same advice to my children. The thing is that they were also wrong. Because for some people, learning needs to be hands-on. You need to see the impact of your work closer to the point where you are doing it. And you need to see the paycheck and the promotions and, well, your future.

I was in my second year of college when I realized I loved manufacturing and could accomplish more by starting my career than sitting in a classroom. I entered into the sales side of the business in Wisconsin. I would leave the house every day bright and early to make sales calls. I found it fascinating seeing locks, water meters, motorcycles, and guidance systems being made from the ground up. Each machine shop I entered was either a screw machine shop with a very strong cutting oil "aroma," or a CNC (computer numerical control) shop with a differing water-based coolant smell.

At the end of the day, I made the drive home. Upon arrival, I learned that my suit had absorbed these industrial olfactory identifiers, not necessarily appreciated by my better half. "You smell like a machine shop," she would say. To me, it was the smell of money, opportunity, and the pride of helping customers make something useful to the world and our country at large.

Today's shops feature a great deal more mist collection equipment and are cleaner. They no longer have the strong oil smell throughout. But the opportunities? Endless.

My (much) younger brother Erik also worked for Iverson & Company for about seven years. Erik left to go to Chicago Dial Indicator, which he now owns and runs as president. Chicago

Dial is a good example of a small manufacturer competing against some of the giants in the quality control and inspection world.

Everyone in our family is proud of the "Made in America" moniker. We believe in the ingenious and productive means of making things here in the U.S.

MAKING A LIFE IN MANUFACTURING

For years I had a tough time as the only sibling "going the distance" in the family business. There were ample chances for me to move on to other opportunities. As one who always finishes a job and is loyal to the family, I stayed in the positions earned through the years. Then, in 1999, there came a week when I attended a strategic finance seminar at the Harvard Business School. I found that people were interested in what I had to say about running our small family machine tool business. The thing that impacted me the most was a young lady from South America. I mentioned being the only child in the family business. She commented, "Oh, so *you* are the chosen one!"

What? I thought.

"In our country, it is an honor to be the chosen one—to run the family business," she said.

I thought long and hard about this. That one encounter was like signing my own permission slip to continue down what is now my fourth decade in manufacturing. My wife Kathy works with me. I am very proud of her. She accomplishes great things in anything she does. I also feel that way about our three adult children. God has blessed us with seven grandchildren, and I cannot wait to see what endeavors each chooses to follow in life.

Life has been good to us, and manufacturing careers have served us well.

HEAR ME LOUD AND CLEAR–YOUR CHILD'S FUTURE MAY DEPEND ON IT

The parallels between playing sports and succeeding in life and business are too numerous to count. I began coaching and mentoring young people when our children were young. I eventually retired from coaching soccer when my youngest son turned 18, and several of his teammates went on to play Division III soccer. Yet, I still felt compelled to mentor youth. I was fortunate to have mentors when I was young, and I felt a great obligation to pay it forward.

As a parent, you have tremendous influence on your child. They want to make you proud. Finding a match between their God-given gifts, personal interests, and a lifelong career is hard. The way schools teach does not always align with how each child learns. What is good for one child may not be good for another child.

You see, the workplace is changing dramatically. Our educational system continues to struggle to adapt to such changes. Our post-secondary educational system does not offer much of a future for those who either cannot afford to attend or those who do not learn the way higher education teaches. A young person going into debt for an educational offering that is obsolete and not relevant to their needs is painful to witness. We can do better as parents, but we need to understand our child's strengths, interests, and talents. We also need to be open to seeing what the current job market offers and the rapid changes around us.

Through the nonprofit I started, **CHAMPION Now!,** I talk with hundreds, sometimes thousands, of young adults each year. Their voices, concerns, and questions stay with me because they are the next generation of leaders and makers—people who will turn ideas into products used by millions of people around the world. Unfortunately, reaching you, the parents, is not easy. I hope this book opens your minds and inspires meaningful conversations with your child. Their lifelong path to success may depend on that one dynamic!

I have given presentations at conferences across the country in front of young people faced with the same decisions as your child. I also became involved in a Leadership Forum at Union Station in Washington. On my way to one of these meetings in Washington, I myself became inspired. I thought, *How do I coin a slogan or an organization to change people's perceptions?* I had already pitched a television idea, but that alone did not seem to be enough.

There had to be a message alongside anything that talked about manufacturing. While scribbling on a napkin on a plane, I toyed with the words: CHANGE – MANUFACTURING – PERCEPTIONS. After all, that is the dilemma. Somehow, I came up with C-H-M-P. I then found my way to the word C-H-A-M-P-I-O-N. It stands for Change How American Manufacturing's Perceived In Our Nation.

I added the "Now" to the name to initiate action to move—immediately. In other words, there is a crisis in our country, which is that no one thinks, is exposed to, or is encouraged to pursue a career in manufacturing. As a result, our workers, managers, and owners are getting older.

There is no succession plan.

TIM TUMANIC:
WHEN PARENTS STAND UNITED

For more than 40 years, I traveled throughout the Midwest selling machine tools. I started in Wisconsin, and this state keeps coming up in my book for its unique ability to make manufacturing a priority—and the opportunity it brings to Packer fans throughout the state.

I worked for my uncle until late 1980. Before I left, a gentleman joined Custom Products by the name of Tim Tumanic. He is now the owner of JR Machine. Tim talks about the powerful impact parents have when they show a united front in a child's growth and success. Much of what Tim speaks about relates to my situation as a young person growing up.

> **Tim Tumanic's thoughts:**
> As parents, educate yourself about what's out there. What jobs are out there where your son or daughter doesn't have to saddle themselves with a $100,000 student loan—and where they can bring home the type of pay that will enable them to live a good, healthy life?
>
> I see so many of these student loans, and it just sickens me. And that's because the [students] haven't had the guidance. Our program has been successful, but I don't think it's been as successful as it could be because that starts at home. That's where I see the gap in pointing kids in the right direction.
>
> *It really starts at home. Parents have to ask themselves, 'Am I doing everything I can to help educate my son and daughter about some of the*

opportunities in the past as they're in high school?
Am I doing enough to point them
in the right direction?'

I think a lot of it has to do with one-parent families or fatherless homes. The whole thing falls on one parent, the mother, right? She's got to do the laundry, she's got to feed the kids, she's got to go to work every day. And then, oh yeah, she's got to make sure they're doing what they're supposed to be doing in school, and that their grades are alright. We can live with that, but what are they going to do when they get out of school? That's a lot for one person.

Unfortunately, my marriage ended in a divorce when our son was in high school. Divorce always affects kids. But we were united in his growth. We never let our differences be known to him.

I think when we stay close to our kids and guide them in vocation, we ultimately help set them up for success. I look out our window and I see all these new trucks, and I see all these young people buying homes. That means they're committed to this area. They're committed to us. I get more satisfaction out of that than anything else. It's paying dividends, that's for sure.

THE COLLEGE ADMISSIONS SCANDAL

One of the most concerning ethical issues I see in parents' role in higher education surfaced with the college admissions scandal in the U.S. In March 2019, 53 parents were accused of bribing administrators to gain favor for entrance into college. The Justice

Department established the code name "Operation Varsity Blues" for the investigation of parents that allegedly paid over $25 million in bribes between 2011-2018. Rick William Singer,[2] the organizer of the scheme, was working under the company names Key Worldwide Foundation and The Edge College & Career Network.

The thought that parents would sabotage their sons' and daughters' integrity to get them into the school of their choice is insane. We need to empower our children to find their own way and motivate them to work hard.

Education in this country needs a reset.

While the current four-to-five-year university model offers value to those who seek careers that require a diploma with a specific knowledge base, the vast majority of students on the job market need a skill set over a parchment noting a degree. The cost of a college education has risen above and beyond what the market requires. Students are lured with the illusion that a college degree is the ONLY path to success.

That is simply no longer the case.

THE WAY YOU SEE THE WORLD MAKES THE BIGGEST DIFFERENCE

How you see the world determines your child's path in life.

For example, what if your child chose a career in manufacturing and then was asked to participate in a signing day with notable media recognition? Would you and they be more excited about the road ahead?

I think most people would say "yes." I would.

Well, in Henrico County Public Schools in Virginia, that's exactly what Director of Career and Technical Education (CTE)

Mac Beaton did. He honored technical education graduates by having them sign letters of intent for employment. This is similar to high school athletes committing to their chosen college on National Signing Day. It's like an ESPN moment for kids in technical fields.

When I spoke as a keynote speaker for NC3 (National Coalition of Community Colleges) in 2019, I also learned of the National CTE Letter of Intent Signing Day to celebrate high school graduates' intentions to further their education in the skilled trade professions. Clark Coco and Tina Blair of Clayton Tatro Washburn Tech in Topeka, Kansas, held the first CTE Letter of Intent Signing Day in 2014. The event has grown exponentially ever since. Last year, 62 schools participated, with over 5,000 students signing letters of intent, with ceremonies tied together by live, nationwide simulcasts.

SKILLSUSA is an organization that also acknowledges National Signing Day each year and is one of the organizations leading the way nationally in not only competitions but also ele-

vating the careers for these young people. (www.skillsusa.org)

Manufacturing is the best-kept secret, yet it *is* one of America's greatest opportunities—one of her Greatest Champions. Next up, we'll take a look at the surprising facts, highlights, and myths of manufacturing, why it is so crucial to our country's future, and our culture's profound—and surprising—influence on manufacturing, especially for young people.

Your role as a parent is crucial to your child's success. Understanding how the changes going on in our culture, educational system, and job market affect your child is more complex than ever. Good news: how you approach these changes may expand significantly as you dive into the pages of this book. More importantly, the conversations you have with your child after reading this may change their lives for the better and invite the ultimate game-changing question: "Why not?"

MANUFACTURING AS YOUR CHILD'S CAREER CHOICE

"...so when I hear people go, 'You guys make your product outside the U.S.' Really? You buy products [made] outside the U.S.? Stop buying it outside the U.S. and we can start making it in the U.S."

—Tony Schumacher,
NHRA Top Fuel Champion

The U.S. manufactures just under 20 percent of the world's goods. Yet, our culture often gives the impression we aren't a manufacturing populace and that manufacturing is not important. Time to *wake up*. Our culture needs to be engaged in *where* things are made, *how* things are made, and *why* it is important for us to care.

So, what exactly is manufacturing? Here's the definition according to Merriam-Webster.

MANUFACTURE:

1. *Something made from raw materials by hand or by machinery*
2. *The process of making wares by hand or by machinery especially when carried on systematically with division of labor. b: a productive industry using mechanical power and machinery*
3. *The act or process of producing something*

You might say, "Isn't that obvious?" Of course, manufacturing creates things. But my explanation goes further than the products that are the lifeblood of any manufacturer. It includes components like:

Manufacturing create$ Opportunities
Manufacturing create$ Jobs
Manufacturing create$ Careers
Manufacturing create$ Wealth
Manufacturing create$ Stability

Much of the media likes to say we have become a service-based country. I disagree. The U.S. manufacturing economic engine is the eighth-largest economy in the world. We still manufacture approximately one-fifth of the world's goods. Does that sound like manufacturing is dead?

The truth is that manufacturing is on the rise. Called reshoring, consumers and manufacturers alike are realizing the advantages of making products closer to home. According to *Forbes*, as of July 2020, 69 percent of manufacturers were actively looking to bring production back to North America.[1] The Reshoring Institute reveals that 69.4 percent of Americans prefer products that are made in the U.S.[2]

NICOLE WOLTER: YOU ARE THE #1 MOST IMPORTANT MENTOR TO YOUR CHILD, SO SHOW THEM THE WORLD

The biggest challenge for U.S. manufacturers is creating an adequate supply of talent to make it happen. The biggest challenge for parents is to see manufacturing as one of their children's greatest opportunities. Here's the inside story of Nicole Wolter, who talks about transitioning into her father's manufacturing company during the 2009 Great Recession.

Nicole Wolter's thoughts:
Mine was a very unconventional start to a career. I actually left college in 2008-2009, right during the Great Recession. I needed a job. My dad originally, right before I left, said that the company—HM Manufacturing—was not doing so well. He thought maybe I'd be a good fit to kind of re-energize the company and maybe start doing some sales because we didn't really have a sales team.

So, I show up on the company doorstep and my dad goes, 'Now?' and I say, 'Yeah.' I mean, what else was I supposed to do? I was fired from a previous job, and I knew I would not be able to get a job anywhere. It was September 2009, and things were not going so well for the country. I did finally convince him to just give me a start. The best thing that my dad did with me was to start me from scratch. I could have gone into sales, but it wouldn't have served a purpose, at least for the long term. I needed to start from the ground up. And so that is what I did.

I started with shipping and receiving. I learned how we got the boxes in, how we put them into the system, how we sorted and looked for material, and how parts were received in from plating and then moved through to the assembly stage. Then I went on to inventory and inventory maintenance. I learned what we inventoried and how we inventory certain items. Once I understood that portion and how to read CAD drawings, I finally went into the office. I learned how to do the payroll and put in job costing. I picked it up really quickly because I remembered doing it from high school, and I've always been very computer-savvy. I have an extremely good memory. I like to self-start, learn, understand, grasp, and ask questions.

I've always been very intuitive. I love to ask questions, especially when things don't add up. And I think it was a very good thing for me to be this outside person in manufacturing, because I came in almost like a consultant, but a very naive and green consultant. It was just me asking a lot of questions and suggesting other ways to approach things. I was hearing, *Well, that's how we've always done it*, and for me, that is my biggest pet peeve.

It freaks me out because I hate the status quo, and I hate wasting time.

Did I underestimate or overestimate
my transition from a non-manufacturing life
to a manufacturing career?
I think it's a mixture of all of it.

I felt I didn't belong in the industry because I didn't know anything. I didn't know how a machine worked. I didn't know how certain machines were supposed to cut material or what products were made from them. Of course, now I do. I have put in a lot of work and effort to make sure that I knew every aspect of the business and manufacturing so I could have intelligent conversations. I'm so glad I put myself through CAD/ SOLIDWORKS® classes, machining classes, and even became a member of manufacturing associations. Meeting others in the space, learning from them, and networking has made all the difference in my career.

Since manufacturing has changed my life in such an amazing way, and the industry as a whole has been incredible to me, I wanted to give back to the community and show others how great manufacturing is, give them a different perspective about it through internships. During these paid internships, these students started to like it (manufacturing careers). McHenry High School has a great system for manufacturing. Giving some of these students a chance not only helped them with upgrading their skill set, but it helped us, too. I have a young shop that ranges from 18-32 years old, and most of my team in the shop has come from this internship, that eventually turned into an apprenticeship program and, finally, a full-time job offer and career. One of my team members has skilled themselves all the way to being my shop manager. He runs the whole shop and is only 32. I think it's just giving these kids an opportunity, and working with them as well is a great thing.

As far as the shop goes, I've seen now are that people are waking up to understand that technology can be a blessing. I think robotics is going to play a large role. I've seen so many people with robots that are running lights-out operations, and they are showing us that it's possible for smaller shops. This is teaching us that technology and staff are the way of the future. After dealing with COVID, I'm seeing a huge resurgence of U.S.-made products and needing the local supply chain. We should be bringing all this stuff back to the U.S. and giving opportunities to American workers. Not only is manufacturing great for the economy, it's necessary for the community and the American people that are looking for reliable careers.

We really need to start paying better attention to the college narrative. We need to start getting these students and young adults to understand that they do have other options besides going to college and going into debt. Not everyone should or wants to go to college, and that's OK. We need to let them know it's OK. They shouldn't be ashamed of that path. Manufacturing offers great careers and pathways with the ability to move up in a company and positions. That should be encouraged and nurtured.

With Gen Z, they're looking for a career, and they're looking for something that they want to do and things that they love. Gen Z is all about changing for the betterment of society, and they believe in choices. As long as we can continue to be vocal and showcase what we do at our companies and be visible on social media, I think it's going to start working on all the parents, the kids, the educators, and it'll be a great thing. We, as owners, need to be available and be willing to take on green talent.

I think a lot of people are so wound up with success, and what success looks like, that no one really looks at failure. And I can't tell you how many times I've failed and continued to struggle. And I continue to learn every day. Like I said, I'm still somewhat new when it comes to a lot of manufacturing practices, but I still read, take classes, and throw myself into discussions to keep growing as a manufacturer and as a business owner. I think people should know that it's OK to continue learning. It's OK to not know things. It's OK to fail. It's a great growth plan, essentially.

I think the best thing that you could do as an owner, as a person that's very high up in their career, is to give back. Mentor others, especially students who just have no idea what they want to do. I'm proud of that. I'm proud that I was able to give back because if I could just impact a few more students that have no direction or don't know what they want to do, I'd be happy to just guide them and offer them a chance at any position in my company, to just try it, to just give them a voice and give them a path. I think that would make all the difference because, at times, when I look at my career, I wish I had that earlier on.

MANUFACTURING CREATE$ OPPORTUNITIES

Here's a story about the day I went on TV and was publicly humiliated by a well-known personality. My response to her, however, is the best way I can show you the opportunities in manufacturing.

In March 2009, I was invited to talk for five minutes on the "Monster and Money" television show in Chicago. My high school teammate Don Dupree was the producer and knew of my manufacturing expertise. It was a live broadcast on Channel 2 Chicago local TV—at a very early time in the morning—somewhere around 5:40 a.m. I talked about my **CHAMPION Now!** organization, how it promoted manufacturing careers, and that manufacturing was in need of young talent.

I doubt I had adequate coffee intake that morning. There were four hosts on the show: ex-Chicago Bear and sportscaster Dan Jiggetts, radio personality Mike North, Mike Hegedus of Hegedus World, and financial expert Terry Savage.

I wasn't cued into what questions were going to be asked or how the interview was going to go. I mentioned my organization and how I had become a self-proclaimed advocate for manufacturing jobs. Mike North talked about how manufacturing companies had moved to the suburbs, and Dan Jiggetts said that growing up, he heard that manufacturing jobs were good-paying jobs. Then came the comment I never saw coming from Terry Savage, when she said: "I find it very counterintuitive that you are sitting here saying that today there are jobs available and that we should tell young people to pursue careers in manufacturing!"

Needless to say, I was floored. Talk about being put on the spot! The answer I gave was simple: "Terry, there are some manufacturing jobs that cannot leave American soil—defense and medical to name a few. We will always have to make the most complex, advanced, and most proprietary products in our country."

The component of the response that I left out was how the aging population in manufacturing exceeds the number of products and jobs leaving for China. Although it is true that a great deal of low-cost products and processes are going to China, with automation and advanced production techniques and equipment, we can compete globally.

With each recession we've had, many of the Baby Boomers working in manufacturing postponed their retirement, but the catastrophic flow of retirees out of manufacturing is inevitable. During 2020 and the height of the COVID-19 pandemic, we learned of our dependence on products manufactured by other countries. When we needed PPE equipment (masks and shields, for example), we learned that most of this came from China. We as a country were scrambling for PPE equipment, to protect those who were on the frontlines taking care of our infected population.

Making products in our country creates opportunities.

MANUFACTURING CREATE$ JOBS

The Boomer labor force has been declining by 2.2 million on average each year since 2010, or about 5,900 daily.[3] The average age of a manufacturing employee is well into their mid-40s. According to the Manufacturing Institute, by 2030, nearly 4 million manufacturing jobs likely need to be filled. The skills gap is expected to result in 2.1 million of those jobs going unfilled.[4] This is at a time when unemployment has hovered around 3.7 percent.[5]

At the same time, the media, high school counselors, and many parents preach to not go into manufacturing-related fields.

Those of us in the industry have an obligation to correct the course that seems to be set. For manufacturing to drive the financial stability of our country and all those employed by it, we need to encourage the brightest, most energetic, and passionate to go into the manufacturing field.

It is no secret that many American manufacturers got complacent and fell asleep at the switch. My dad told me that deliveries in the machine tool business got to the point where it took 12 to 24 months to get a very basic standard machine tool in the mid-1960s and 1970s. This opened the door to aggressive machine tool builders from Japan and Taiwan to have more competitively priced products, as well as in-stock deliveries. Machine tool builders in these countries saw an awesome opportunity. They seized the moment. As a result, the machine tool business was never the same in the U.S.

Many would say that the weak manufacturing sector is now to a point of posing an extreme risk to our national defense. What would happen if we went to war with some of the countries that we now consider our allies? Many of these could be the same countries that supply machine tools to make our defense mechanisms. We might not be able to keep these machine tools operational in order to supply our arsenal of defense to our military. A strong machine tool foundation in our country is vital. With all the problems we've faced throughout the pandemic, our culture is starting to realize we need to manufacture more in the U.S. The supply chain deficiencies have become scarily apparent and exposed our country's vulnerabilities in the global marketplace.

The automotive industry also became apathetic from the standpoint of quality. We made inferior products and just expected U.S. consumers to not only accept it, but also to pay more for it. We did not listen to what the consumer wanted, expected, and needed. Japanese car companies came in with reasonably priced, economical automobiles that featured more miles to the gallon. The American automotive executive allowed products to be designed, built, and manufactured that were primarily status-defining luxury cars that cost more and were inefficient.

Now we have executives like Elon Musk at Tesla who think differently. Not only has he introduced a more efficient car and battery, but he also will lead the automotive giant into new, more responsible and responsive designs to build cars in the future.

Our industries suffered from not listening to consumers in both cases. It would be worse yet if we didn't learn from our mistakes as a culture, and instead became less competitive and less responsive to market demands. We need to be more responsible in developing and attracting the next generation of manufacturing workers, employees, and leaders.

A close friend recently texted me this news flash: "GM drops four-year degree requirement for many jobs, will focus on skills!" They are also focusing on women and people of color, both of whom are vastly underrepresented in the manufacturing sector.[6] This is incredible news!

I find the success of Tesla very exciting, as well as the technological gains in their electric cars and autonomous driving. I think of the freedom that my father would have had if he had

 lived another five years or so. My father had macular degeneration to the point that he gave up driving for good the last five to eight years of his life. He loved cars and driving, not to mention the independence it gave him. While I think the trend is a

long time coming, I find this to be a welcome wake up call for the U.S. auto industry. All the major automotive brands are playing catch-up at this point, but it will pay dividends for the earth as we try to reduce emissions and address climate change in the world. Being less dependent on fossil fuels will certainly help our world.

TONY SCHUMACHER ON WHICH COMES FIRST: MADE IN AMERICA OR BUY IN AMERICA?

In this section, we take a look at U.S.-made goods through the eyes of someone who puts his life on the line driving a car built with parts manufactured in the U.S.

I was at a Mother's Day brunch with my extended family when my sister Amy mentioned that a friend from work was moving into our subdivision. She thought the husband did something with racing but she wasn't totally sure. So, I mentioned that I would stop in and say hello. Not long after the family had moved in, I knocked on the door and introduced myself. As it turns out, they were a young couple with the last name Schumacher, and Tony was a drag racer. Over the years, we became very good friends, and it was awesome to see Tony grow and become so accomplished. At the time of this writing, he is an eight-time NHRA (National Hot Rod Association) champion.[7] (At one point, Tony held the speed record of 336 MPH).[8]

Besides owning Don Schumacher Racing (DSR), his father also owns Schumacher Electric. Schumacher Electric is known as a first-class battery charger manufacturer. Tony became the winningest Top Fuel driver in NHRA history.

Tony Schumacher's thoughts:

Now, if Americans, as buyers, would walk into a store and only buy the stuff made in America, we'd be great. We would be wonderful. But they go in and they want the cheapest price too.

When I hear people go, 'You guys make your product outside the U.S.' Really, you buy products made outside the U.S.? Stop buying it from outside the U.S., and we can start making it in the U.S. It costs more to hire an American than it does to hire someone in China. We still save a ton of money, even with the shipping and all the containers, the taxes, everything coming in.

As buyers, we need to make the conscious choice that it's here that we want to be part of. Stop being so, *We're trying to save money*. It comes full circle. If we spend the money in the U.S., we all get paid more, everything goes up. The value of everything we do is good. I'm not making anything up. We can make America great again, we just got to do it right. We got to start being responsible as buyers, buying a product right here, so people who own companies can start making stuff here, because we want to. And guess what? If I want to go overseas and make stuff, don't buy it. Maybe you'll force me to do it. I think it's important that we take a little responsibility as the buyer.

While speaking to engineers at Boeing, I told this story. If I am going to get in my race car that goes 330 miles per hour, and I'm about to start it, and my crew chief leans over and goes, 'I've got great news for you. This car's built in China and Mexico. I just saved your dad a ton of money,' my response would be, 'I have great news for you. You can drive. I'm not getting in that car.' The place went nuts.

On a very bright note, there are innovative programs making a difference in how manufacturing is perceived in the U.S. The Science, Technology, Engineering, and Math (STEM) and Project Lead the Way initiatives are making their way into high schools. Project Lead the Way allows for high school youth to learn with their hands and makes the connection between book knowledge and project-based learning.

Robotics and For Inspiration and Recognition of Science and Technology (FIRST) robotic team competitions teach young people decision-making skills as a means of developing the much-needed troubleshooting tasks used in any manufacturing field or career.

Around 1994, I followed fellow machine tool sales professional Tim Doran's lead to do presentations at local high schools. In our presentations, we encouraged students to attend our trade show, the International Manufacturing Technology Show (IMTS), held every two years in downtown Chicago. IMTS is like the Disney World of the machine tool and manufacturing industries. For many years, attendees had to be over 18, which did very little to attract the next generation of workers. Since the 1990s, IMTS has welcomed young people with their Student Summit. This was a much-needed change.  Any parent that attends this event would have their eyes opened to what might be possible for their child in the way of an exciting and high-paying career.

Having said that, the biggest threat to manufacturing is the lack of skilled workers.

As the Reshoring Movement progresses, the new administration removes the regulations, taxes, and other hindrances that impede manufacturing companies from competing in a global market. We must address the lack of employees to allow the manufacturing renaissance to bring prosperity back to the U.S. and the middle class of America. This means more training, more opportunities, more programs, and *more jobs*.

MANUFACTURING CREATE$ CAREERS

As we went into late 2021 and early 2022, the supply chain became a disaster. Shipments of products from Eastern Asia were taking much more time than previously anticipated. We found ourselves yearning for our favorite products, food items, Christmas presents, and more. Cars could not be built because of the lack of computer microchips. Deliveries for everything were pushed back longer than anything I had ever experienced in my lifetime. The fact that 75 percent of microchips are made outside the U.S. could be an omen for our standard of living. The *60 Minutes* episode from May 2, 2021, brings this dilemma to the forefront talking about how this will affect us all.

 If that wasn't enough of a challenge, then came the "Great Resignation." In December of 2021, 308,000 workers left manufacturing employment, while that month, there were 433,000 hires. The previous months saw 294,000 (November), 298,000 (October), and 324,000 (September) workers leave manufacturing employment, when three years prior to the pandemic attrition each month averaged between 225,000 and 300,000.

In 2000, the average age of a manufacturing worker was 40.5 years of age. Twenty-two years later, that number has risen to 44.2, compared to retail where the average age is 37.7 years of age.[9]

We have been preaching that Baby Boomers were near retirement and that the "silver tsunami" of retirements was coming. As mentioned earlier, the Boomer labor force has been declining by 2.2 million on average each year.[10]

Additionally, millennials had a collective epiphany as they were fed up with the work-life balance, or lack thereof. In Europe, there seems to be a better understanding of how to balance things out. Travel in Europe in August, and you will find that plants are shut down for an entire month while the rest of the world waits for their return.

The truth is that manufacturing isn't just a job. Manufacturing is a great career where your child can experience many opportunities: steady career growth, leadership growth, a learning path to expand their skills and make more money, and access to advanced technology to be a programmer, work with robotics, or do data analysis.

MANUFACTURING CREATE$ WEALTH

Historically, if you look at any leading nation in the world, you will find that they have economic success. In order for each country to prosper, manufacturing is at the core of their sustained prosperity.

My immediate and my extended family have done well in the manufacturing sector. We have all owned nice homes, driven nice cars, provided for our families, and saved money for that "rainy day." These are all possible with hard work, determination, and taking advantage of great opportunities. Starting with my grandfather, many have taken this path. Some took a more direct path, while others had to find it in a more cumbersome fashion (that was me). However, despite that, I was in the groove by age 22. When I look back at my 42-year career, I am thankful, grateful, and proud. Going forward, I intend to yell this from the mountaintops so others can accomplish the same.

My dad repeated something that a peer told him decades ago: "I never wanted to be a millionaire; I just wanted to make a good living for my family." Ironically, not only did my father become a millionaire, but so did several of our career-long employees in the profit-sharing plan.

MANUFACTURING CREATE$ STABILITY

Manufacturing creates wealth, and wealth creates stability. The more you learn in manufacturing, the more value you add to your company and yourself.

In today's job market, young people compete with other applicants for the same job openings in the same sector. We are producing lots of lawyers, accountants, and other traditional careerists. Meanwhile, all things technical are getting fewer and fewer applicants. Companies are realizing they don't necessarily need a new employee to have a degree; a skill set is more important. Manufacturing creates stability because simple supply and demand proves it to be the case.

I hope that this chapter has inspired a newfound appreciation for the significance of manufacturing and our country's place using a global perspective. Automation is a means to build an economy that needs even more skilled workers, not less.

Chapter 3 will present stories from those who reinforce the **CHAMPION Now!** spirit by changing perceptions through plant tours, podcasts, talk radio, and TV programs. They are my heroes. Collectively, we can build a better tomorrow for the U.S. and a more skilled workforce.

Just as important, as a parent you are the key to opening the door for your child so they discover the best debt-free career path for themselves.

THE BRIDGE TO MANUFACTURING, CONSTRUCTION, AND OTHER PATHS

"They keep going down this road like sheep to a slaughter, man. Everybody told me I couldn't have a shop and that American manufacturing was dead and I was like, 'I'm different.'"

—Titan Gilroy,
CEO, TITANS of CNC

The U.S. manufacturing industry is thriving and enjoys the promise of even greater growth and prosperity ahead. In fact, 90 percent of manufacturing companies recently surveyed feel positive about their own company outlook. The statistics hold the promise of new prosperity, benefiting our global competitiveness, economic growth, and communities across the country. But there is one huge threat to the future of U.S. manufacturing: the large deficit of skilled workers to fill open positions, up to 2.1 million unfilled jobs by 2030."[1]

Not only do your children have great opportunities in manufacturing, but there are other industries to consider that are closely connected with manufacturing. Many companies are not able to build what they need to fulfill orders because of a lack of manpower. Consider these careers. These are the 2021 median salaries (not including benefits) from the U.S. Bureau of Labor and Statistics website:

CNC Operator	$46,240.00
Welder	$47,010.00
Precision Machinist	$47,730.00
Carpenter	$48,260.00
Sheet Metal Workers	$53,440.00
Tool & Die Worker	$57,000.00
Plumbers	$59,880.00
Electrician	$60,040.00
CNC Programmer	$62,360.00
Production Supervisor	$67,330.00

You might wonder: Why didn't I know about these career options? I have a story about that.

There is a TV commercial from MB Financial Bank. The lead character is walking through his machine shop, talking about his company to the banker. While the shop owner is rattling off various aspects of his CNC (computerized numerically controlled) lathe, his coordinate-measuring machine, and his press brakes, the MB Financial banker stays quiet during the entire 30-second spot.

This type of commercial speaks volumes about our culture, where few in the general populace understand the full potential of manufacturing.

When people ask me what I do, it's hard coming up with a concise response sometimes. Will they have some clue as to what I am talking about? Or will they act politely interested with the *deer in the headlights* stare while thinking to themselves about the unglamorous perception that we have grown all too familiar with?

Companies like Gillette and Harley-Davidson are changing the game on this. They've started to share the pride of making quality products in America. Some of their commercials talk about the company competing globally, with American workers making a quality product.

WHY CNC ROCKS!

We have already covered how important manufacturing is to this country. What we haven't covered is how absolutely awesome today's manufacturing technology is! CNC operators are one reason why.

The next generation has been brought up in a digital environment. Your kids text rather than pick up a phone. They play computer games rather than go outside and play a pick-up game of soccer, football, baseball, or hockey (unless, of course, it is organized ball). Many get a phone around age eight or nine. There are computers in grammar school. Given our digital culture, why aren't kids lining up for careers in manufacturing? They have all the innate capabilities to be successful in manufacturing from a very young age.

The answer is back to the **CHAMPION Now!** message. The perception is that they can't make good money in manufacturing. It is not a safe or clean environment. It is not for smart students. It's not an honorable profession.

The facts disprove these perceptions. According to the National Association of Manufacturing (NAM), in 2021, manufacturing workers in the U.S. earned $95,990 on average, including pay and benefits. Workers in all private nonfarm industries earned $81,308 on average.[2] We need to change these perceptions, not only in young people, but also their parents, grandparents, media, and guidance counselors. That is the difficult task.

More TV shows, commercials, news reports, plant tours, and focused programs to educate guidance counselors will make you more aware of your children's choices.

The term CNC Rocks is a slogan I came up with through **CHAMPION Now!** to convey that manufacturing is a great place to be. It is exciting. The CNC portion of the industry is pertinent to youth. This slogan spoke to me because it speaks the language of young people.

DO YOUR HOMEWORK ABOUT THEIR CAREER OPTIONS

Whether your child goes into manufacturing or some related field, doing your homework pays off. Making assumptions doesn't. I think you'll find the following myths about manufacturing helpful. Both the websites for Marketing4Manufacturers[3] & The Manufacturing Institute (NAM) say it best:

Myth: Manufacturing jobs are disappearing, and the ones that exist don't require many skills. Fact: There are an estimated 350,000 manufacturing jobs unfilled today. More than 80% of manufacturing companies have reported shortages in skilled production workers from entry level on up. Since machines are increasingly computer-controlled, the jobs that need to be filled are for programmers, operators, and maintenance workers. Highly skilled maintenance workers can earn more than $100k per year.

Myth: Free trade agreements hurt U.S. manufacturing. Fact: About half of all manufactured goods exported from the U.S. went to countries with which we had free trade agreements. U.S. manufacturers in 2015 had a $412.7 billion surplus with countries with which we had free trade agreements versus the $639.6 billion deficit they had with countries without agreements.

Myth: U.S. manufacturers can't compete with cheap, overseas labor. Fact: Over the past 25 years, the export of U.S.-manufactured products has quadrupled. Also, manufacturers fund more than 75% of all private sector research and development in the country, creating more innovation than any other sector. With the large growth the manufacturing industry has experienced and its focus on innovation, U.S. manufacturers have become more "lean" and automated, which is helping them become more competitive in the global market.

Myth: Manufacturing jobs in the U.S. are disappearing, and they don't pay well.
Fact: In 2020, millions of manufacturing employees made, on average, $92,832/year, including benefits. In addition, nearly 4.0 million more manufacturing jobs are expected to become available by 2030.

Myth: There aren't many "small" manufacturing firms in the U.S. anymore.
Fact: The vast majority of manufacturing firms in the U.S. are small. In other words, there are 239,651 manufacturing firms in the U.S. with fewer than 500 employees. Furthermore, 74.3% of these small manufacturing firms have less than 20 employees. It's also interesting to note that manufacturers have one of the highest percentages of workers who are eligible for employer-provided health benefits—95%!

Myth: Manufacturing isn't a big part of the U.S. economy anymore.
Fact: In 2021, U.S. manufacturing contributed $2.77 trillion to the economy and accounted for approximately 8-10% of the total workforce. Additionally, in 2020 manufacturing accounted for over 10.8% of GDP in the economy. For every $1.00 spent in manufacturing, another $2.68 is added to the economy. That is the highest multiplier effect of any economic sector. In addition, for every one worker in manufacturing, there are another four employees hired elsewhere.

DO WE HAVE SOMETHING TO LEARN FROM JAPAN AND EUROPE'S CAREER CULTURES?

We can learn so much from different cultures, particularly in Europe, which embrace manufacturing careers and tradespeople. Somehow our culture changed dramatically in the 1980s when the recession caused many changes in the U.S. Inflation and interest rates went through the roof. The first wave of outsourcing overseas started. Someone came up with the notion that our country would be based on a service-based economy, as many manufacturing plants closed. Apprenticeship programs were closed in many manufacturing companies.

This was a very short-term philosophy.

My father taught me long ago to always make decisions based on the long-term outlook. His financial mindset was based on that approach. He based his strategy on developing personnel and employees on that idea. Often, investors in the U.S. as a whole look for quick returns. We have gone to a more disposable way of life as consumers, which, in turn, is counter-productive to the long-term philosophy adopted by successful countries like Japan.

There are other parts of the world whose cost of living exceeds ours. Recently, our gas prices have reached all-time highs. We are starting to contend with issues that countries like Germany did many decades ago. Yet they have found a way to embrace manufacturing in their culture. The U.S. can learn a great deal from others and change its inherent culture, including how we view careers, success, and the value of apprenticeships for young people.

VIRGINIA ROUNDS: YOUR VIEW OF APPRENTICESHIPS IS ABOUT TO DRAMATICALLY CHANGE

Speaking of apprenticeships, meet Virginia Rounds from the German American Chamber of Commerce (GACC). She points out how multi-generational families have succeeded in manufacturing, as well as the advantage of apprenticeships in the German culture.

> **Virginia Rounds's thoughts:**
>
> At GACC Midwest, the Apprenticeship Networks team manages and advises on apprenticeship programs throughout our territory. We work with other German American Chambers of Commerce across the U.S. to do it in other regions as well.
>
> According to the definition of the U.S. Department of Labor (DOL), an apprenticeship has five aspects. One, the apprentice is an employee, and that's the primary relationship. Second, they receive structured on-the-job training. They also have related technical instruction, which is in a classroom, or in some cases, a book or online training that covers the theory part of it that is connected and coordinated with that the on-the-job learning. The apprentice's wages increase as skills increase. The apprentice earns a recognized industry credential at the end. That's the definition of 'apprenticeship.'
>
> On a side note, some people are calling things 'apprenticeships' that aren't. I saw a company that was taking college grads, then giving them a job and calling that an apprenticeship. That's just an entry-level job. An

internship, on the other hand, is related to (and hopefully coordinated with) what that intern is studying at school but has no specific credential coming out of the internship.

The German apprenticeship model covers all of those things that I just described from the DOL definition of apprenticeship. We typically talk about three aspects of the German-style apprenticeships that are a little bit different. One is that the training content is defined for a particular profession. There's a consortium of industry and education experts that get together and decide what skills and knowledge are needed for this profession generally. All apprentices receive training on these, regardless of location or employer: somebody in the south of Germany is learning the same topics as somebody in the north of Germany for that apprenticeship. This means that an apprentice has a credential that's incredibly portable. They can go to really any employer, and the employer will know they have learned x, y, and z.

The second aspect that creates portability is that all German apprenticeships have comprehensive exams at the end that cover the major topics that the apprentice was expected to learn. The apprentice can then prove that they earned it, and potential employers have an objective measure to be sure that the apprentice has learned the skills.

In the U.S., employers are more free to pick and choose the content of most apprenticeships. It is flexible for the employer, but it is really much less transparent when that apprentice wants to take that credential someplace else. A new employer often doesn't know for sure what the apprentice actually learned.

The final difference in Germany is that the person who is the trainer, the mentor of the apprentice, is expected to have their own credential. They need to learn how to teach. Teaching isn't something that you can just automatically do because you're a subject matter expert. Germany has training courses to teach these mentors how to better pass on their knowledge. And, as we all remember from our own school days, having a good teacher can make an incredible difference.

All three of those aspects are things that we have brought to our apprenticeship programs here in the United States.

Our apprentices that study to be, say, mechatronics technicians, all learn at least the minimum core competencies, whether they're in Florida, Ohio, Michigan, or Illinois. Some employers and some colleges teach more, and that's fine! They all take an exam at the end, and it's all the same exam each year, regardless of their location. Again, we do that so that the employers can measure those skills.

In terms of the trainer qualification, we have also implemented a 'train the trainer' course, which has been adapted from the international model from Germany. This really gives those tools to those trainers, to those mentors, so they can more effectively pass on their knowledge.

*We're really excited to see
the growing interest in apprenticeships.
This is not a new concept here in the U.S.—we
have had apprenticeships in the U.S. as long as
the U.S. has been here—but it had lost a lot of
momentum in previous decades.*

There are a couple of reasons for that. I'm going to really focus my remarks on apprenticeships for manufacturing because that's the primary area in which we are helping companies with their apprenticeship programs.

A couple of things happened in manufacturing in the '70s and '80s, and one was offshoring (manufacturing moving to other countries). We lost manufacturing jobs, and we had an oversupply of skilled technicians that were looking for jobs, so employers were in the lucky position to be able to scoop up skilled technicians just off the market. Because they had plenty of people, they were also able to do loose ad hoc training. There was plenty of time to identify potential, and for the new person to learn from the more skilled person. You didn't have the need for fully structured apprenticeships.

At the same time, manufacturing was seen as a less attractive career once people saw the layoffs. Our entire education system started talking about the importance of going to four-year colleges, treating it like a panacea for whatever job problems they had. 'Everything will be fine if you just go to a four-year college. You'll earn so much more.'

Now we are starting to see changes in this attitude. People are starting to realize that so few people who start four-year college actually finish it. A small percentage of people who do finish four-year college get a job in their field. The cost has also skyrocketed so much that the levels of debt that people are getting into for this supposedly magical college degree are just incredible. It's a heavy burden on them for decades, as opposed to being a lever to become more successful. It's just not right for everyone.

Community colleges, with or without an accompanying apprenticeship, are increasingly presented as an alternative to a four-year college, and we definitely support that.

Not all apprenticeships include community college coursework for their classroom training, but the ones that we work with do. We have set that as a requirement for all of our programs because we do want apprentices to have a transferable academic credential so that they can have more choices.

We are still working on making people realize that apprenticeships and modern manufacturing careers can be truly great opportunities. Manufacturing careers aren't about pressing a button or pulling a lever all day: pretty much any easy task like this has already been automated. Today the machinery costs millions of dollars and is controlled by high-tech control systems, and so manufacturers need people knowledgeable enough to step in when things are too hard for computers to do.

At the same time, manufacturing is facing a so-called 'silver tsunami' where the skilled technicians are retiring or will be soon.

When I talk to manufacturers, I usually ask: Is your big retirement wave coming in five or ten years? Before the pandemic, more of them were saying five, and now some are saying it's already hit.

Manufacturers can't find these people on the open market anymore and cannot continue 'poaching' them from the company across the street, because the company across the street is not going to have them either. We see that employers are really starting to think, *Our method for getting the skilled technicians that we've been using for the past 30 years is no longer working. We have to do something different.* With apprenticeships, they're able to train up their own sustainable pipeline of skilled talent, skilled talent that is incredibly valuable and valued.

We are trying to change the dialogue on manufacturing as a career with potential, as well as the acceptance of any non-desk career. There's the assumption among certain circles, including the one I grew up in, that everyone goes to a four-year college, and if people don't go, it is because they aren't smart enough to go. For other groups, a four-year college has been aspirational, and they've spent 25 or more years hearing that college is the one key to success. It's just such a shame because there is so much more out there for great careers with upward mobility beyond sitting at a desk.

What's been exciting is that we have been able to win over teachers and counselors at high schools, as they are just such important influencers. Another thing about teachers and counselors is that they all went to four-year colleges. They all have a successful career having gone to a four-year college. It's completely understandable that they would see that as a great path. It's really been great to see them visit the companies that we work with and to see the success that our apprentices have. We give them concrete examples from their own network of people that they know with an apprenticeship or see how successful they can be with an apprenticeship.

We do talk to so many people who tell us things like, 'Oh my gosh, I wish I would have known about this. This is such a great deal. This is such a great opportunity. This would have been perfect for my older child who never likes to sit at a desk.'

Look at what it means in terms of earning. You finish your four-year degree, and how much of that money goes towards student loan payments? Look at what that can mean if you are A) earning more, which you can when you come out of an apprenticeship, and B) don't have that debt. Suddenly, this $300-a-month student loan payment is just gone. There's $2 billion in student loan debt, which is a number people can't even conceptualize. When it comes right down to it, I'm paying this much in rent. I paid this much for my car. I can either spend that $300 a month on my student loan debt, or I can spend it on something for myself.

On the other hand, we also have quite a few apprentices from families where four-year college was expected, but they and their parents were wise enough to recognize that there are many paths to success.

One group with a lot more potential is women. This is true for manufacturing in general, in which women are underrepresented. Interestingly, our women apprentices tend to have above-average success in their fields. One young woman pointed out to me that her social skills were a strong advantage; she became friendly with so many machine operators, and they called her over more quickly when things went wrong, so she was able to fix things faster. There's a long way to go still, but we're starting to see apprenticeships attracting promising women to these careers.

There needs to be better connection and communication about the potential for apprenticeships—and manufacturing careers in general—between the manufacturer side and the parent/guidance counselor/student side. I wish parents and guidance counselors knew more about the types of things that go on in manufacturing and what that can mean. I wish manufacturers would open up more.

The professionals that some of our apprentices are training to become are doing things like programming control systems. They're troubleshooting complex systems with 20 different moving parts or 10 machines talking to each other. They might be designing and building a special tool to help another team save hours of time. High-tech manufacturing may be making anything: breakfast cereal, medical devices, motors, or toothpaste tubes. All of these industrial systems are incredibly complex, and all of them need to be maintained and repaired.

We need to have more communication, more visits, more field trips, more career days, more examples of what manufacturing is, so people can be aware of those possibilities. I want every day to be a manufacturing day. Every day HAS to be manufacturing day!

$40K/YEAR WITH STUDENT LOANS

- Monthly Net Pay (after taxes): **$2,616**
- Cell Phone (w/ Unlimited Data T-Mobile): $70
- Rent for Studio: $1,000
- Internet (Comcast): $30
- Car Payment: $350
- Car Insurance: $100
- Gas for Car: $100
- Student Loan Payment: $350
- Health Insurance: $120
- Food: $200
- Leftover at end of month: **$296**

$45K/YEAR AVG AFTER ICATT

- Monthly Net Pay (after taxes): **$2,930**
- Cell Phone (w/ Unlimited Data T-Mobile): $70
- Rent for Studio: $1,000
- Internet (Comcast): $30
- Car Payment: $350
- Car Insurance: $100
- Gas for Car: $100
- ~~Student Loan Payment: $350~~
- Health Insurance: $120
- Food: $200
- Leftover at end of month: **$960**

ICATT APPRENTICESHIP PROGRAM

RAND HAAS: MANUFACTURING INTERNSHIPS ARE MAKING A DIFFERENCE

Next up, meet Rand Haas. He'll talk to you about his Manufacturing Careers Internship Program (MCIP) program. In Rand's first internship group, I took two of the ten and hired both full-time. One still remains with Iverson & Company. The internship program is vital in bringing along young people towards manufacturing careers, and in some ways, can be combined with an apprenticeship program that I call an "ApprInternship." Rand's program is by far one of the best that I've seen.

Rand Haas's thoughts:

The Manufacturing Careers Internship Program (MCIP), developed by Business and Career Services (BCS) in 2011, has been recognized as one of the most effective and innovative workforce development programs in the United States. It received the innovation award from the State of Illinois as one of the most innovative workforce programs in the state, with more than 70 percent of the participants who completed the program now successfully employed. It also has been cited by the Brookings Institute and the Aspen Institute out of Washington, DC, as a 'best practice' workforce development program.

Designed to address the critical need for younger workers in the manufacturing sector, the MCIP has three major goals:

Help employers identify, vet, and hire motivated, out-of-school youths ages 18–24.
Help young adults learn about manufacturing careers and start a successful career path.
Change the perception of manufacturing and promote it as a highly desirable career.

The MCIP is funded through the Illinois Department of Commerce and Economic Opportunity (DCEO), by a federal WIOA grant from the US Department of Labor. It starts with a Career Exploration Camp that leads directly to an internship. BCS serves as the employer of record during the internship and covers wages and liability and worker's comp insurance. Participating employers interview and select interns prior to the internship and can hire them at no charge upon completion.

The Career Exploration Camp is one of the reasons for the success of this program. One issue that was identified early in the program's development was that many young adults entering the program had no clear career goals and lacked training and skills to start a career in manufacturing. We found many young adults finished their high school with no clear career direction or didn't know what was expected of them in their workplace. Before the internships, BCS brings all the participants together in a classroom setting on work readiness training during the Career Exploration Camp, which includes:

- Tours of local area manufacturers to learn about careers and skills required.
- The opportunity to earn 10-hour OSHA and forklift driving safety certifications.
- Emphasis on work-readiness, including attendance, accountability, and problem-solving.
- Emphasis on learning shop, math, and communication skills.
- Résumé preparation and interviewing skills.

There was a group out of Denver, Colorado, that did a study of over 1,500 companies. They asked the HR departments, 'What are the soft skills you look for when you hire and promote?'

The seven attributes they found to be almost universally desired by HR departments are: Attitude, Attendance, Ambition, Accountability, Acceptance, Appreciation, and Appearance. In addition, the eighth A is 'Ask.' Those eight As have become the basis of our boot camp.

These soft skills are covered in-depth during the work-readiness camp. The same soft skills are reinforced when we go out and visit several different manufacturing companies in the area. During the tours, the participants will ask the owner or the general manager, 'What do you look for when you hire or when you promote?' or 'Is attendance important? Is attitude important?' These young adults hear the same message repeatedly from different sources during the boot camp. At the end of the training, we see a changed attitude and improved attendance.

The program can also provide a forklift driving certification and a 10-hour OSHA (safety) certification. The importance of these certifications is to make them safer, as well as give them a nominal skill in forklift driving. It also helps their self-esteem. Many young adults don't have these certifications when they're just out of school and looking for a job. This gives the interns an edge to start a career path.

The young adults are quick to realize the value of a strong work ethic and industry certifications. It helps build self-confidence that they can achieve something. Other parts of the program include shop math, conflict resolution, financial literacy, and business communication skills.

At the end of boot camp, candidates interview with participating employers. We call it Internship Selection Day. The purpose of this is to help the interns learn how to do a job interview prior to the internship selection day; we do mock interviews. We videotape them. We help write their résumé and prepare them for the all-important question, 'Tell me about yourself…' After intensive preparation, the employers come in and interview all the interns.

The intern selection process is similar to a job fair. It's a private job fair for just the employers and the interns in the program. Every intern has about 15 minutes with each employer. At the end of selection day, each employer writes down their top three or four interns that they would consider hiring. The interns write down their top three or four employers. This creates buy-in. After the interviews, the staff sits down and places interns at the location that best suits them.

What are the results?
- More than 300 companies have participated.
- Over 900 interns have completed the program.
- More than 75 percent of the interns completing the MCIP are now employed or pursuing post-secondary education and training.
- More than 85 percent of those hired after the internship have stayed with the company six months or more.

Employers play a huge role in the success of the MCIP. BCS has been doing this since 2011, and we are constantly surprised at the commitment manufacturers make to the success of the MCIP. It's amazing. Their goal is to design and/or build quality products for their customers. And yet, they also willingly accept the role of a corporate citizen. Even if the internship may not work out the first time, the manufacturers are willing to try it again.

The good news is that the perception of manufacturing is changing. Some high schools in the Chicagoland area are offering manufacturing classes as part of their Advanced Placement curriculum. Enrollment in these classes is up. It just takes time. Internship programs like the MCIP help turn potential into reality.

TITAN GILROY: TITAN TV, TITAN MANUFACTURING, AND THE ACADEMY

I have been fascinated by a significant new force in manufacturing: Titan Gilroy. He is bridging the gap between television and technical education in innovative ways. You will love his show! You can see from his remarks that there are many paths to success for your children.

Titan Gilroy's thoughts:

My name is Titan Gilroy, and I am an American manufacturer. I started this company in 2005, after 10 years of working for different shops. I entered the industry without even knowing what a machine shop was. I started by working on parts for Siemens and NASA in a prototype custom-shop atmosphere in the Bay Area. I've always loved making things. Ever since I was a kid, I've been very creative. I didn't have money, so I built my own toys, I built my own surfboards in Hawaii, and I painted the beauty I saw around me.

I took to manufacturing naturally. It's a cool story. I owned a machine shop at 35 years old. Around the same time, I met with my grandmother for the first time. She showed me a picture of my grandfather, who had been a machine shop foreman at Boeing (I had no idea.) Later, I met my other grandfather for the first time—and he had been a machinist for Chrysler! I walked into the trade for nine bucks an hour and never knew the heritage of great machinists in my family before me.

I grew up in Hawaii fighting and being the only white kid in my neighborhood. I went from scrapping on the streets and getting in hundreds of fights because I didn't back down when people picked on me, to being one of the top fighters in the U.S. and fighting for Top Rank Boxing. Fast forward… and when the path toward a future in boxing ended, I took all of my aggression and my competitive nature and devoted myself to the CNC machines that I was working on.

Other people would sit there and push a button. I was more curious. *How fast can this thing go? How can we make the surface finishes better? How can we run more parts and compete?*

If you solve problems for the right people and make them money, you can be incredibly successful. It's about striving for perfection. You have to be proud of the quality that you are producing and blow people's minds and expectations out of the water. I want my customers to *love* the parts I make for them. I get comments all the time that the parts look like jewelry! That's what it's all about: having pride in your workmanship.

After solving huge problems in the industry and making a name for myself and the company, the global recession in 2008 took it all away. I almost lost the shop.

Every day for a year, I sat on the edge of a massive local bridge, taking in the vastness of God's beauty and praying for the company to be saved. Ultimately, the shop was able to continue, but something was different. My perspective changed, and, after seeing 50,000 shops close, I had a fire in my heart for the industry like never before. That's when I knew I had to do something and developed the idea for a TV show (TITANS of CNC), which would be the only national television show featuring CNC machining. I wanted to inspire people with the possibilities that manufacturing has to offer. I wanted to tell the stories of great companies and open the doors to an industry that no one knows anything about. I needed a way to start closing the 'awareness gap' for this great industry. It still plays on MAVTV and is continually growing and bringing new people into our sphere of influence. Even with the TV show, I knew that more had to be done, and I dedicated myself to CNC education. In the third season of the TV show, the State of California asked me to develop a CNC program inside of San Quentin Prison. We documented the entire process by bringing cameras in where they had never been allowed to go before. This led me to develop an advanced curriculum for CNC machining and create true change in the industry that has been desperately needed for decades. My focus has been education ever since. I haven't lost faith in the industry, but I've learned to harness my attention and focus it on creating things that truly matter.

After the third season of the TV show, I fully dedicated myself to creating a comprehensive curriculum for

CAD, CAM, and CNC. This revolutionary platform is called 'The TITANS of CNC: Academy.' It is the most advanced CNC curriculum ever developed. The bottom line is this: There is a real problem in this trade right now. Everyone wants to talk about the 'skills gap,' but in reality... we are dealing with one of the greatest 'awareness gaps' ever seen. And even when awareness is achieved, there is no advanced curriculum to support the training that students need. Currently, students simply aren't learning enough. They aren't learning through repetition. They only make a couple of parts as individuals and spend most of their time working in teams, which is not how the industry operates. I've looked at the problem, and they are simply not making enough parts to be successful. Not only that, they're not running the types of parts that matter to the industry that will hire them.

Teachers and instructors are not sufficiently resourced, so even the 'advanced' classes are simply not even close to being truly advanced. They're still pushing the basic philosophies that were taught 20-30 years ago. That's why I put out so many videos and so much content because instead of just talking about it, we're doing it.

Why is our curriculum different? We make what was once complicated easy. We embrace technology and teach how to use it efficiently. Our tutorials take you from the first step of designing a part on the computer, to holding the same finished part in your hand. We've standardized materials and standardized tooling, and we do things in a way that progresses students rapidly. They learn through repetition. Everyone is picking it up. We have 6-year-old kids, 13-year-old kids, 40-year-old machinists, people of all ages entering or shifting positions within the trade. We have 160,000 students all over the world, in 170 countries, and over 2,500 schools. Even established shops are picking it up and advancing their capabilities and efficiency, making payroll easier, giving raises, hiring, and buying machines. It's all changing, but one of the reasons it's all changing is because I buckled down and started working and doing what I knew needed to be done.

One thing that I realized was, *Wait, there's no 'national curriculum.'* There are people trying to make money off of this type of training, and that is actually a big problem. Everybody 'talks the talk,' but who sees through all the platitudes and empty promises? If you're a principal or a dean of a school and you want to have a super elite CNC education program, what do you do? The truth is, you have to go find somebody who's great at manufacturing and is willing to teach for the money that you're willing to pay. Nobody is teaching the teachers. Nobody is saying, 'Hey, you're doing it wrong.' Everybody's too scared to say what needs to be said, but that fear is pushing us further and further behind on the global manufacturing stage, and we can't allow it any longer.

I did not build this platform out of selfish necessity. If I simply wanted to make money, I could have stayed at a shop producing parts for the largest aerospace companies in the world. I'm doing what I'm doing because I'm sick and tired of seeing what has happened to our country and what is currently happening to our kids. We're not competing. We're not teaching our kids to compete. I've been to all these schools. I haven't seen a single one where I thought, *Man, this is awesome!* and that is a tragedy. These are beautiful machines, but the educational programs are horrible.

Going to college is awesome, but not everybody has the same opportunity. There are people like myself who never had the resources, the time, or the opportunity. There are so many people like me who are creative and love to work with their hands. Manufacturing opens doors for those people: 'If I can figure out and solve some of these problems, I can actually make good money.'

Our curriculum is free, and it's the most advanced. We have millions of followers on our social media platforms hungry for the educational and entertaining content we put out.

The Academy has become the glue for in-house training. Machine shops have created schools within their facilities using our free education system. They meet in their spare time: on a Monday night, on a Friday evening, or on a Saturday morning. They teach the trade to the people in their company and community, as 90 percent of them open their doors to the public. You can learn this trade using our curriculum and it's an absolutely *free* education! These shops then turn around and hire the very people they've trained when they need to expand their teams. They're learning in weeks what previously would've taken years in a school environment.

We continue to develop new curriculum for aspects of manufacturing in addition to CNC machining. We've launched the Aerospace Academy, focused on high-end difficult parts with real-world applications in rockets, engines, and flight components. We have launched the Grinding Academy, which intimately teaches the art of high-precision CNC grinding to reach tolerances measured in microns. We have curriculum for additive production, 3D metal printing using extrusion and powder bed machines... We are showing the world of wire and sinker EDM. Our passion for teaching all aspects of manufacturing isn't slowing down, and, in fact, we're mashing the gas pedal to the floor because this country *needs* it.

We've even launched a new social site dedicated to manufacturing called CNC Expert. This is another revolutionary platform that allows individuals to achieve actual certification for each part they've designed, programmed, and CNC machined from our Academy series. It also gives users a visual home on the web to showcase their certifications, personal projects, pictures, info, and videos of work they've done. It allows users to connect with each other to solve problems, review job opportunities, and is effectively turning a disconnected global manufacturing community into a tight global manufacturing family.

Everybody else out there is stuck for months or even years trying to prepare students to be effective in their jobs. I'm saying this is actually pretty damn easy. I understand that it may be complicated to some people, but I'm not going to say that to your face. I've taken what was once difficult and simplified it. I leave you a little trail of crumbs. Follow the crumbs. Don't think about it... just repeat... and you're going to have success.

Everybody told me I couldn't have a shop, that American manufacturing was dead. But I'm different. I didn't learn from textbooks; I learned by doing and through putting in the work. Do I have a different way of doing things? Sure. Was it hard? Yeah, but look, now I'm talking to you. We've had a national TV show. We've made crazy aerospace parts for the world's top rocket companies. But I look out into the world, and I see the current state of education...

As a leader in manufacturing, I'm bewildered at the fact that nobody's ever fixed it or solved it. They keep going down this road, like sheep to the slaughter. Man! Nobody's changing. I'm like, *What the heck is going on?* I have dedicated myself to education to make a difference. If you want to step into this trade and do something big, then surround yourself with talented people and put in the work. It is up to you to make it happen!

To learn more about TITANS of CNC, head to www.titansofcnc.com.

MAYBE A PICTURE IS WORTH A THOUSAND WORDS!

It is time to make manufacturing and the other "skilled trades" cool!

During the pandemic, following the example of individuals like Titan Gilroy, I decided to produce video content to explain some basic manufacturing concepts to those wanting to know more. This could be an industry member who wants to use videos for potential employees or for their existing workforce not directly involved in making things, like an accountant, receptionist, shipping and receiving clerk, or anyone who needs to know more about manufacturing in general.

Check out this video explaining some basic manufacturing concepts. It's a great video for you to watch *with* your child. Educators can also use these videos to introduce or augment manufacturing programs to new or existing students. These contain great content for all to see! The name is CNC Rocks Virtual Manufacturing Camp.

As parents, we don't want young people to lose sight of following their passion. What they love to do is MOST important. If they enjoy making things, designing things, and working with their hands, then they are naturals for the manufacturing world. Many manufacturing companies pay their employees to go to school to further their education. This alone should be an intriguing concept to parents.

Manufacturing companies have gotten very good at mentoring young people. Many of them are 50+ years old and have a genuine concern for who is going to learn what they already know. They want to pass on their skill sets, talents, and knowledge to the next generation. There is an alarming shortage in manufacturing and other related fields.

All this to say: Your son or daughter has a great opportunity to enter a stable, interesting, long-lasting career. One compelling reason why?

Technology, as you'll see in the next chapter.

4

TECHNOLOGY DRIVES MANUFACTURING

"...and then I saw the CNC machines, and then I saw them running, and I was like,
they take this raw piece of aluminum. You put it into this machine, it cuts it down, it takes away from it. But now it's worth 10 to 1,000 times more expensive than what you just bought it for. *It blew my mind."*

—Andrew Crowe,
Founder of the New American Manufacturing Renaissance

Technology has changed our lives forever. The younger generations are practically born with cell phones in their hands. Watch how intuitively a toddler knows to swipe a screen left or right. iPads are yesterday's television sets with *Sesame Street* episodes or *Tom & Jerry* cartoons (does Tom *ever* outsmart Jerry?). Digital natives need a parallel to the manufacturing arena.

When I entered the manufacturing world in 1980, computerization was just beginning. Heck, when I entered college in 1977, computers were just being introduced to the student population. I remember taking a Fortran class at Florida State University (FSU) that at least led me down the path of what would be known, decades later, as "coding."

Today, manufacturing is entering the Fourth Industrial Revolution (or Industry 4.0). The digital transformation is modernizing manufacturing with things like robotics, programming, data analysis, cloud computing, edge computing, and sensor technology.

I even find myself programming a computerized lathe for customers who have never truly entered the technologically savvy age of manufacturing. It is very gratifying to see their world open up with increased efficiencies and productivity. Parents today find themselves embracing smartphones and apps. Children and grandchildren find themselves reverse-mentoring their parents and grandparents with how technology can work for them.

So, let's drift back to earlier comments about young toddlers learning to swipe a smartphone to see photos. That circumstance then leads to surfing the web and Facebook posts and immersion into social media mania. Why then are the careers that feature computerized, highly technological CNC-controlled devices and automation in manufacturing so foreign to people?

It is not that your child is making a conscious decision *not* to pursue these careers. Instead, both you and your child simply do not know what you both do not know!

The responsibility lies on us—the manufacturers, parents, teachers, and guidance counselors to ready them for their future. That means showing you the real story behind manufacturing.

MARK HIBNER OF PALATINE HIGH SCHOOL: THE MAGIC IS GOING TO HAPPEN

Mark Hibner is one of the best technology education teachers in Illinois. His insights highlight how technology is driving manufacturing.

> **Mark Hibner's thoughts:**
>
> I've been an educator for 20 years. In my fourth year of teaching, I was fortunate to be offered a leadership role as an Applied Technology Department Chair. The following year, I became the District Chair. It was a great opportunity to be in those leadership roles early in my career. A few years later, working with the Applied Technology Department Chairs, we successfully implemented the Project Lead the Way engineering pathway of study in all five high schools in our district. Soon after, I worked with educators, manufacturers, professional organizations, and the community college to implement the manufacturing pathway of study. It's hard to believe the Engineering and Manufacturing programs have been up and running for over 10 years.
>
> We've changed the face of what the Applied Technology Department looks like. We've introduced

new career pathways and advanced technology into the lab, which helped establish the persona and perception of what the Applied Technology Department is today.

I have a very diverse classroom. Several students come to class having a variety of home-life challenges. For instance, some students are being raised by single parents that work the night shift. As a result, those students are left at home taking care of their younger siblings. Other students work 40 hours or more to help support their families. These are a couple of obstacles students may face that challenge their social and emotional well-being.

In the past several years, I've heard a lot of debate on whether or not students should attend a four-year college. Manufacturers need highly trained and educated employees. Young adults need to be challenged with extending their learning so they can add value to a company. It's advantageous when manufacturing companies and the student work together to develop a plan on what education is best for both sides. Some companies provide in-house training, and others pay for students to complete an apprenticeship that leads to an associate degree. Other companies will pay for students to complete a bachelor's degree. In order to have the best workforce, some type of higher education and training must take place.

I think the mindset needs to be: *Here you are in high school. You gained this interest in manufacturing, so what is your next step? What are you going to do to pursue a career in manufacturing? Are you interested in going straight into the workforce, attending college, or enlisting in the military? If you are interested in the armed forces, are you aware the military has occupational jobs to become a machinist or a welder?*

Educators should take responsibility for informing students of the opportunities available post-graduation. Numerous approaches exist to obtaining higher education and training in manufacturing. One option is to find employment with a company that sends their employees for training at a professional organization, such as the Technology & Manufacturing Association. A second option is to apply for an apprenticeship with a company or a community college, such as Harper College. A third option is to pursue a bachelor's degree at colleges that focus on manufacturing, such as Illinois State University, Bradley University, and Northern Illinois University.

With numerous opportunities post-graduation, educators should be able to inform students of the path that is right for them. I feel it is the responsibility of the Applied Technology teacher to market, promote, and educate all stakeholders about the awesome opportunities that exist in taking Applied Technology classes. Marketing starts with selling a quality product and quality service to our students. It's just like a business. If you're not selling a quality product or service, you're not getting the business. On the flip side, when providing exciting and worthwhile education to students, they promote the classes. They recruit for you.

For parents, the Applied Technology teacher must promote all the benefits manufacturing companies are willing to offer their children. Parents need to be invited to attend events at manufacturing companies. They need to hear from industry professionals what it is like to have a rewarding career in manufacturing. They need to see how safe, clean, and advanced manufacturing environments are. They need to see the opportunity for advancement.

In addition, it's important to educate counselors, administrators, and other teachers about your course offerings. You have to invite them to walk through your labs, see the projects students make, and observe the skills they develop. Also, you need to inform them about the awesome career opportunities and all the benefits companies are willing to offer. I believe when you accomplish that level of communication, the magic is going to happen. Students will be provided with opportunities for growth in a rewarding career. Parents will trust their child pursuing a manufacturing career. Educators will support students going into manufacturing. Manufacturers will hire talented students. As a result, we will build a stronger workforce, community, and economy.

Our youngest son is a gamer. This is not a world I understand. My generation doesn't. So, let's talk about the gaming world.

A 2011 article claims that 91 percent of kids between 2 and 17 are playing video games. You would think that this is the solution staring at us in the face. Industry members should take advantage of this trend. One of the most difficult, most sought-after, and most competitive careers that young people seek is programming video games. Why not turn that into a job as a CNC programmer on a shop floor? This connection is not at all farfetched. It is just a matter of connecting the dots for this sector with a skill set that is aligned with their interests. The population of children who play video games is growing and has been boosted in large part by kids between the ages of two and five.

Here are some important facts to note about the video game industry[1]:

- The gaming industry is expected to reach $337 billion in revenue by 2027.
- There will be more than 3 billion video gamers around the world by 2023.
- The average gamer is 34 years old.
- 70 percent of gamers are age 18 or older.
- 60 percent of Americans play video games daily.
- 45 percent of US gamers are women.
- 70 percent of parents believe video games have a positive influence on their children's lives.

Here is information from another 2022 article by Victor Yaney about the interest many gamers have when they decide on careers[2]:

Are game developers in demand? All signs point to yes—but it shocked us to learn that jobs for game developers and game designers have shown a strong decline since 2014 with a 65% drop in the number of postings. However, searches for gaming jobs have remained relatively constant since 2014. Searches for 'game developer' have even grown by 50%, which shows there is interest from job seekers. Our team examined the job market outlook related to the overall gaming industry and found some interesting patterns to signal strong growth for jobs in gaming.

The next intriguing thought is the trend that the developer career set is very highly sought after, but the number of postings for openings is freefalling, dropping 65 percent while the interest is increasing by 50 percent. This is leading to an army of disappointed talented young adults with coding skills. This is where the manufacturing arena needs to step in and educate, inform, and inspire!

ANDREW CROWE: WHEN PARENTS DON'T SEE THE MANUFACTURING PATH

Sometimes parents don't understand the manufacturing path. Andrew Crowe shares this story about a student and his parents' perceptions about manufacturing:

Andrew Crowe's thoughts:
I had a potential student that emailed me about a video of mine that he saw online. In the email he was really excited to learn more about the trade and learn more about manufacturing because of what he saw me do and say in the video. I talked about how it could change your life. I told him about how they are high paying, with over 2.8 million careers open at the time. How you can literally take anything that you can think of in your mind, turn it into a solid model, telling a machine how to make that out of metal. Then the machine will do it for you. It just really blew his mind.

So we set up a tour. As we're going through the shop, he's looking at these CNC machines and seeing their capabilities and watching them run. I can just see the fireworks going off in his head. We were really creating a bond. He was a junior at the time. He stayed in touch via email and sent me machining videos. He asked all these questions. I was really fostering this relationship. I was fostering his mind, and trying to channel him into becoming a machinist, and then a programmer. Showing him the different career paths that he could take to eventually become an engineer and work for DOD—Department of Defense (his main goal). Eventually, he just stopped. There wasn't a slowdown. There was a complete stop.

I reached back to the kid. I said, 'Hey man, it's coming up on graduation your senior year. We've been working towards this thing. Are you still going to come? I haven't seen your application.'

He told me that he was considering it. He was really loving it. It was time to throw in for college scholarships.

 His mother told him it was not a good idea, because he'd be staring at a screen all day pressing buttons. So, I told him, 'You already stare at a screen all day pressing buttons. You might as well get paid for it!'

The future of manufacturing is going towards more CNC, robotics, and automated processes. This requires more programmers and more tech-savvy young people looking for good-paying careers. Let's dive into what these careers look like now that we have indicated the people who can fill them! Your child could be taking advantage of that need—and the increasingly fascinating careers and salaries that they offer.

AUTOMATION: JUMP ON BOARD BEFORE IT'S TOO LATE!

While we may have fewer people in the manufacturing workforce, we will have higher-paying jobs. Because we are competitive in global markets, our production in this country will expand and result in an increase in higher-paying, more skill-based jobs.

Robot installations worldwide totaled 3,020,000 in 2020, which doubled since 2014. Throughout the world, countries have embraced robotic automation to different levels. Those with an aging working population have done more so than others. In 2017, the United States had 14.5 percent of the population over the age of 65, while Japan conversely had 28 percent over 65. Both countries have been included in the "silver tsunami" metaphor, alluding to the tidal wave of pending retirements. This will explain, in part, Japan's notably higher ratio when compared to the U.S. in the following data set.[3]

The following scores represent the number of robot installations per 10,000 workers. Korea (932), Singapore (605), Japan (390), Germany (371), Sweden (289), Hong Kong (275), U.S. (255), and China (246). What is interesting about China's ranking is the extreme size of its workforce. Its rank is lower than one would think, but it still employs the largest number of robot installations in the world.[4]

Rick Romell from the *Milwaukee Journal Sentinel* writes:

After overseeing a huge survey of employers worldwide on the impact of automation, Manpower Group has a calming message for workers worried about the digitized future: Don't fear the robot. Among the employers polled, only 10 percent told Manpower Group that automation would prompt headcount reductions over the next two years, the Milwaukee-based staffing company said. Twice that share—20 percent—said they expect to add workers because of increased use of digital technology. Two-thirds of the employers, meanwhile, said automation would have no effect on their staffing levels over the next two years. The findings come from a survey conducted in October of 19,718 employers across 42 countries and 6 industry sectors. The results vary by country and occupational group. US employers were among the most optimistic, with 25 percent saying automation will increase their head count in the near term.[5]

One of the most noticeable technological gains has been the emergence and adoption of 3D printing. The introduction and adoption of 3D printing led to the term "additive manufacturing," rendering all other conventional manufacturing to be back-labeled as "subtractive manufacturing."

Many schools are now employing 3D printing in the classroom, which, looking back, could be the single most technological gain responsible for bringing young people into the manufacturing fold. Not only is 3D printing employed in industrial production and R&D rooms, but it has also gained momentum among hobbyists and tinkerers alike. Makerspaces are popping up with CAD classes through local libraries with waiting lists to attend their classes. This is a significant movement that will have a positive impact for decades to come.

With technology gains that are tangible, relevant, and approachable (like 3D printing), we will dive into the next subject in Chapter 5: money. Now that you have a reason to be enamored with manufacturing, we will explore the financial justification of an alternative educational path into manufacturing employment.

The return on education (ROE) for college is not justifiable. Many of our youth are focusing on majors designed for careers that are saturated with graduates in the marketplace. Meanwhile, the manufacturing sector has a tremendous void with way too many openings and way too few applicants.

But you are already winning. Just knowing manufacturing is an option for your children puts you miles ahead.

ROE—YOUR CHILD'S RETURN ON EDUCATION

*"Right now, no one is really accountable
for student outcomes.
It's graduation rates."*

—Vince Bertram,
Former President, Project Lead the Way

How am I (or my child) going to afford college? This is the question, right?

Let's say you have three children. Each one is different. One may be among the 13 percent who have a passion, go to college, and then practice in that field. Fine. But what if the other children aren't? Then you have to ask: What can you do with $10,000? It could be a down payment on a house or a payment to a vocational school, or an investment in their small business. It could augment their lives because they've chosen a life path or profession with a salary that does not allow for any extras.

If you burn through thousands of dollars in cash and the child gets what they want, that's fine. If it means that much to you, then great. But if it doesn't serve them? What if this investment is *not* appreciated? What if one side thinks it is good for them, and the other side doesn't? There is often a disconnect between the parent and the child on what is best for their child's career or the educational path to get to it. This book is designed to get the conversation going early on about what is possible and appropriate for the young person based on his or her talents, desires and dreams, and passion.

Tethering your child for three, five, even twelve years because they didn't have the head start they deserved, or they were held back by financial burdens, is not the best way to go. In the end, you will have to look in the mirror and admit you were part of that.

Many people who can't afford to finance college feel emotional pain when money is actually the issue.

The real success factor, though, doesn't require money. It requires engagement. Engage with your child to find the best path. Engaging is free. Start with the conversation starters in the middle of this book. Engage with business leaders like myself who offer opportunities for youth. Let's chat about the mom who came up to me after one of my talks. Let's call her Betty. With tears streaming down her face, Betty told me she had thought there was no future for her son, but after my talk she knew her son could be successful even though he wasn't going to a four-year college.

Betty was over the moon. She discovered all was not lost. Betty suddenly saw a way through—and it wasn't a last resort. It was a great opportunity for her son and his future.

In business, we look at the return on investment (ROI). This is a basic concept. If I put $100 into an investment, I am looking to get more than $100 out of it. ROI is basic, simple, and practical. This should apply to education too!

Ask: What is my Return on Education (ROE)? ROE is about more than money. It is about your children's time and future. It aligns with what they have studied (most likely with your time and money) and what they will get back in terms of money, happiness, and satisfaction in their career.

In this chapter, I am not trying to convince anyone **not** to go to college. Rather, I will open your eyes to compelling facts about attending college and how to assess this really big decision. Key factors include:

- The job market
- The institution's educational model
- Our culture
- The affordability of college
- Lifelong opportunities
- The market demand for your child's career choice

MORE OPTIONS, MORE SUCCESS

How many young people can afford the college of their choice? How many parents have to take out a second mortgage on the house to pay for our child's post-secondary education? Can your child get accepted into the college of their choice? Can they adequately navigate the very competitive college acceptance process? Will they be taking out student loans that may put them in a hole they cannot get out of? Could this lead to them moving back in with you because of the economic burden that the student loans created? (Now I have your attention.)

There are many alternative educational paths that lead to very productive and financially rewarding careers.

Many technical and community colleges offer two-year degrees costing a fraction of four-year university degrees. As a result, students enter into the workforce making $50,000-$60,000 a year and have a very short payback on their educational costs.

The four-year degree student is wallowing in debt after having paid $160,000-$200,000 (or more) for their education. Your child will have a decade or more of trying to pay back these costs. They may also have a difficult time finding a job and differentiating themselves from others with the same degree. With unemployment now at around the 3.6 percent mark, and experienced individuals willing to work for less, there is a reverse competitive market for the employer.

The irony is that manufacturing companies have to bring in engineers from Europe, India, and other countries because of the lack of domestic skilled workers. Some manufacturers cannot expand their business due to the lack of talent.

There is a significant demand for talent and skill, not necessarily diplomas.

MORE OPTIONS, MORE OPPORTUNITIES

Author Charles Sykes challenges us all to rethink the typical education advice in his book *Fail U: The False Promise of Higher Education*. Here are highlights Sykes points out[1]:

The cost of a college degree has increased by 1,125 percent since 1978 (four times the rate of inflation).

Total student debt has surpassed $1.4 trillion.

Nearly two-thirds of all college students must borrow to study. The average student graduates with more than $30,000 in debt.

What, then, can we learn from these facts? Sykes describes a vision of higher education as "being one that is affordable, more productive, and better suited to meet the needs of a diverse range of students and that will actually be useful in their future careers and lives."

Sykes points to private education as the equivalent of buying a BMW every year and driving it off a cliff. He cites many private colleges like Duke University, Dartmouth College, Wesleyan University, Boston College, and Southern Methodist that command more than $60,000 a year.

In *Fail U,* Sykes also shares that student loan debts exceed both the nation's total credit card and auto loan debt. The delinquency rate on student loans is higher than the delinquency rate on credit cards, auto loans, and home mortgages.

A survey of 30,000 alumni by the Gallup-Purdue index found that only 38 percent of recent college graduates strongly agree that their degree was worth the cost. Only a third of graduates with student debt think their education was worth the price tag.

Their skepticism is understandable. A study by Rich Richard Vetter and Christopher Denhard found that there are more college graduates working in retail jobs than there are soldiers in the U.S. Army, and more janitors with bachelor's degrees than chemists. Only one-third of students entering four-year institutions earn a bachelor's degree in four years. Barely two-thirds of college students finish within six years.[2]

MY STORY ABOUT GOING TO COLLEGE

I witnessed the dubiously ineffective educational model first-hand. From 1977 to 1983, I attended five different universities. In each case, I decided that the educational model in my youth was ineffective. I found the current methodology and learning to be extremely boring at the time. I had trouble focusing in the classroom. The terrible lack of challenge and effectiveness was not consistent with my learning style.

One late night, while sitting in my thermal dynamics class at Marquette, I had an epiphany. Listening to the teacher drone on, I realized that Kathy and our two young children were at home alone again without me—why? Several times a week, I would arrive home after midnight. Why was I doing that to our family? At the time, I already had a full-time job. I had more engineering background and education than my job would ultimately require. I was selling machine tools. I was fascinated with making parts, not designing the machine tool itself. In retrospect, I would probably have been best served learning to program a CNC machine tool—but that technology was just emerging in the industry.

I realized that my young family was suffering from my absence more than the benefits (economic or otherwise) of furthering my education. I decided, in that instant, to go home and quit college. I also came to the realization that maybe I was more concerned with what people thought than about the impact education would have on my life. The only person whose opinion I cared about was Kathy's. She agreed it was up to me whether I finished school or not. That was my last college class.

CONSIDER THE NUMBERS: THEY DON'T LIE (SHOCKING REVELATIONS AHEAD)

Millions of young students come out of school with a mountain of debt from loans. The independent finance-advisory company Comet estimates $1.379 trillion in student debt. Just to explain the gravity of this number, let me share some of the statistics from Lifehealth.

That money is not only owed by young people fresh out of college but also by borrowers who have been out of school for a decade or more. The standard repayment timetable for federal loans is 10 years, but research suggests it actually takes four-year degree holders an average of 19.7 years to pay off their loans.

Here are the top statistics on the student loan debt landscape in 2018:

- Current U.S. student loan debt = est. $1.4 trillion
- 1 in 4 Americans have student loan debt, an estimated 44 million people
- Average student loan debt amount = $37,172
- Average student loan payment = $393/month

In the past decade, total U.S. student loan debt has surpassed credit card debt and auto loan debt. In the third quarter of 2017, Americans owed $810 billion on their credit cards and

$1.21 trillion in auto loans. Currently, U.S. student loan obligations are larger than both, trailing only mortgages in scope and impact. Student loan debt has ballooned in the past few decades, primarily because the costs associated with higher education—tuition, fees, housing, and books—have grown much faster than family incomes.

The College Board has tracked costs at public and private universities since 1971. When the organization first started monitoring prices, the average cost of one year at a public university was $1,410 ($8,450 in 2017 dollars). That was 15.6 percent of the median household income of $9,027 and manageable for many families without going into debt.

Fast forward to 2018, and the picture is very different. Today, the average cost of one year at a public university is $20,770, which is 35.2 percent of the median household income of $59,039. That could be why more than 70 percent of bachelor's degree recipients emerge from college today with substantial student loan debt and why many find themselves in need of loan consolidation and refinancing.[3]

There is a lesson here. Maybe we need to stop and think about the ROE on a college education: the time it takes, the costs, and how soon a young person can be in the working world making money rather than spending it on education. Starting out a career with a boulder of seemingly insurmountable financial responsibility on their shoulders is putting a huge strain on our child's futures. Couple the current debt with the new direction of companies like General Motors, who are rethinking college diploma requirements for their hiring practices, and there's a lot to think about.

THE #1 BEST-KEPT SECRET: HIGH SCHOOL MANUFACTURING PROGRAMS

In 2011, the SME Education Foundation, led by my friend and **CHAMPION Now!** Board member, Rodney Grover, developed the PRIME initiative, which stands for Partnership Response In Manufacturing Education.

The PRIME initiative engages manufacturing companies in the building of high school manufacturing technology programs in their own communities. PRIME provides a platform for manufacturers to charitably contribute to their own community while fostering their future workforce. The program, which is now in 26 states, gives high school students the opportunity to gain the skills to immediately find employment, provides financial support to the school for equipment and curriculum updates, and offers summer camp programming for middle school students in the district. In addition, the SME Education Foundation provides access to scholarship funds for graduating PRIME school students.

DR. LAZ LOPEZ: "BE RELEVANT"

Dr. Laz Lopez, previously the principal at Wheeling High School in Wheeling, Illinois, is another force making a difference for young people. He says high schools need to do a better job of meeting the needs of students and local employers. His vision at Wheeling High School has gained him respect from parents, administrators, and industry members alike. Wheeling High School was one of the very first PRIME High Schools, as designated by SME. Dr. Lopez currently serves as the Associate Superintendent of Township High School District 214.

Laz Lopez's thoughts:

As a school principal, my goal was to ensure that we are relevant. The value of a high school diploma is widely questioned. One of the strategies the high school leader can use is through the authentic and relevant experiences students can have that give the community insight into the school and into the value it's offering.

If you have an increased number of students being employed in the community as a result of the work that's happening in the high school—as well as those earning professional degrees or credentials in demand and returning to the community to work—that is a direct validation of the quality of the school.

A high school can serve as a lever for broader economic development. I think this is a unique perspective. As an engine for economic development, principals need to develop deep ties with employers and understand the business climate of their community. We did this at Wheeling High School. We found that our community had the third-largest concentration of manufacturers in the entire country.

There was nothing the school was doing to help meet the needs of that particular employer group, or that industry. In my meetings with employers, they stated, 'We have a shortage of qualified individuals applying for and even considering this as a well-paying career.' There seemed to be a mismatch between these local opportunities and the fact that many of our residents were living in poverty. The school could play a role in making the connection to local employment more directly.

The initial efforts were to respond to the immediate need. Keep in mind that, at that time, we were still in the midst of the Great Recession. A lot of people thought I was crazy for trying to create a manufacturing lab at a time when everyone was saying, 'We're supposed to be only about college-ready or college-bound students. Why are you going backward instead of forward?' Where I did get support was from the Economic Development Office in the Village of Wheeling. They have all of these manufacturers who they're trying to serve and support, and they understood if they could not deliver on a talent pipeline locally, they could consider relocating. Their encouragement and validation helped me move forward.

Our entire public education system, from a lens of accountability, focuses on trying to ensure that our schools are graduating students who are ready for college. This was a result of a loss in our belief that earning a high school diploma actually meant something.

A multitude of assessments were introduced, and the focus of the entire K-12 system narrowed for over a decade on testing and test scores. And while that is one valid measure, it is not the only measure of student potential for success. In that process, we got rid of everything and anything not directly contributing to test scores, and the central focus of school leaders has been on, *Can my kids score a certain number on a standardized test?* So, you're correct in the sense that the end goal is an assumption that if we can get all the students high enough test scores, all of them are going to college, and that is the right path.

However, as any parent knows, students are more than just a single test score given on a single day. 'Redefining Ready,' adopted by the National Superintendents Association, attempts to counter this assumption by redefining the way we should be holding schools accountable. Utilizing multiple measures, students can show readiness for both college and career.

We've structured the comprehensive high school academic program, and all coursework, around each of the 16 national career clusters along representative career pathways that encourages all students to engage in work-based learning experiences prior to graduation.

The apprenticeship program at District 214 was started to provide a high-quality work-based learning experience for students. The program provides opportunities in over a dozen occupations that allows students to have paid employment while gaining employment experience in their area of interest, as well as beginning to build a professional network for themselves.

One of these apprentice-able occupations is Construction and Building Systems, where students gain experience on both commercial and residential projects under a general contractor. Apprentices are involved in all aspects of architectural design to do hands-on work in the trades.

Another is Industrial Manufacturing Technician. Students are employed with local manufacturing employers while learning about workplace safety, set-up for production run, operating equipment according to the production schedule, and producing products that contribute to the business goals.

Whether it's the students who are tearing down the walls or operating equipment, each experience affirms their career choice. Is this what they want to do with their life? We should make sure that high school is the place where students are able to discover that future.

The application of manufacturing challenges students in math and science beyond the theoretical to real-world projects.

Wheeling High School was selected as one of 15 schools in the nation that prepared components for the International Space Station in partnership with NASA. The tolerance for manufacturing the parts was less than a human hair. There is no room for error when you're working with NASA. The application of skills, technical and interpersonal, to actually produce these brackets and handles with real-world consequences was incredible. That project, which will impact the students and teachers involved for a lifetime and provide education to them, is applicable to other teams and industries.

The process of developing a product is also replicated through our 'Robot Rumble.' Students begin with a hunk of metal. They design and build remote-controlled robots that are going to combat other student-built robots at a regional competition. The result is that bringing all these experiences to scale gives students a real opportunity to authentically discover their future.

THE COMMUNITY COLLEGE CAREER TRACK

In reading about Thomas Snyder and his career at Ivy Tech, an Indiana institute known for technical education excellence, I learned of his passion for the community college's alternative path to success for its students.

Over the decades working in the manufacturing sector, I have found that Snyder's comment about employers being willing to pay for night-class training for their employees to be spot-on. This is a win-win for both parties.

This is what Synder has to say about community college: "Nothing can hide the fact that community college is the smart higher education choice for an increasing number of students. Professional certificates and associate degrees have become the favorite gateways to many of today's and tomorrow's best jobs."[4]

Some of Snyder's commentary adds that going to community college in lieu of the first two years of a four-year university is a viable alternate path. He goes on to say that a degree from an elite college may not hold the same mystique and impact it once had, adding:

> **Thomas Snyder's thoughts:**
> Conversely, there is strong evidence that community college can accelerate your bachelor's degree attainment and/or quickly put you on a desirable career path. Not for the first time in the nation's history, the American dream stands in need of reinvention and renewal. The process of reinventing and renewing the American dream will be a complicated one with many elements, but there is no doubt the community colleges will remain at the center of the story over the years ahead.

SHEYENNE KREAMER: A VALEDICTORIAN CHOOSES MANUFACTURING

When I was in high school, I was often bored. (Keep in mind this was before computers.) Nonetheless, I was capable of AP coursework. There are young people that, despite their intellect, do not learn in the conventional manner. That was me.

Next up is a story of someone who also fits this same storyline. Sheyenne Kreamer was introduced to me by my friend Eileen Bild from OTEL Network, who handles the **CHAMPION Now!** ROKU Channel. Manufacturing is not just for those deemed unsuccessful in conventional careers. Manufacturing is for those who can find success in anything they choose.

> **Sheyenne Kreamer's thoughts:**
> I was valedictorian of my high school class. And as I was kind of struggling through the process of trying to determine what I wanted to do after high school, there were a lot of well-meaning people who I kept saying, 'Oh, you're going to be eligible for scholarships. You need to go on to college.' And I had a well-meaning parent who was sure that I needed to go to college and learn electrical engineering. That's where all the money was going to be. Somehow, that didn't feel right to me. It did not make me happy.
>
> *I was extremely happy the day that our high school brought in a recruiter from a major manufacturing company. She actually showed up with a video talking about career opportunities for women in manufacturing.*

They were trying to bring more women into manufacturing. They were trying to diversify the workforce. I watched that video, and I talked to the recruiter afterward. I just said, 'You know what? What a cool way to be able to get hands-on doing something where you're actually creating stuff.' It was a three-year apprenticeship program that would allow me to work in all these different departments, on the manufacturing floor, and in different office departments as well.

[Internships] just make so much sense because our young people are confused, especially today. I saw an article on LinkedIn recently that said that we are living in a generation of the most depressed young people that we've ever seen since people started recording this kind of information. Of course, a lot of it has to do with the pandemic we've all come through and all of that. If we're not spending a little bit more time earlier on in the high school years... Really, I mean, I swear, guidance counselors are pushed to the wall. I'm not blaming them for any of this whatsoever because some of the problem does exist with our trade organizations. If they're not coming out to the career fairs to shake hands with and explain about the opportunities that exist to these students, they're as much to blame as anybody.

The guidance counselors are getting measured by how many kids go to college. That is just a fact. There's not as much internal incentive to be exposing them to things like manufacturing. I think it's a crime because more kids would go there if they knew what the opportunity looks like.

I am a big advocate for alternative career paths. Pursuing those alternative career paths earlier can end up saving a lot of frustration later on. They say that 76 percent of all college students this year have thought about dropping out. That's just because they're all stressed out and anxious these days. So, it's like, Okay, so why do we think that the only lucrative career paths are by going directly into a four-year college?

For a young person who's struggling with all these things, I say, 'Oh my goodness, ask somebody in your school to try to find some tradespeople, whether it's in manufacturing, automotive, construction, whatever. Ask them to hook you up directly with some of these people, even if it's just a site visit where some of these people are working. You can actually see what they do and how they do it. That is one of the best ways that you can explore for yourself instead of just letting everybody else make the decisions for you.'

DO THE MATH TO FIND A $250,000 DIFFERENCE

This is a sample of two students. One goes to college for four to five years, taking out loans or using money other than a gift from mom and dad. The other goes to a two-year school for a fraction of the cost and goes out into the working world two to three years sooner, making good money!

What this shows is that, in year 12 (7 years after graduation), a person with a four-year degree is still $130,000 in debt. The two-year vocational student in year 12 has a surplus of $90,000. *This is almost a quarter-million-dollar difference between the two.* This assumes that only 20 percent of a person's wage can be used to pay back the principal, while the vocational graduate makes 25 percent less per year, which may not be the case at all.

4-5 year college degree				2 year vocational degree		
	Tuition/Income	cost/paycheck			Tuition/Income	cost/paycheck
Year 1	$(50,000.00)			Year 1	$(20,000.00)	
Year 2	$(50,000.00)			Year 2	$(20,000.00)	$(40,000.00)
Year 3	$(50,000.00)			Year 3	$50,000.00	$10,000.00
Year 4	$(50,000.00)			Year 4	$50,000.00	$10,000.00
Year 5	$(50,000.00)	$(250,000.00)		Year 5	$50,000.00	$10,000.00
Year 6	$75,000.00	$15,000.00		Year 6	$50,000.00	$10,000.00
Year 7	$75,000.00	$15,000.00		Year 7	$75,000.00	$15,000.00
Year 8	$75,000.00	$15,000.00		Year 8	$75,000.00	$15,000.00
Year 9	$75,000.00	$15,000.00		Year 9	$75,000.00	$15,000.00
Year 10	$100,000.00	$20,000.00		Year 10	$75,000.00	$15,000.00
Year 11	$100,000.00	$20,000.00		Year 11	$75,000.00	$15,000.00
Year 12	$100,000.00	$20,000.00		Year 12	$75,000.00	$15,000.00
	$(130,000.00) NET				**$90,000.00 NET**	

Assuming that only 20% of a person's wage can be used to pay back principal

If you include the financial model to take the $250,000 gift, deduct the $40,000 and instead invest the balance of $210,000 in a conservative investment, then the justification goes to an entirely different level. Now the two-year student has enough money to start his or her own business. At a rate of return of 5 percent re-invested, the two-year student would have $325,800.00 to fund a start-up, pay cash for a house, or re-invest in stocks. Add the $90,000 to that, and you are approaching a half-a-million-dollar nest egg for someone who is quite young and only went to a trade school for two years.

CHAMPION YOUR CHILD

Enough about the financial side of life. The fact is you and your child are the true champions. Your child is young and has their whole life ahead of them. In the next chapter, you'll discover ideas on how to "own" your awesome responsibility of helping them find their passion and creating a path toward achieving it. Help them find what makes them happy and support them in following that path. If they work hard enough, eventually they will make the money necessary to sustain a career. The financial rewards are the icing on the cake. Ultimately, their satisfaction and self-worth will carry them the distance through life.

In our next chapter, we will consider and contemplate the awesome responsibility of parenting. Our culture has introduced so many challenges for our children. We have to work hard at preparing them for success in life. Sometimes this means redefining our perspectives and perceptions. This book is meant to inspire conversations early.

Know your child's passions. Inspire their journey. Champion them. Research a potential match for your child in a broad range of possibilities, including manufacturing, construction, and other debt-free paths.

TEN WAYS TO OWN THE AWESOME RESPONSIBILITY OF INSPIRING YOUR CHILD TO FIND THEIR PASSION!

"Why did the eleventh one work?
Well, I learned from those 10.
I don't want to be known for 10 failed companies
but one good one.
But those 10 got me to the last one that worked."

—Craig Rabin, Founder, Airhook

O ur culture today often expects conformity, especially for young people, but you need to summon the courage and confidence to help your child make their way in the world. In fact, that's the point: Show them the world. If your daughter is good with numbers, one son is good with making things, and your other son is good at working outdoors, each one demands a different plan.

We should never be disappointed in our kids if they are true to themselves. But disappointment goes both ways. Maybe those who are disappointed in children who don't follow the path they want are, in the end, disappointed in themselves as parents.

The key is "seeing" your child.

Take a page from your own book: When you find something that excites you, it energizes you to excel. You know the money follows. Here are 10 ideas to help you, as a parent, guide your children toward a career that embraces their passions.

1. LEARN ABOUT YOUR CHILD

One of the people who inspired me is the same person who founded the Reshoring Initiative®. Harry Moser influenced many in the boardroom and C-suite offices to turn the spreadsheets inside out and consider the full cost of ownership when making decisions on where to make your goods.

Here's what Harry has to say about choosing a career and balancing this with their passion. From a parent's perspective, Harry's words resonate greatly!

> **Harry Moser's thoughts:**
> As a country, we need to give young people encouragement and permission to find their passion. Explore

how young people can do this effectively. Take a look at skills assessments, the high schools that are doing this well, why some guidance counselors are doing this well and some aren't. How do you know if you are a good fit for manufacturing? How about listing the traits manufacturers look for in people (respect, curiosity, hunger to learn, diligence, problem-solving, etc.) and the strengths one should sharpen (goal setting, listening, etc.)?

Both Harry's passion for informing students about manufacturing careers and his reshoring efforts were more inspiring than anyone else I had come to know. According to Harry, the future is all in your child's hands, but your input and support are paramount. He says: "Get a career that will pay for you and your family. Develop a passion for that career. Pursue your other passions using the time and money generated by your career. Work entitles you to what you earn and desire."

Dana Ward, inventor of PreHeels and founder and president of Barefoot Scientist, is another manufacturing leader who points out that it can be difficult to embrace all the characteristics that make a person unique. This is where learning about your child really comes into play. She says:

Dana Ward's thoughts:

I know that growing up, there was so much homogeny to fit in, be cool, etc., and I really tried hard to always be true to myself.

I think it's a good thing that individualism is much more celebrated today than it was when I was young (almost to a fault, actually, but let's focus on the good right now).

Think about it this way: If you're so used to trying to fit in—passively going along for the ride or even just pursuing the path that someone said you're supposed to take without thinking for yourself for a moment—you might be missing out on a class that's more interesting, an internship that's more inspiring, a project that's more lucrative, or a career that's more personalized to you.

And it's OK to not know what you want to study, or what you want to do for a living (hey, I'm still evolving!). Make sure that you actually take a few moments to think about it before you set off on some path because society tells you it's a good one. Think about your strengths and passions and consider future employment trends. Consider you. Be an individual. Think for yourself. And if you're trying to help someone else find their career path in this wacky world—whether a parent, counselor, writer, mentor, or friend—perhaps you see something in that person that they don't see themselves, so share it.

Remember that the re-education process from individuals and parents to mentors and teachers to society and media takes way too long and is on an extreme delay. Think for yourself. Do your own research. Find the best strategy for you.

Many young people get exposed to various subjects and concepts during their high school experience. Often, this informs their career and the things they really love to do.

RYAN POHL:
CHALLENGE YOUR PERCEPTIONS

In the late 2000s, I stumbled across Praeco Skills founder Ryan Pohl. His company focuses on training and development in the skilled trades. His website aims to change the perception of manufacturing. Aha! This was the exact same goal I had. This insightful leader, workforce advocate, and father talks about the skills shortage and the powerful influence parents have over the trajectory of their children's lives.

Ryan Pohl's thoughts:

One of the things we do is go onsite or via a webinar, and we teach apprenticeship-level classes primarily in advanced manufacturing. The main thing that we do is build customized systematic training programs for industry. A lot of companies struggle to add structure to their training programs and provide systematic and measurable, customized training programs to industries.

At the end of the day, we need individual business leaders in particular, parents, and business leaders to stay the course and see it through.

Challenge your own perceptions as a parent. Many of us, even in my generation, were hit with the very strong messaging that success only lies in college. That's just flat-out not true. We have to challenge our own perceptions. It's uncomfortable. I still see a lot of friends who've got kids that are about to go off to college, with no real direction. I ask them, 'For what?'

'To get a degree,' they say.

'In what?'

'Well, it doesn't matter, just some sort of degree so they can get a good job.'

Well, why are you going to go $70,000 in debt for something you don't even know you'll use? It just makes them uncomfortable to think about other alternatives.

So, I'd say challenge your own perceptions. Read and research, even if that means you've got to do things that are a little uncomfortable. Call some local shops and say, 'Hey, I've got an 18-year-old son or daughter. They're interested; I want to understand what you do. Do you have any opportunities? Do you guys give tours? Anything like that?'

Maybe go out of your comfort zone a little bit. If you know a shop owner somewhere, ask for a tour. Ask for more knowledge like you would for a college.

If a kid says, 'Hey, I'm thinking about going to this particular college,' what's the first thing they do? Well, let's go take a tour, right? Request a tour of a shop! Why not? Shops should do the same thing. If they know a kid, invite them for a tour. These models are there. We just need to apply them to what we already do.

Challenge your own perceptions of things and be willing to make yourself a little uncomfortable for the sake of your child.

2. WHAT DID YOUR CHILD
ALWAYS LOVE TO DO?

Craig Rabin is a modern-day inventor and entrepreneur who took a chance, followed his passion, and successfully brought a product to market called the Airhook. The Airhook is a product that you take on a plane with you, allowing you to hang your coat, mount your electronic device for viewing, or hold a drink—all while your tray is in the upright position.

Craig explained the origins of his unconventional path:

Craig Rabin's thoughts:
My guidance counselor had absolutely no clue what to tell me! For me, what has worked when there is an unknown is to ask for help. I remember thinking how hard it was to figure out what I wanted to be. I didn't fit that norm. I didn't need a guidance counselor telling me that, especially someone who didn't know what it was that I was talking about. It wasn't until I started asking people I looked up to how they got there and what advice they had for me [that things started to change].

I wasn't a super book-smart person. To be honest, my brother, who is five years older than me, is a frickin' genius. Coming up after him, there was a lot of pressure to be smart. That forced me to be street-smart, always coming up with different things to fill that void. I was in the library for hours.

It was hard for me to figure out what I wanted to be. All I knew was I liked the idea of owning a business in developing markets.

Craig was a techy geek early on. He is a very gentle soul and genuine to the core. During the early days of internet and web design, he was entrepreneurially driven, and I used to pay him hourly to do work on my company website. He would come over to the house, and the two of us would huddle around my laptop while Craig did HTML code. Eventually, Craig got hired at Microsoft and moved out to Washington. "Years went by. I was 30; I was single and experiencing a third-of-a-life crisis. I had a great corporate job at Microsoft. *Do I try my hand at being an entrepreneur?* I decided I wanted to take one more chance."

As a result, Craig was one of the first contestants on Steve Harvey's 2017 show "Funderdome." It had some similarities to "Shark Tank," which had already aired for eight years. Craig won the first round and the $20,000 prize, making him the very first winner on the show. I think part of what drove Craig to succeed is that he realized what he loved to do in his life.

I had this notebook of ideas for different products and concepts. My pivot in the road was 3D printing. I could get a machine in my house that could do the prototyping. So, I bought one, and for a year, taught myself how to use it. I thought of Airhook when I was sitting on an airplane and had no idea where to hang my sport coat. Inventing it was amazing. I had to relearn geometry.

As he commented later:

Craig Rabin's thoughts:
The only piece that didn't air on 'Funderdome' was the cancer ribbon that I wear. That was because we make

a donation on every Airhook in honor of my mother who passed away from cancer in 2016. We want to be that leader. Even the smallest brands and companies can help change the world. Cancer is something we all have to fight together. I want to continue to fight for other people. It's been a really rewarding part of this journey. Every sale represents one step closer to a cure for cancer. It boils down to that. It gives my team and me a push forward. Every day, we're accomplishing something for the greater good.

In my many conversations with young people, they are often quick to admit that they are not the smartest sibling in their family, much like Craig Rabin's story. These young people are bright and talented and, equally as important, they are dedicated, motivated, and driven.

Young people need to toss away inhibitions about what they consider to be their limitations. As parents, we need to help them focus on their strengths. Knowing your limitations and understanding how to compensate for them is important, but your confidence and persona going forward depends on you knowing who you are and what your passion is. This gives you the recipe for success.

3. CHALLENGE YOUR CHILD TO COMMIT TO THEIR DREAMS

Throughout most of my education, I was bored; I wasn't challenged. There was way too much theory. I always tried to enjoy everything I did, though: the social scene, athletics, and, for a while, academics.

Outside of school, I worked most of my junior and senior years. I played football and soccer and excelled in the latter as the leading scorer on the team. Most nights that I worked, I got home around 1:00 a.m. and had to be up at 6:30 a.m. for school. My AP Physics teacher (nicknamed Boo Boo) told me one day that I would be academically ineligible for Friday's soccer match, as I had scored a 50 on my test. (Needless to say, I had worked a lot that week before.) Now, he had my attention!

I would not and could not let my soccer teammates down. I asked my teacher when our next test was, and he said, "Thursday."

"What would I have to make on the test to be eligible?" I asked. I added, "Would you grade it that afternoon to see if I could play?"

He agreed and said I would have to make a 95 in order to play.

"OK, then. Deal."

Boo Boo was stunned at my confidence and matter-of-fact statement. "You really think you can do that?" he asked.

"I know I can. It's all about priorities. I will have to take some shifts off at work, but I *will* get the grade."

That Friday, Boo Boo gave me my test back—on the top of the test was the grade: 97. He shook his head in disbelief.

Friday's game, I started at center forward—disaster averted. Boo Boo challenged me. Even if he didn't understand his role, he made it real for me. He was awesome. He cared.

As for me, I was committed to my dream of playing soccer. It taught me that if I believed in what I was doing, I would somehow always come out on top. This also taught me the value of making sure not to disappoint my teammates, those who are depending on you.

(This concept will carry through your child's team at work in their career too.)

Thank you, Boo Boo.

LEIGH COGLIANESE MCCONNELL: THE MAGIC OF LOVING YOUR CAREER

I often get asked to speak to high school and college students. Twice I ended up on the same panel with Leigh Coglianese McConnell, manager of training and education for the Technology and Manufacturing Association (TMA). Here is a young woman who was a great student and who chose her career path, bypassing college. Like me, she also found it difficult to learn in the conventional class environment.

> **Leigh's Coglianese McConnell's thoughts:**
> I probably could've gotten a scholarship, but I just didn't want to go to school to figure it out. I kind of wanted to know first before heading into college. I entered the workforce, and I did a lot of random jobs: retail, worked in a locker room, I was a nanny, and I cleaned houses. I was really fortunate enough to have someone ask me if I'd ever considered manufacturing as a career. Prior to that, I really didn't know what I was doing in the world, or what my purpose here was.
>
> On the machining side, there are not as many females there. However, I do believe that's changing, especially to see the work I do with high school students and our precision machining competition. There are a lot of girls that are competing in there, and they're also placing. They're accepting their awards in dresses with long nails.

I just think that's super cool and super empowering. I think they end up empowering one another as well.

When I was in high school, I took a dual credit class 'Intro to Engineering.' I took it for one day because I was the only woman in the class and probably the only individual under the age of 30. My first day in class, the instructor picked on me the whole time and wanted me to know all the answers. I didn't know a single one.

Don't worry about the outside world and what they're telling you. There's nothing wrong with not going to college immediately after high school. There's no expiration date on when an individual can go to college, so put that completely out of your thought process.

[If I were a parent of a high school student,] I would strongly encourage them to enter the workforce and figure out what they want to do and what they enjoy prior to making a decision to go to school. Then, of course, after that, I would recommend they consider manufacturing. But don't be afraid to do what everybody else *isn't* doing. Don't feel like you have to fit inside a box because nobody does. Usually, the ones that are more successful are the ones that venture outside the box. The first thing I would recommend is to go on YouTube.

I hated school ever since first grade. I don't know what it was, but I never liked it. I always gave it my all, I was honor roll every semester. I just wasn't a fan of school. I think even if my mom and dad did save money, it wouldn't have been my first option. I didn't understand why my generation was pushed so hard into college. I was very fortunate to see other people. I kind of caught on to the fact that a lot of people were going to college, and they weren't necessarily getting the jobs that they had gone to get the degree for.

I've never once wondered what would have happened if I did go to college. Maybe that's just because I feel like I'm just as successful as my siblings who did go to college. I don't believe there would have been a difference in my life, except that I would not be happy as I am today.

I'm a huge science and math nerd, and I felt like every year, we learned the same thing in science: the structure of an animal cell and the structure of a plant cell.

We just kept learning the same material over and over again. I wouldn't say it was the way I was taught, but I just felt like there was so much out there that they weren't teaching us. Loving science and loving math, I honestly thought the only things I could do with those two was teach math or teach science. I was not aware of any other careers at that time of my life associated with the two.

There's a lot of people that probably should have gone into manufacturing and never considered it because they don't know what's out there. Nobody tells them about it. I tell everyone.

4. INSPIRE YOUR CHILD
TO CHOOSE OPTIMISM

You already met Dana Ward; however, you may not know she worked as a producer and interviewer of Hollywood stars on the red carpet as part of the founding team for Clevver Media. Just like some of the others I am writing about, she then crossed over to the manufacturing industry when she developed her dream product called PreHeels. From a young age, she noticed opportunities to improve things and little details that others didn't see, and thus, the idea of innovation was very important to Dana and her co-founder ahead of their PreHeels blister prevention spray product launch in 2016. Since then, her company evolved into a broader brand, Barefoot Scientist, and her premium products line the shelves of big box stores like Ulta Beauty, Costco, and Walmart. In 2022, Dana's company was acquired and joined the portfolio of leading beauty brand Japonesque for the next stage of company growth. Dana found the Greatest Champion within herself through manufacturing. One person with an idea made something that, along the way, became an incredible success story.

> **Dana Ward's thoughts:**
> "I'm looking forward to the next steps in our company journey, and certainly proud of the hard work we did to get there. To go from a single product company to a new, full collection brand was no simple feat," she says. "Continuing development on the original formulation plus R&D for new product innovations as we expanded to Barefoot Scientist felt like we were running two companies for a transitional period of time. For our initial product release, we chose to 'soft launch' via a popular

crowdfunding platform to validate interest, test the audience, garner reactions, get customer feedback, etc.—an important survey step in any entrepreneurial strategy in whatever format or platform you choose. If you listen, someone will tell you what they think. We went on to pass $3 million in sales our first year, and we've continued to optimize and innovate as we grow."

Dana's enthusiasm and "get it done" attitude were key to her success. "I'm a pretty optimistic person, and I think that's important—at least to me—in entrepreneurship. Sometimes it feels that if it can go wrong, it will go wrong, so you need to be able to keep your head down and keep working through the storm in hopes that the sun eventually comes out to shine."

She adds, "I think it's important to understand why you're choosing to launch something. Don't do it just because it is trendy or the cool thing to do. Entrepreneurship is not for everyone. It can be extremely difficult on your mind, body, and soul. It requires sacrifice, self-motivation, and calculated risks. Just be honest with yourself about the reason you're building a product or business, and ask yourself how it is new or better than what already exists in the market."

Inspiring your child to choose optimism is a great way for them to come up with "new or better" ideas for themselves and, like Dana, for others.

5. SHOW YOUR CHILD
HOW TO MAKE THEIR OWN PATH

Our children's lives are a journey. (Gosh, *all* our lives are a journey, aren't they?) Carrie J. Kurczynski demonstrates this as she shares how hands-on learning led her to engineering, manufacturing, and a career at General Electric (GE). As Carrie recounts:

> **Carrie J. Kurczynski's thoughts:**
> I was lucky to have hands-on teachers who taught us to 'see' the theory, not just memorize it. In high school, I remember my physics teacher laid on a table with a board across her stomach and challenged students to hit the board with a bat to teach the dispersion of energy.
>
> When I was in college, again, our physics teacher dropped a stuffed gorilla and marble from the ceiling of the lecture hall at the same time to demonstrate terminal velocity.
>
> GE saw my experience working in the machine shop at Purdue. They saw that my senior project was being a part of the Mini Baja team and my hobbies included working on motorcycles. They directed me to apply for a field engineering position, where I ended up spending the first five years at customer sites leading teams in tearing down and inspecting steam turbines.

6. HELP YOUR CHILD TRUST THEIR GUT

When I was deciding what to study in college, I was naïve. My mom had given me a nice camera for high school graduation. Upon entering general studies at Florida State University (FSU),

I considered both photography and psychology as majors and subsequent careers.

I soon came to the realization that, not only are there a limited number of opportunities for those positions, the pay was somewhat limiting.

When I thought about psychology as a major, I realized that in order to succeed in that field, most people went on to grad school. Despite the fact that it was a fascinating subject, the thought of sitting and listening to people's problems all day long quickly deterred me from pursuing that major.

And then came my strong suit—math and science. I decided that if I was to go into engineering, FSU was probably not the strongest choice at the time for that subject. I then decided to transfer to the University of Wisconsin-Madison. I was now at a strong engineering school, and I determined that I could still satisfy my interests in photography in a way that was not a career choice.

My college career took many turns. I transferred several more times as I struggled to find the right fit for me. This was further complicated by the fact that my girlfriend at the time was still in Florida. Long-distance relationships are very difficult to manage, to put it mildly. Pursuing our relationship led me to transfer back to the University of Florida in Gainesville, get engaged, and move back north to Wisconsin. There I took a job in my uncle's machine shop and went to Marquette University for engineering classes in the evening. You already heard in the previous chapter about the night I quit college (five times is the charm!).

You see, I knew my earning goals and my strong math and science aptitude were a great match for one of the family businesses in manufacturing. Even though I did not finish mechanical engineering school, the background that I accumulated along the way was more than enough.

Looking back, I have no regrets. I trusted my gut.

7. GIVE THEM PERMISSION TO FOLLOW THEIR HEART

As Kathy and I became serious and close to getting engaged, Kathy indicated there was one person I had to meet to get his approval—her best friend from high school, Frank Frangie. Frank was like a big brother to her. Fortunately, he approved. Forty-two years later, we are fortunate to have a very blessed marriage and life together. I could not have found a better partner, supporter, and spouse. As the following remarks by Frank reveal, following your heart applies to career paths in much the same way it does in finding a life partner. In both cases, you need to trust your gut instinct, risk your heart fearlessly and commit 100%.

Here's what Frank shared with me:

> **Frank Frangie's thoughts:**
> I knew very early on, at that bank, that that wasn't me. I was going to be a sportswriter, and it wasn't ever about the money. That was never the plan. Hell, I grew up without any money. We lived in a 900-square-foot home. I just realized that the banking thing wasn't for me. I got out of that pretty quickly. The most interesting career change was the one from sports writing to broadcasting. That was the one I never saw coming.

After a stint in sports writing, Frank got the chance to do radio and loved it. He did both jobs until 1993.

He advises young people to do the following:

> Before anything else: Find your passion. If you find something you love doing, you'll never work a day in your life. Wake up in the morning passionate. Go to bed at night passionate. Drive around during the day passionate. Think about it at lunch passionately. Make yourself not think about it at church, you're so passionate about it. Find something you're *that* passionate about.

I wondered what would have happened if Frank had stayed at the bank. I think he would never have had the stories he shared with me—his eyes on fire thinking about the exciting experiences he had. Looking in my rearview mirror, I can honestly say that I followed my passion, too. So much so that it led me to writing this book and the opportunity to share my passion for youth, manufacturing, and readers like you who care about those things too.

TOM MCSHEEHY: SMARTER THAN YOU THINK

A lot of people don't think they are smart. Part of the reason is that they only look at one aspect of themselves, IQ, which is based on linguistic intelligence and mathematical or logical intelligence. According to Teaching Heart Institute founder Tom McSheehy, however, there are at least six other ways to display intelligence that IQ testing doesn't measure. These include:

- Movement intelligence or kinesthetic
- Spatial or visual intelligence
- Interpersonal, or the ability to get along and work with others

- Intrapersonal, or the ability to self-reflect, go inward, and set goals
- Naturalist, or the ability to understand nature and the connections within nature
- Musical ability

Ready to be amazed? Here's what he has to say about our innate forms of intelligence.

Tom McSheehy's thoughts:

We really need to broaden our definition of intelligence. There are so many people walking around like me who think they are not smart. I thought that the only reason that I got good grades was that I worked very hard. It wasn't until I was 38 years old that I realized I was intelligent when I was young, just not in reading or writing. I struggled a lot in those areas. It pains me to listen to people say, 'He's smart' or 'she's smart,' as if other children and teenagers aren't smart. All people are smart, but in different ways.

Encouraging young people to explore their different intelligences—and then pursue those that interest them most—also gives them room to breathe. Helping students find their areas of intelligence is so connected to mental health.

Because when we are seen and valued for our strengths and areas of intelligence in classrooms, we feel valued and a part of the classroom team and belong. When we focus on kids' strengths, they naturally want to work on their weaknesses. When you focus on their weaknesses and what they can't do, they get discouraged and shut down and go away or get very angry. We need to change the way we see students in terms of their intelligence. We don't spend time in schools talking about purpose with middle or high school students. Sometimes our purpose is connected to areas of intelligence, and sometimes it is connected to areas where we struggle or encounter pain. It is very important for students to explore their purpose on this earth.

8. ENCOURAGE YOUR CHILD TO ASK FOR HELP

Craig Rabin points out that asking for help is important. He's right. It is not a sign of weakness, but a sign of great intelligence. Encouraging your children to set aside their egos (like me, when I'm lost and need directions!) is one of the greatest pieces of advice you can give. Because if you don't ask, you don't get. That's a fact.

Craig says: "When you find that thing you love and you don't look at the clock, it's fantastic." Given that, isn't it worth looking for answers outside of yourself? He goes on to say, "It's always harder to ask for help than it is to give help. Failure is good as long as you learn from it. If you can turn your failure into learning, you can turn it into success. I've had 11 companies. Why did the eleventh one work? Well, I learned from those 10. I don't want to be known for 10 failed companies, but one good one. But those 10 got me to the last one that worked."

9. TEACH YOUR CHILD TO OVER-PREPARE, THEN GO WITH THE FLOW

In Chapter 2, Tony Schumacher talked about making products in America and the choice we make by purchasing products made outside this country. Here, Tony talks about how each young person should make a conscious decision about how to advance their young lives to the next level as they near graduation. Having the support of parents makes all the difference in the world.

> **Tony Schumacher's thoughts:**
> I think my favorite expression that I use is just to over-prepare, and then go with the flow. Too many people show up and just wing it. If you showed up for a test, just winging it, you wouldn't be very good at it. I think what that entails is, number one, choose your job. Don't let it *choose you. Choose it.* Figure out what you want to do. If you won the lottery, what would make you wake up and be happy every day? Then you learn it. Don't learn it like you're trying to get an 'A,' learn it like you've got two brakes on a car with two car seats in the back seat, and it has to work. Learn it that well. It has to be done right.
>
> If you can do your job like that, you'll be proud. Everyone around you will be proud, and let me tell you something, man, when you do a good job, your friends want to do a good job, and so will everyone around you. It starts the world in a better place. I just think we're in a little bit opposite position right now. We need to fix it.

10. STRIVE FOR CHARACTER

Earlier in this book, you read Ryan Pohl's interview. Ryan introduced me to someone who runs a school in Pennsylvania that brings dreams to young men by way of a technical education that leads to high-paying careers. Mike Rounds is the President of Williamson College of the Trades. Mike emphasizes that seeing your child as a whole person will help them thrive. Recognizing this balance is important for all of us.

> **Mike Rounds's thoughts:**
> I've become a firm believer that it takes a real investment in a young person to get them to really change their trajectory in life. As important as it is to train young people in specific skills that they can take to the workforce, it is even more important to train them that values like integrity and discipline, showing up on time, being reliable, and knowing how to be a good leader are really the keys to success. Character is at the heart of it and is probably the biggest thing that will make a difference for a young man (or woman) moving forward, regardless of what career path that they decide on.
>
> Inspire the young person in your life to see themselves as a whole person: their passions, dreams, strengths, weaknesses, goals, past experiences, and future accomplishments.

* * *

In the next chapter, you'll get a front-row seat to a party many people don't think they're invited to: a manufacturing career. But don't wait for your child to get invited. Let them make their own path to a career that leans into their strengths and future success.

MANUFACTURING WELCOMES PEOPLE OF ALL BACKGROUNDS

*"St. Louis city is 85% Black and I don't see
10 Black people (on the shop floor).
Or if I do see 10 Black people, they are the
janitors."*

—Andrew Crowe,
Founder, New American Manufacturing Renaissance

As a young person, I was always fascinated with athletics. I could never play enough ball, no matter what it was. Baseball, football, kickball, soccer, it did not matter. I was fast and loved to run. When I started playing baseball, I usually played shortstop or left field. While I could not hit worth a lick, I could usually field and throw fairly well, and those positions suited my skill set. Our third baseman that year was named Bruce; he played next to me when I played short. We would sit on the bench together waiting for both of our times to go up to the plate to bat.

One game, we were sitting in the first base side dugout, and Bruce started a conversation. "A friend of mine hit a home run here last week over the wall," while he pointed to the right field outfield wall. (Keep in mind we were 10 or 11 years old at this point, in the late 1960s, so hitting a baseball that far was reason to take notice.) I'm not sure why, but I responded with: "Oh, was he colored?" In the South, the term "colored" was used for decades but, unbeknownst to me, the African American community did not approve of being referred to this way.

In a very matter-of-fact way, Bruce responded to me, "No, he was Black."

That moment in my life was all-changing. I am not even sure what I said to Bruce after that. I do know that was the last moment that I referred to any Black person as "colored." That was over 50 years ago. I cannot tell you Bruce's last name. I cannot tell you where life took Bruce beyond our time on the Knights of Columbus baseball team. I do know that I owe Bruce a word of gratitude and thanks. He taught me a valuable lesson that I did not even know I needed. So, if you are out there, Bruce, thank you for this life lesson. What I thought was a casual conversation made a profound impact on my worldview. Little did I know!

As a 10-year-old, I was taught a lesson that I wasn't respecting someone who was different than me. Although I did not know I was not being respectful, my teammate gently let me know. I want to do the same for our industry, in the same way. We are in need of new blood in our industry and our industry has a void of people of color within our ranks. We need to start thinking differently, just like I was directed to so many decades ago. There are people of all different ethnicities eager for opportunity. They probably do not know anything about manufacturing careers. Take the initiative to introduce manufacturing careers to those who would otherwise never know. They just might be your next great hire, and you might just change a life for the better!

You might be thinking, *Sure, you can say that people shouldn't wait for an invitation, Terry, but you're a middle-aged white guy.* You're right, I am, but I also know what I'm talking about here. Manufacturing is a great career for people of all cultural backgrounds for one simple reason. We need the best and the brightest—that means your child!

Throughout this book, you have read about some fascinating people. Each has an interesting story about how they discovered and nurtured the Greatest Champion inside them. But what about the plethora of young people who may not have the support or confidence to find their way—especially in the field of manufacturing?

In 2020, this country underwent a racial awakening. Unfortunately, this movement did not transfer to the ranks of manufacturing, where there are too few people of color. While I made a significant push to highlight the need for more women in our companies in my first book, I failed to highlight the need to include people of color and other diverse backgrounds. In this second book, I am committed to doing a better job by showing that good-paying careers are there for the taking.

According to the book *Made in Illinois: A Modern Playbook for Manufacturers to Compete and Win*, the State of Illinois has 64 Black-owned companies out of some 13,000 manufacturers in the state.[1] If this is not a shocking statistic, I am not sure what is. Something needs to change in order to bring the manufacturing dream to more people!

I often ponder why there are not more people of color in manufacturing, a career path that has so much to offer.

One of the best movies I have ever seen speaks to the impact of a group of Black women on the NASA space program in the 1960s. The movie *Hidden Figures* is nothing short of amazing and inspiring. This movie highlights the significant accomplishments that these women made. Set in the 1960s, people recognized back then that the bias and racism was wrong. Here we are, so many years later, and we still have far to go. It shows the bias that still prevails, a bias we are long overdue to eradicate from our culture. There multiple correlations between the young women in the movie and the messages included in this book. The movie offers versions of the role models of Katherine Johnson (played by Taraji P. Henson), Mary W. Jackson (played by Janelle Monáe), and Dorothy Vaughn (played by Octavia Spencer). Even though this movie took place decades ago, the situation of these skilled women reflects a problem that is still ongoing: the lack of representation of women, and Black women in particular, in technical fields.

In the rest of this chapter, you'll see the many opportunities in manufacturing for women and people of color, plus those with disabilities, from different backgrounds, and even young people with challenging life stories seeking a second chance at success.

PARENTS, ENCOURAGE YOUR DAUGHTERS TO STEP INTO THE LIGHT!

Sometimes, even those who already are in the manufacturing sector are pushing their sons and daughters onto another path. That is true of Nicole Wolter's father. Despite finding success in manufacturing with HM Manufacturing, Nicole's father had a different kind of dream for his daughter. Often destiny has its own plan and, at times, it prevails. Some great things are just meant to be and cannot be altered. Nicole says:

> **Nicole Wolter's thoughts:**
> I don't want to knock the industry. I think it was always available for women to get into it. I just think that as a woman, it's just not something that you look towards for a career. It's not the typical career path. You don't say, 'I want to be in manufacturing.' You usually say, 'I want to be in marketing, business, a lawyer, a doctor, or in public relations,' things like that. Even in the household I grew up in, with my dad owning a manufacturing company, they wanted me to go be a doctor or a lawyer. I definitely had an aptitude for being a lawyer. But they wanted me to do something completely out of the industry, which is very interesting.
>
> My dad didn't really want me at the company. That was never the foresight. At that time, he had a business partner, and that partner had a son who was working for the company. So it's very telling how even my own dad really didn't see me as a person to work there. My mom kept pushing, 'Why doesn't she just learn a little something? Give her some skills.' But I also didn't push the envelope

either. It's not like I said, 'Yes, I want to go work for you.' I just saw it like everyone else sees it: dirty, grimy manufacturing. It's not a sexy industry. It's not a very appealing industry. But that was in the '90s and so much has changed since then, including the industry itself. And it's a shame because the company was always state of the art; I just never fully appreciated it. However, there is also the cool factor. And as a teenager and a young adult in college, manufacturing just didn't scream cool. Now, in today's age, it's a vibe.

Today, I'm seeing more women in the industry. Young women are starting to take a second look because they realize it is not just running a machine. I think that has just been the biggest misconception, that manufacturing is just machinery. I mean, there's so much more we know about accounting, quoting/estimating, sales, marketing, social media/video content, purchasing. There's just so much to engineering, R&D, and inspection/quality. The list is endless, and I think now with LinkedIn and social media, people are able to see manufacturing for all the different varietals. I think that's going to make such an impression on everybody else.

Why are there so few women in manufacturing?

It is a rarity that I talk to a woman involved in the manufacturing or engineering part of the business. There is a tremendous amount of good that comes from bringing in a labor pool that looks at things differently. Why not draw from areas of the workforce where we have not done so in the past?

Our family has been blessed with strong women—from my mom, my wife, both my younger sisters, my cousins, and my daughter (and my daughters-in-law). Having said that, I don't understand why there aren't more women in our industry. Are men too biased to allow them to become significant in our manufacturing companies? I would like to think that is not the case. I do know that when you meet a woman in manufacturing, she is commonly strong, very determined, and driven to succeed. There aren't enough stories to tell, however, I will do my best to share those who have inspired me. Nicole's story above was certainly one!

Going back a few years, I went to visit a machine shop closing that was a GE division where they machined turbine blades. We had sold them a very high-end CNC surface grinder that I was interested in.

When I arrived, a young woman answered at the window. "I didn't know you were going to be here!" she said.

At first, I thought someone was behind me until I realized the lobby was too small for anyone else to have walked in. "Oh, OK," I said in a confused manner. We exchanged small talk until she escorted me to the shop. She asked someone else to take me to the machine. On the way back, I asked my chaperone, "Help me out; what is her name?! I know that I know her, but I cannot place her name."

"Carrie," he said.

"How about her married or maiden name?"

"Kurczynski," he said. I still could not figure it out.

As I was taking my photos and videos of the machine, she walked back to check on me. "Help me out here," I said. "I know that we know one another, but how? What is your maiden name?"

"Johnson," she said.

"Ken and Muff are your parents!" I loudly said.

At the same time, we said, "Kingswood!" That is the church that Kathy and I attend. We've known Carrie and her parents for Carrie's entire life.

CARRIE J. KURCZYNSKI:
PARENT INFLUENCE IS KEY!

I knew Carrie went into engineering, but I rarely had a chance to talk to her about her interests, education, or career. Shortly after our impromptu meeting, I called and asked her to be interviewed for my book. I asked her how she made her way into engineering, then ultimately manufacturing.

Carrie J. Kurczynski's thoughts:
At a young age, I was taught what you did and how you did it had nothing to do with what was under the hood.

It's hugely related to my parents. When I was 12, we rebuilt my dad's motorcycle. It wasn't our first project; he was always tinkering with something, but it was the project when my dad kindly insisted I should consider engineering—telling me that I would love it. When I reached high school, my mom helped point out all the tech classes so I could better understand the school side of engineering. Since math and the sciences had always come easy to me, she didn't want me to think it would all be easy.

When I finally got my driver's license, my dad wouldn't let me take the car out until I could prove I could change the oil and change a tire. Ironically, the only time I have ever needed to change a tire was on my way to a wedding as the maid of honor. I was already dressed for the ceremony when I heard the tire blow. Lucky for me, it was right in front of a mechanic shop, and they offered to change it before I could assess what was going on. I knew I needed to let them, as my heels and dress were not going to survive me doing it myself. But I called my dad and vented my frustrations at needing to accept help when I could have handled it.

While I liked all the hands-on projects, enjoyed my technical classes and found that math and science came easy, I was diagnosed with ADD and a slight form of dyslexia, mostly with numbers, at a young age. In high school, I was able to control or work around it with minimal accommodations. Sometimes I would lose points on tests or homework because I switched a number here or there but nothing that affected my overall semester grades. But I was worried about getting in over my head in college. With the help of my parents, we were able to look into what accommodations were available at a college level. It turned out that Purdue had many more resources available than I even ended up needing, but they were always there if I asked.

Our (high school) graduating class had 1,065 students. If I had to guess, maybe, easily 10 percent of the women had the ability to do it (go into engineering). I can only remember three or four who did—there could have been more. After college, a lot of companies tried to get me to go in the direction of technical sales. It would have been twice the salary, but I couldn't imagine not getting dirty on the shop floor or sitting in some office eight to ten hours a day. It almost felt like they thought I enjoyed getting dressed up in the suit and heels and putting on makeup. No thank you!

I had spent my last year of college career on campus 12 to 13 hours a day, bouncing between classes, labs, and the machine shop. Sitting still just was not for me and heels weren't for me (well, not boring back ones and certainly not every day). When I started learning what a field in engineering was, I was hooked. There was no other option for me and not once in any of the conversations did anyone care that I was a girl. All they cared about was that the long hours, hard work, and technical issues wouldn't stop me from pushing forward.

I would tell young women to drop the notion that being female has anything to do with what makes you happy or what you want to do in life. Don't compare yourself to the guy down the street or another girl or your siblings. Do the best you can do and do what makes you happy. Ask questions! Just because no one else has asked something doesn't mean they aren't wondering also. You would be surprised how many people just don't want to talk. I don't know if I never cared what other people thought or if at some point, I just stopped worrying about it, but I've always sort of ended up doing my own thing (for better or worse). You can come with me or not.

I was lucky. I was brought up to believe that what you did and how you did it had nothing to do with what was under the hood. Maybe that is a little blunt, but my work and work ethic was what counted. I wasn't always the best, but I worked my butt off. In school, it was the same way. I didn't always have the best grades, but I worked hard. And now I work for a great company and they support me, not only as an engineer but also a mom and a wife—no need to pick one over another.

Right around the same time of our meeting, I saw a GE commercial about a young woman inventor named Molly. As I watched it, I could not help but make the correlation between "Molly" in the GE commercial and the nonfictional real-life Carrie, who worked for GE. I texted Carrie and told her about the commercial and the uncanny connection of her working for GE making turbine blades. Wow, some coincidences are just too timely to be anything short of "a sign." GE has shown up as a leader in trying to make a statement in commercials for the role of women in its manufacturing workforce.

A PARENT'S MANTRA: "YES, YOU CAN"

This empowerment of a young daughter is one of the greatest gifts we can give her. Hopefully, there will be more women entering into the ranks of STEM (Science, Technology, Engineering and Math) or STEAM (Science, Technology, Engineering, Arts, and Math) fields going forward. Dana Ward (whom we talked about in Chapter Six) shares her parents' influence on her path to success. She says:

> **Dana Ward's thoughts:**
> I think it is key to understand that failure is just a normal part of life because, as an entrepreneur, you're going to experience failures of varying degrees throughout the journey. You need to be okay with it or work towards accepting it. I try to consciously address an issue quickly, learn from it, and move on. You cannot allow failure, or even fear of failure, to paralyze you. No one has time for that!
> Something that you should always try to make time for—and this is just me preaching, but for others who are

motivated by value, it can be helpful too—is to support others in their endeavors. At some point, you'll need help from your network, friends, family and even strangers, so put out what you'd like to receive. If you support someone for who they are, ask how you can support... or if you like an idea or product, then buy it and review it.

I give a lot of credit to my parents for helping structure a healthy mindset; they really were responsible for teaching me at a young age that I could do anything that I wanted to do. I mean, I'm pretty sure that if I decided that I wanted to become an astronaut and go to space tomorrow, I would find a way to make it happen (even if logically and logistically that means buying a ticket for when a public flight is available!). Find that confidence and hold on to it tightly. Inevitably, you'll need it.

STEPPING UP TO ENCOURAGE GIRLS AND MINORITIES TO GO INTO STEM

Colorado certainly seems to keep surfacing as a state that is doing all the right things when it comes to STEM and getting more young people involved in coursework and activities. Monte Whaley writes about various contributions that are making a difference in their state.

Monte Whaley's thoughts:
In Denver Public Schools (DPS), $10 million in bond funds are supplying laptops for 9,000 students in 2017. The effort is aimed at encouraging girls and minorities to pursue careers in STEM fields, DPS officials said. Many businesses, nonprofits, and individuals

are stepping up to help cash-strapped families meet their back-to-school needs. More than 400 volunteers donated their time to help run the Action Center school supply giveaway in Jefferson County (Jeffco). They sorted supplies and stuffed backpacks and then formed a well-oiled machine to check IDs and match students with the appropriate school gear during the week-long event. One of the biggest donors to the Jeffco effort is local home builder Cardel Homes, which began donating as many as 3,000 backpacks a year to the Action Center in 2014.[2]

SHE WANTED TO BE A WELDER

When I was working with Milwaukee Area Technical College, I would present during their "Heavy Metal Tour." Each year, they have manufacturing companies talk to high school students. Based on my suggestion, they asked me to present to the students prior to talking to the manufacturers. By having an understanding of the opportunities *first*, they will be way more engaged and likely to ask intelligent questions. A young woman approached me after my presentation. This time it was presenting more of a statement and dilemma.

"Mr. Iverson, I want to be a welder," she stated.

"That's awesome!" I said.

"But my parents are not sure that they want me to pursue this. What should I do?" she continued.

"Well, do you enjoy it?"

"Absolutely!" she said without hesitation.

"Well then, I would educate them on all the opportunities in that field."

Here is a perfect example of parents that are basing their influence on perceptions that are antiquated. Hopefully, this young lady was able to have a meaningful conversation about her passion and what the welding profession had to offer her.

Sometimes we try to protect our children from what we think is not in their best interest, only to find out we may be impeding them from fulfilling their dreams.

YOUR DAUGHTER NEEDS TO HEAR
THIS FROM YOU

While working with Palatine High School, I wanted to figure out a way to encourage young people to enter into Project Lead The Way classes. I met with Mark Hibner, their instructor, and let him pick the top 10 students to be ambassadors around the school. I came up with a poster program that would be the marketing campaign for the class. The poster would feature photos of young people in their high school activities, as well as photos of them in potential future manufacturing-related activities. The tagline on the posters was "They were Champions THEN and they are **CHAMPIONs Now!**" I also designed **CHAMPION Now!** shirts and provided them with fabric pens. Each of the students was given the task of getting all of their peers to sign the shirt. The front of the shirt said **CHAMPION Now!**, while the back coined my Manufacturing Create$™ slogan.

Wouldn't you know that two of the young ladies took the challenge and ran with it! They were *really* engaged in the task, getting many signatures. This is the type of program that could revolutionize Project Lead The Way programs throughout the country.

Manufacturers need engineers with degrees for their designs, innovation, patents, and more. However, manufacturing's needs are far more than just that. There are many young people who cannot forge that path. They can still make their own path to success, just in a different way. This is one of the best messages you can give your daughters.

How can we, as a culture, continue to ignore the talents and energy that women offer?

"Women make up about 29 percent of the manufacturing workforce despite filling 47 percent of the positions in the overall workforce, according to the Manufacturing Institute. While there have been periods of growth and decline, the dynamic is mostly unchanged since 1970, when women held 27 percent of the manufacturing jobs. "[3]

We have elevated the stories of so many successful women in this book: Nicole, Sheyenne, Dana, Leigh, Carrie, and Kathleen. Each had conversations with their parents and chose a passion and a path. All of us as parents should have an informed point of view in order to give our children the best advice for them given their interests, passion, and changes in the educational sector and job market.

Think about the young lady who approached me at MATC, describing her struggle with getting her parents to accept her passion for welding. What would you do with your daughter? How would you react? Would you take time to be informed prior to that discussion?

PEOPLE WITH DISABILITIES ARE WELCOME

While Rand Haas' internship program has been awesome for at-risk youth, there is a group not represented that might also be a perfect match for manufacturing careers: children and adults with disabilities and special needs. Inclusion can mean many different things for many groups of people. What if someone led the way to advocate for their opportunities?

Recently a group of manufacturing individuals met with the FMA (Fabricators & Manufacturers Association) about holding a camp for just such an under-represented group. FMA has a series of awesome camps named "Nut Bolts & Thingamajigs" (NBT). Each year, it runs hundreds of camps around the country. In the summer of 2022, it ran a "Manufacturing Inclusion Camp" for special needs individuals and those with disabilities.

Some of these individuals have superior attention to detail and are better at rote mechanical tasks than others who might have a shorter attention span. Their capability of focus is exceedingly high compared to the general population. Wouldn't this opportunity be music to the ears of special needs parents? Many parents are ill-informed about manufacturing opportunities. Parents of special needs and disabled children are even more in the dark. FMA is shedding light on this brave new world that many are unaware of.

Ed Dernulc, Director of the Foundation at the FMA, explains the following:

Ed Dernulc's thoughts:
I would say their main objectives are as follows: 1) give manufacturers another option when it comes to human resources, which is a major issue in most companies; and 2) drive individuals with special needs into the industry. The best way to describe an employee with special needs is it may take longer for the training process to take hold, but once it does, you have an employee for life. This helps develop the social, economic, and career spheres for the client. We believe this is a great source of employment

for the industry and the individuals are great candidates to provide a strong workforce for many companies.

NBT proposes a three-year plan to adapt its successful manufacturing summer camp model to be inclusive of young people with disabilities. The first year will focus on program design and methodology, with a second year for a small pilot of one camp to test the methodology, and the third year a larger program launch. Both the pilot and launch will include a modest yet effective evaluation. After the three-year grant period, NBT intends to be ready for a larger program launch.

While NBT offers camps nationwide, it will build out this program in the Chicago area, near its home base and closest partner organizations. NBT will rely on partner experts to ensure inclusivity in the program design. These non-profits have decades of experience helping people with disabilities secure employment and lead integrated lives.

NBT will work with partner high schools and technical colleges with both fabrication labs and special needs programs. These will likely be Wheeling High School, Lake Park High School in Roselle, or Maine South in Park Ridge. Harper College or Elgin Community College, all longstanding NBT partners, would be the technical partners. After the first three years, NBT expects to expand to Wisconsin or Indiana due to close proximity and then grow even further from there.

The takeaway: Be open to alternative career paths for your children. Nothing is more important than our child's well-being, happiness, and future.

Over 50 years ago, I was fortunate enough to have my mom believe that a private education was something I needed going into junior and senior high school. The Bolles School was one of the few non-faith-based private schools in Jacksonville, Florida, with an excellent reputation. After discussions with my dad, he agreed to pay for tuition. Somehow, I was able to test well enough to get in. This was one of the best decisions my parents made for my future. Environment is everything. Bolles is the epitome of an environment that challenged me in all sorts of ways and allowed me to flourish academically, socially, athletically, and in character.

One of the first students I met was Cathy Randle. Cathy was one of the hardest-working people I knew. Over the decades, I kept in touch with both her and her husband Jerry (Hurst), and periodically would be introduced to her children. I have always identified with Cathy in many ways, starting with her work ethic in the industrial sales profession.

CATHY HURST: RECOGNIZING THE MENTAL HEALTH OF OUR YOUNG ADULT CHILDREN AND ASKING "WHAT ARE YOU PASSIONATE ABOUT?"

After a successful sales career and her son's path to the NFL, Cathy became the director of the Hayden Hurst Family Foundation. Triggered by her son's terrifying mental health crisis, Cathy uses the organization as a platform to address the stigma of mental health issues for teens and athletes. Get ready to inspire the young people in your life with these eye-opening stories from Cathy about her son and his challenge as an NFL player, her path to helping youth, and the importance of their mental health and happiness in our complicated world. Cathy shared:

Cathy Hurst's thoughts:

Jerry and I have two children. It was kind of funny when I told my in-laws I was pregnant. They were shocked because they thought I was always going to be a career person and that I would never really consider having children.

Our daughter is a very old soul, if you will. She was always so mature for her age and just followed a path. Then our son Hayden came. It was like night and day. He was always on, never stopped, and still is that way today. He always tested us as adults and tried us all the time. It was great for us as parents to have each other. I can't imagine being a single mom trying to raise Hayden because there were times when I would just put my hands up and say, 'I don't know what to do.'

Jerry would be the strong one. We really worked together as a team to raise both our children. That is so critical for kids, and I know not every child in this world has that blessing and that opportunity. So we wanted to do our best with what we knew. There's no manual that says *this is how you raise kids*. Sometimes it's just you with your gut feeling on what to do.

Jerry and I balanced each other out, trying to figure out how to work with these two kids. We weren't perfect. We had good days and bad days. To me, that's also what parenting is about. I always tell people, 'You can't send them back to the hospital. They're part of you.' It's something that you can't give up on. You just have to keep experimenting and trying different things.

I always made time for the kids. I adjusted my work schedule as far as travel if there was a big game or something going on I knew about. Luckily, my job allowed me the opportunity to do that.

Jerry was a teacher and had the summers off with the kids. We called it 'Camp Jerry.' One year, he actually took a year off and was Mr. Mom. He always says it was one of the hardest years of his life because it's just so demanding. That's why I was not a stay-at-home mom because I knew I needed that adult connection and to have the outside connection with work so that when I came home, I appreciated my kids and enjoyed them more. I want to work; I enjoy that. It gives me pleasure, not that being a parent it doesn't, but I like that balance in my life.

Back to the kids.

Kylie enjoyed other activities more than she enjoyed schoolwork. She chose to go to Santa Fe Community College, so she could hopefully transfer into the University of Florida after her two years of an AA degree. It was never easy for Kylie. But she was like the 'Little Engine That Could.' She just kept driving, and she wouldn't give up. She got into the University of Florida and then took a year to get into veterinary school. It just finally clicked. She just loved learning and having to figure things out.

Of course, she had this younger brother that was always successful in whatever sport he picked up. She always felt like the underdog. Even though we tried very hard to give both our kids equal time, she had to go to summer baseball games where we were traveling with Hayden. She was always having to give up what she wanted to do.

Hayden was not the studious one. That's what I tell Kylie all the time. He could never have taken the same path she did. There's no way. He would not sit in the classroom that long. They were just two totally different kids—and adults now.

Whatever sport Hayden attempted, he just had a God-given ability. A lot of parents said, 'What do we do with our seven-year-old to get him to be like Hayden? What camps do I have to take him to? What workout program does he have to do?' It was a natural-born ability. Hayden was blessed with that. In middle school and in high school, he kind of took it for granted. When he had the opportunity to get drafted in baseball with the Pirates, and he went off to the minor leagues. It was then that everything came to light for him.

He was away from home for the first time in his life. He was an 18-year-old among 25-year-olds. It was overwhelming for him. He started struggling mentally with the game. He couldn't feel the ball in his hand. He developed 'the yips,' not being able to throw like he used to. He was worrying about what other people were thinking about him, like a coach standing there or another player. Where once he was the star athlete, his life had now changed. He would just go to his dorm room at the minor league facility and sit in the dark.

Of course, we were four hours away. We could hear sadness in his voice. There were times when Jerry would just take a trip down there and go play golf with him and try to get his mind off of it.

Scott Elarton, a pitching coach, worked with him early in the morning before anybody else got up. When Hayden just couldn't get it together, he would say, 'What do you miss? What are you passionate about?'

And Hayden said, 'I really thought a lot about football.' This was after two and a half years in the minor leagues.

'Well, go play football,' Scott replied.

Before he could do that, however, Hayden hit a wall.

One in five people has mental health issues. Some say that it's five in five. And I agree with that because I think each one of us, at some point or another in our lives, has anxiety or depression or the blues, and we don't know how to deal with things. Even this pitching coach admitted to us through email that he had struggled in baseball. He had struggled with pitching, and when he saw Hayden, it probably gave flashbacks to him that he didn't have a mentor or someone to help him.

Scott wanted to help Hayden. I got to meet Scott when Hayden was playing football in South Carolina. When he came, he extended his hand to me. He's 6'7" tall and I said, 'Oh no, I have to have a hug.' He was taken aback, and I said, 'No, you saved my son's life, I have to hug *you*.' It was a beautiful moment because he realized that he had a significant impact on Hayden.

So it's a blessing, the people God puts in your life, even if it's for a moment, for a day; it's beautiful, and we have to remember that.

Hayden was embarrassed about his mental state. He didn't want to disappoint us because he'd always been that shining star, that great athlete. He found it difficult to come to us and say, 'I can explain what's going on in my head, but I can't pitch anymore.' Thank goodness Scott gave him the strength and stood with him when he told (his dad) Jerry, 'I want to play football.' I have to admit, I was not a very good parent because I was always like, *Oh, stick with it, you'll figure it out.*

So after an unsuccessful spring training in 2015, Hayden decided to 'retire' from baseball and play college football. He contacted a friend on the University of South Carolina football team, who relayed the information to head coach Steve Spurrier. In a matter of months, Hayden was afforded a walk-on position at South Carolina. By early May 2015, he was a member of the Gamecock football team.

At first, I thought he was crazy when he was going to go play football. I've told him on numerous occasions, 'I was wrong, and as a parent, sometimes, we aren't right, and we do make mistakes ourselves.' It's good to let kids know you're not perfect and you make mistakes also.

In early January 2016, after a night of drinking and drugs, Hayden attempted to take his life by cutting his wrists. The vices were a way of hiding the failure he felt after being unsuccessful in baseball, and the switch to football did not allay his alcohol and drug use. Fortunately, he was able to call a friend, a nursing student at the University of South Carolina, and she rushed over, stopped the bleeding, and called 911. Hayden was transported to the local hospital and put on suicide watch and confined to the psychiatric ward for 72 hours. We were allowed to see him for five minutes the first time we arrived when they had him confined to a small room. He was mortified about what he had done and sat silently. He wanted us to get him out, but by law, he was there for the 72-hour period.

We said, 'This is beyond Mom and Dad's control or saving you. You did something, and you have to serve the consequences.' I would say that was probably one of the hardest things in my life, not being able to save him. He says today that that was probably one of the best experiences of his life because he never wants to be there again. That gives him the strength to fight through any challenge that he has moving forward.

Sometimes kids need the hard knocks. They need to realize life is not perfect. Everything is not going to go their way. What happens when these kids leave school and you can't protect them anymore and they get into a job? Are you going to go see their boss and say, 'I can't believe you did that to my son or daughter?'

Hayden played three years at South Carolina, became team captain, and unanimous first-team All-SEC tight end. He was then drafted in the first round of the 2018 NFL draft by the Baltimore Ravens. He wanted to start a foundation focused on mental health and suicide prevention. He was aiming it toward adolescents because he felt like the earlier kids were trained, or had resources, then they could understand what goes on in your brain and what causes the emotions. It causes things that you can't necessarily see or touch.

I quit working in my sales career and helped run the Hayden Hurst Family Foundation for him. Jerry helped with major events. I took it like one of my sales jobs! I wasn't afraid to reach out to other foundations to pick their brains to see how we could make a difference and change lives. We've been doing this since November of 2018. We focused our work on three cities: Jacksonville; Baltimore, Maryland; and Columbia, South Carolina, where Hayden went to college.

We did a campaign called 'The Critical Catch Campaign' in Baltimore with an organization called BTST Services, which is Better Tomorrow Start Today. They do an outpatient mental health facility for young people. We went to four inner-city schools. Hayden and Chris Simon, the CEO of BTST Services, talked to the kids. The kids were amazed because here is this NFL football player sitting in front of them, talking about his anxiety and depression. Then you have the fact that his uncle and cousin had died by suicide because they also struggled with depression and anxiety.

We've just got to equip these kids with more tools to handle life and deter them from choosing suicide or feeling like there's no alternative for them.

With everything going on today, we have to help these young people be able to handle life. It's so sad that, even though we've talked about COVID and how many people have died, we need to look at the number of people that have died by suicide, whether it's a child, a military veteran, or a veterinarian. I've seen the statistics. It's incredible. We need to help these young people realize that tomorrow can be a better day and it's okay not to be okay.

I've learned with this foundation and hearing from trained mental health professionals that you must be able to be flexible and understand that your child may not be just like you, and what you're trying to teach them may not always be the only answer. That's what I've learned to say to kids: 'Wow, I'm sorry you feel that way.' Whereas we were raised with *Listen, it's this way or the highway.*

 I've learned to be more fluid and flexible as I've aged. I wish sometimes I could go back to my 30s with the knowledge that we have now and try to re-parent. I think I probably would be doing things a little differently.

GANGS & DRUG ABUSE: THE KILLER OF DREAMS, FUTURES, AND LIVES

There are positive and negative influences for youth in this country. Many times, employers have told me that the interview process goes great until the drug test is scheduled, and, low and behold, that is the last time the prospective employee interacts with the employer.

As I shared in Chapter 3, one of Rand Haas' internship programs is for people with very real issues. We're talking about living in areas of Chicago that have gang fights. According to Rand,

One intern says he doesn't need OSHA, he ducks bullets at night. We've actually had an intern that was killed in a gang war the day before he was going to start his internship. Hunger is a real issue for these young people. There's no food on the table, they're starving. That's why the MCIP program is great for those kids.

Rand is making a statement about some young people whose influences are beyond description and understanding. Most of us can't comprehend what these young people go through. Having said this, I have dived into some of the crossroads of gangs, drugs, and manufacturing in communities.

The MAPI Foundation analyzed the intersection of the current drug crisis and manufacturing to understand the risk it poses to the sector's long-term health. Three findings stand out in its report "Ignorance Isn't Bliss: The Impact of Opioids on Manufacturing." Counties seeing the highest drug-related deaths intersect in an alarming way with manufacturing. The drug crisis is accelerating in communities with large manufacturing workforces. If the trend continues unchecked, the report continues, it will have profound effects on manufacturing in the future.[4]

Above, Cathy Hurst spoke of the importance of parents' awareness of our children's mental health. This is never more relevant than during the COVID-19 pandemic of 2020-2022. The national survey on drug use and mental health in 2020 confirms how much of a negative impact the pandemic had on young people in particular. This survey showed a rise in not only drug abuse, but also mental health struggles and suicide. The pandemic does not allow the survey findings from 2020 to be applied directly today, but the statistics cannot be ignored.

According to the 2020 data, among adults aged 18 or older:

- 4.9 percent had serious thoughts of suicide,
- 1.3 percent had made a suicide plan, and
- 0.5 percent had attempted suicide in the past year.

People of mixed ethnicity 18 or older scored twice the percentage of having serious thoughts of suicide, almost 3 times the percentage made a suicide plan, and over twice the percentage attempted suicide, when compared to adults aged 18 or older.

The results for adolescents 12 to 17 were even more troubling. When compared to their adult counterparts, twice the percentage had serious thoughts of suicide, over four times the percentage had made a suicide plan, and over five times the percentage had attempted suicide.

These statistics point out that our youth between 12-17, as well as those with mixed ethnicity, have challenges greater than any of us realize. As parents, we need to understand these challenges before they lead to irreversible problems. Knowing our child's passion, and then supporting, empowering and inspiring them into successful careers, just might be the panacea for their future self.

All of us think: *That would never happen in my family!* I can no longer think that way. Every day, I am reminded this is all too close to home.

The opioid addiction is an epidemic destroying our young men and women, one overdose at a time. Employers cannot find workers who can pass a drug test. I was interviewing for manufacturing positions in my company and had two candidates in a row agree to take drug tests but mysteriously not show up for them, and they did not have any contact with me afterward. We cannot comprehend the extent of this issue.

Probably the most eye-opening story I could possibly share is that of a young man, Mikey Santini. He attended school with my youngest son in suburban Chicago. They used to run around together on the soccer field while their older sisters played on the same travel soccer team. This young man was an unbelievable athlete. He was a charismatic person with a smile that would melt the coldest of hearts. You could not help but love him.

This young man got involved in heroin. Try as he may, he could not quit the drug. Tragically, in 2015 at the age of 25, he lost his life to this killer. You could not find a more loving family behind this young man. Mikey had two sisters (Jackie and Jessy), a mom (Geri), and a dad (Bob), who all worshipped the ground he walked on. Everyone loved Mikey. He was just that type of guy. I loved Mikey.

While on a family trip, we all got the word that Mikey had died. Sitting at a dinner table with family all around, we were all hit with shock and sadness. With disbelief, we wondered how something so tragic could happen to one of our best and brightest young people. It doesn't matter where you live, how affluent or poor your family is: We are all at risk due to our kids' dangerous experiments. The reasons they try these things vary. Some feel the need to lessen their painful, uncomfortable, or unpleasant feelings. Others are persuaded by the wrong people.

In a flash, their dreams, futures, and lives are cut tragically short.

I attended this young man's funeral. We all felt a pit in our stomachs and pain in our hearts. The funeral home was packed. Soccer players, coaches, teachers, family, and friends all lined the funeral home. We all felt their loss. The Lake County (Illinois) sheriff spoke at the service. He reminded us that this epidemic scars many families, and that it has to stop. Sadly, this story is not uncommon, even in affluent suburbia in the U.S. High schools now have Naloxone (sold under the name of Narcan), a heroin antidote, in their hallways. How tragic it is that this problem is so prevalent that we need Naloxone in schools.

Once again, we need to offer our young people the best. Watching them succumb to this deadly disease is scary. We need to do whatever we can to interrupt the culture that does little to prevent young people with so much promise from ending their lives. Their lives are cut short by sophisticated drug cartels and ineffective policies and programs that are not treating this epidemic like the public health crisis that it is.

In the pain, we also find hope.

ANDREW CROWE: SECOND CHANCES

Andrew Crowe explores his unconventional path to manufacturing. Second chances are not always given or earned easily. Andrew is one of the fortunate few who took full advantage of his second chance through superior attitude, effort, and determination. Be prepared to pause and take note about not waiting for your children to get an acceptance letter or invitation to join a profession. Rather, encourage them to make their own way forward with courage, confidence, and commitment no matter what their circumstances have been!

> **Andrew Crowe's thoughts:**
> I was raised in St. Louis. It's a typical inner-city youth story. Whether you're Black, brown, white, or other, it doesn't matter typically when you're in an inner city with a sector that has jobs that have been leaving. All American inner cities have been dying. I had a

single-parent household. My mother raised me and my brothers and sisters. She was literally always working. That gave me two things. It gave me a lot of time to get into stuff. And it also gave me an outlook on life that I didn't want to be like her.

I love and admire my mother, but I knew that there had to be something better than just slaving every day at three different jobs to barely make ends meet. We'd have lights with no running water, or we'd have food in the refrigerator, but we wouldn't have lights. I saw how hard my mom worked and that the American dream wasn't really panning out for her.

My options, or so I thought at the time, were limited to my experiences and the things that I saw every day.

My school wasn't funded to the point where we had a STEM lab. We didn't have speakers who came in and told us about different career pathways. What I saw around me was that the people that were not struggling day to day were the people whose *parents* weren't struggling day to day.

I naturally gravitated towards the street. It was never to be diabolical. It was always with a mindset of helping my mom out and not becoming like her. That was the only avenue that I saw that could get me there. Because of that, I made some adverse decisions in my life. Before I was 18, I was a two-time felon. I was a teenage father, and I didn't really have much of an outlook still.

The people on the streets were the only people that have hired me with a felony on my record. I was in that cycle of jail, I guess, worthless existence, meaningless, just going through the motions.

I got tired of going through the motions, and I got tired of not feeling like I was important. And I got tired of being the example that I was to my son. More importantly, I woke up one day and I said, 'I don't know what I want to be, but I know what I don't want to be anymore.'

I reached out to my network: 'I'm looking for a legal job that I can get as a felon. I will humble myself. I don't care if I'm shoveling shit at the zoo. I will be the best one I can be.' I got a library card at the same time and started reading books. I started reading *Think and Grow Rich*. I started reading Wallace D. Wattles self-help books, and all these different books that help you shift your mindset. I still didn't have a career path or anything that I thought I was good at, but I just had a different mindset.

A lady that was close to the family reached out to me. She said, 'Hey, I got a job for you.'

I walk into this place, and I sit across from the gentleman. He hands me a machinist test. 'I got two job openings. One's for machinist, and one's for saw operator. A machinist pays this, saw operator pays this, and saw operator pays less.' So, I want to be a machinist, not knowing what it was, having no idea what it was at all. This was also during the same time as the recession. There were no jobs really available for anybody. You know what I'm saying? (Let alone a two-time felon that had no experience in the fields.)

That's where manufacturing was different, where it weathered that storm and was still paying. At the time, it was $19 an hour, or $22 for the machining, and then $15 an hour for the saw job, which was almost 2 to 3 times the minimum wage at the time. It was still really appealing to me. I was like, 'Oh, I got to do this!'

I saw manual machines first when we went into the manual department, and I was like, Wow. *My mind just exploded!*

I saw the CNC machines. I saw them running. I was like, *You take this raw piece of aluminum. You put it into this machine, it cuts it down, it takes away from it. Now it's worth 10 to 1,000 times more than what you just bought it as.* It blew my mind!

I felt a fire light inside of me. Oh my God, I had never seen or even thought about where things were made. Now that I'm around it, I don't want to leave it. I just became the best saw man that I knew how to be. I'd make sure the cuts were proper. I would go drop off the material at all of the CNC machines, so first shift was set. I started seeing what their preference was, what their materials were. If they wanted it set up in a corner to the jobs that they had, I would go the extra mile.

After that, as I would leave, third shift going into first shift, I was looking in the parking lot. I'm like, *Damn.* That was the first time I saw a Ducati motorcycle. Then in the locker room, as I'm changing out, and they're dressing in, I'm hearing the conversations are like, 'Oh yeah, I just closed on my lake house.' During the recession, this is crazy. Even before the recession, I had never been around conversations like this. *Damn, I got to get the first shift. I got to be a machinist.* Whatever these people were doing, I needed to be able to do it if they were doing it in a recession and making that type of money.

I started staying after. I would clock out and stay after four hours in the first shift, and just beg people to teach me. YouTube wasn't big. There was no Titan. There were no tutorials. There was nothing online. I bought an old machinist handbook. It was probably four or five versions back. I was buying coffee and doughnuts to have there in the morning for the old machinists when they came in for a shift.

It took maybe a month of them eating my doughnuts and coffee to where one person was like: 'Look, you can stand next to me. Don't ask any questions. When I talk, you write. That's it. When I tell you to do something, you do it. I'm not going to tell you twice.'

That's how I learned manual machines. By the time I had my year anniversary, I was a CNC machinist. I would go home. The notes that I would take, I would compare them to my machinist handbook, and then go through all of that, and try to reteach myself this stuff.

This was the first thing that I had to apply myself. I would go to sleep at night thinking about G-code. I'd wake up early in the morning before the sun, and be excited, *I can't wait to be at work*. You know what I'm saying? I would not get tired at all.

As a Black man in America, we live a different experience. You know what I'm saying? I didn't feel like an American. I felt like a second-class citizen. On top of that, throw the felonies and stuff; I was really down. I didn't feel like I had a meaningful purpose in this country until I became a machinist. It's like, *Yo, if I don't show up to work today, and if I don't cut this stock right, if I don't give it my all, then the jet fighters that are protecting us aren't going to be as good.* You know what I'm saying? For once, I felt like the work that I was doing in my life when I woke up every day actually meant something, not just to me, but America, and my country. It made me feel good as a person for once.

At the end of the day, I knew what the alternative was if I didn't take the shot. If I didn't really give this my all. The only thing that was waiting for me on the other side was death or jail. That was the route that I was going. You know what I'm saying?

It's like, *Damn, this is my second life right here. I got to give it everything I have.*

MANUFACTURING WELCOMES ALL—VONDALE SINGLETON

It does not matter what neighborhood you come from, the color of your skin, your gender, or any other facet of your background. You are America's Greatest Champion, and there is a place for you in manufacturing. Several years ago, I reached out to someone making a difference in the lives of young men on the south side of Chicago. His mentoring program goes under the name of CHAMPS. Of course, the parallels between his organization and the name and focus of my 501(c)3 were too obvious to not make an introduction. His name is Vondale Singleton, and he gives hope on the south side of Chicago, where it is not often found.

Vondale Singleton hails from the inner city of Chicago and grew up in the "housing projects," as he calls them.

Vondale Singleton's thoughts:

We talk about it as if it's some mythical place. But that was a real place for me. It was a frightening place for me. To watch my mom get hooked on drugs at an early age, or at least succumbing to that warfare of drugs that ended her life in 1994. When I was 14, she was only 29. Imagine a 14-year-old burying his mom, and she's 29. She didn't even get a chance to experience life. Yet I had to navigate that and still navigate it, and now I'm almost 40 years old. I'm blessed and I'm fortunate because I would have been another statistic had it not been for my mentor. They eventually came into my life in '97 and really did a very powerful thing by modeling for me a high level of consistency. Many of my peers didn't have a father. But then, many of my peers had real struggles. Mentorship was my lifeline.

I heard a lot about manufacturing in the '80s and '90s. And as the technology boom, I think, has arrived, it has kind of lessened the conversation around manufacturing. I don't know why that is but in our educational field, I think the contents of the fields of study that most of our teachers are pushing these days are more in line with the wave of the future, if you will, right? There are many aspects of manufacturing that touches technology, math, health care, so on and so forth, right? So, I think, to a degree, our educators are at fault for not having the education behind it to be able to share information around it.

Through these stories about young people who have overcome many obstacles, we need to **all** carry the flag and help inspire champions in manufacturing in the next generation, whether they are a:

- Young person who loves working with their hands, making things, and has an interest in a manufacturing career.
- Young person of any gender, color, or background.
- Young person conquering his or her demons by overcoming drug addiction.
- Military veteran trying to make their way back into the workforce.
- Person with disabilities who wants to make a living and be a productive member of our society.

We all must do our best to elevate our youth to become their own **CHAMPION Now!** and, as a result, make our country a better place. In our last chapter, you will walk through a path to success for both you and your child.

CREATE
YOUR PATH OF ACTION
AS A PARENT

"I tell young people: arrive early,
leave late, and tell the truth."

—*Finding America's Greatest Champion:*
Building Prosperity Through Manufacturing,
Mentoring and the Awesome Responsibility of Parenting

J ust as your child has a path of action, you do too! It's your choice: Challenge your child with the talents and gifts they have, or send them to college and say, "Figure it out."

Of course, it all starts with communication. And that's not easy sometimes. However, talking with your child, showing them the possibilities, listening to what makes their heart sing helps them make better decisions about their future. Something as small as encouraging them to go to YouTube to see what a prototype engineer or machinist does goes a long way.

I also wonder if it comes down to long-term parenting vs. short-term parenting. Long-term parenting is hard and messy, but, as a result, you can feel pride in seeing your child create success versus paying for your child's school, and potentially going deep into debt, without doing your due diligence. Relationships run deeper when a parent has invested in the best interests of their child.

One thing is for sure: You're not in this alone. We all need to step up.

Companies need to quit thinking about next quarter's results and think more altruistically about our country's future by way of their employees' future. Adults need to look beyond their own children and consider how to impact others too. Our children need to stop making assumptions and become more self-aware.

Positive influences like guidance counselors, internship programs, job shadowing, and sports teams make a difference, especially when negative influences like drugs, gangs, and over-dependence on technology come into play. We all need to encourage and empower the positives and educate against the negatives. Let's give our young people the best we have. For adults, that means we should volunteer, mentor, and pay it forward by sharing our time, compassion, values, and experience. Not all young people will want and accept what we want to share, but there will be a time when they will need them and embrace them. We all need to be there for the next generation of Champions.

KATHLEEN BURLEY: YOUR CHILD NEEDS TO FIND THEIR CRAFT

Kathleen Burley is a great example of someone who supports future generations. She is the former executive director of the Greater Chicago Advanced Manufacturing Partnership (as of the time of this writing, GCAMP is led by Dawn Curran). Kathleen has long championed young people and has become a strong voice for young girls entering manufacturing. You will love her backstory.

Kathleen Burley's thoughts:

The Greater Chicago Advanced Manufacturing Partnership, or GCAMP, was started in 2010 (formerly the 'Golden Corridor' Advanced Manufacturing Partnership") with a handful of NW suburban manufacturers and Gary Skoog, the director of economic development for Hoffman Estates.

The first event that GCAMP took part in was IMTS 2010 (International Machine Tool Show) by funding buses for local high school students to attend at McCormick Place. Loaded with automation, robotics, and more, IMTS hosts the Smartforce Student Summit, which is the perfect place to introduce students to the amazing, high-tech careers in manufacturing. GCAMP hosts a booth at the IMTS Student Summit, which is held every two years.

GCAMP is a bridge between manufacturing companies and their future workforce. Our work previously focused on the "Golden Corridor," an area which runs along I-90 from O'Hare to Rockford. We originally worked primarily in the Northwest suburbs of Elk Grove Village, Schaumburg, and Hoffman Estates with local manufacturing companies, Harper College, and High School districts 211 and 214, the two largest high school districts in Illinois. GCAMP was instrumental in assisting high school District 211 and high school District 214 in getting manufacturing programs back into the schools. (Note: Both Mark Hibner & Dr. Laz Lopez, who were interviewed in this book, were a big part of the CTE curriculum and programs in each district.) We have helped to place countless students into internships, apprenticeships, and employment positions.

In 2021, GCAMP joined forces with and became a part of the VIA (Valley Industrial Association) and changed their name to The Greater Chicago Advanced Manufacturing Partnership. In large part, this was done to expand GCAMP's reach so that we could help schools in a much larger area and connect with industrial and manufacturing companies to continue finding work-based learning opportunities such as paid internships, student apprenticeships, and employment after graduation for many more students and companies.

*When I was 19 and had just finished up
my freshman year of college, I had no direction
and no idea what I wanted to do. I was told,
"Your mom didn't have the opportunity you have
to go to college, so you need to go."*

There was no talk about what I wanted to do and what interests I may have had. No high school counselor spoke to me about college pathways or potential careers. I went to college anyway because that was what was expected of me to have a career, to support myself.

My freshman year was not very successful, and I was on academic probation. I decided that I would get a full-time job and I was going to let life be my education. I found a job working for a cutting tool distributor, thinking, *This is going to be the most boring job ever.* Now, I cannot believe I am a girl working in the tooling industry. It became interesting to me. I started in shipping & receiving, but quickly moved into inside sales. I was good with customers and I really liked learning, so with that, I became knowledgeable about the tools. It was just cool to learn how things were made.

Fast forward three years later, I ended up buying into a cutting tool company and became VP and managing partner at 22. I never saw manufacturing or knew what it was until I got that first job, and I said, 'This is cool. This is really cool.' And I love the fact that, I mean, well, there were not very many women. And I thought, well, *I could blaze a pathway here. I can be that girl, that woman.*

My mother never went to college. She studied to be a hairdresser, like many women. Back in the '50s and

'60s, they got married and had kids. She did not have an opportunity to go to college, and so the expectation was for me to go because many of my female classmates were going to college; it was expected I would as well. I was not the best student back then, with a lack of direction or motivation (later learning that I had ADHD). There were never conversations as to 'what are your interests?' or 'what do you think you would be good at?' It was always *you're going to college*. I signed up for our local college and said, 'Okay, accounting,' which later became, 'Okay, so I will be an English major, something.' I just picked something.

I think at that age, you just do not know what direction you want to go. You are 18, 19 years old. Bottom line was that without direction or interests, I was not ready, nor did I want to go the college route.

When I talk to companies and they say, 'We want to take this student on and put them through a six-year apprenticeship,' I say, 'So you're going to have to explain this to them. You cannot just tell them that they should do this. You must explain the path better and explain what they're doing.'

Part of the reason that work-based learning experiences and internships as a junior or senior in high school are so important is because we must let them see what manufacturing is all about.

PARENTS: YOUR ACTION PLAN

My wife and I grew up together. We married at 21 and 20, respectively. One thing that we were able to both develop was the art of "futuring." While this was not necessarily fair or enjoyable to our children, it made us better parents and better professionals. Futuring is when you think about the "what ifs" in any scenario in your day or in your life.

While my wife was thinking, *What if this happened, what would I do?*, I was thinking, *What am I missing in any task?* In any scenario, Kathy would be arranging for a Plan B while I was trying to constantly think about how I could do something better, do something more completely.

Having said that, I could not be prouder of our three adult children. They are awesome! And, as you hear so many times, each and every one of them is different. This is so true. Each has their own style and unique skill set.

The mainstay that runs through each of them is honesty. All of them are terrible liars. I am proud of many things; however, I am so very proud of that! Here are a few lessons we have practiced (not always well). Some of these took us awhile to learn as parents!

TEACH HONESTY, HARD WORK, ACCOUNT-ABILITY, AND INDEPENDENCE. These are some of the building blocks our children need to succeed in life. The stronger the foundation, the better prepared they are for life's unexpected curveballs. And yes, life will throw all sorts of things to make it hard. Life is hard. As parents, we need to give our young people the tools to slay whatever dragon is around tomorrow's corner.

ENCOURAGE. Children need to know their options. Too many times, we do not encourage our children to learn something, such as a new skill they want to develop. The more we expose our children to opportunities, the better. I am a big believer that knowing what you *do not* want to do is the first step in learning what you *do want* and ultimately *will* do in life. So many times, I hear young people say, "Well, that was a waste of time." This is not true. Learning what you need to develop, or do not enjoy, is valuable. This is the first step to what you do well and what you enjoy. Internships are the perfect first step.

INSPIRE. By inspiring our children, they can try whatever they need to fail or succeed. Most of us are not innately confident. After all, there is no guarantee they will succeed at everything. Every young person has to be told it is OK to fail because, without that, there is no concept of success and how to reach that pinnacle.

SUPPORT. Inspiring is only half the battle. Young people will fall, and we need to support them with resources and encouragement to get back up. Parents fill this role more than anyone. If there is a missing parent, some young people are very fortunate to have the void filled by others like aunts, uncles, grandparents, coaches, and mentors, among others.

IF YOU ARE A MENTOR OR COACH

EXPECT EXCELLENCE. Push young people to be the best they can. Too many times, we reward children for showing up. While being involved is great, success is not merely measured by being present. Success is measured by results. Unfortunately, there has to be a winner. That is a simple fact.

However, I would say there are no losers. I don't believe in that message. Losing is just the first component to eventually winning. How we teach young people to win and lose is important. When I coached, it wasn't about winning but rather about continual improvement. As long as every player on the team got better each season, our team got better. But improvement doesn't just mean a win/loss record. It is also about learning life lessons and becoming more accountable, more mature, and more independent.

CULTIVATE. So many times, young people are looking for guidance. If we can cultivate the basic skills to be successful in life, the current generation of young people will be called the greatest generation. Maybe they will become the solution generation. I feel that young people have endless potential to become what they want to be. Environment is everything. I learned that at Bolles. We need to cultivate them for success.

More are willing to listen and learn than those willing to mentor. Since I was fortunate to have mentors (besides my father, who was an awesome mentor), I have felt the obligation to "pass this gift forward" and mentor others. So many of our mature adults have talents, and we need to share these with the next generation—beyond our own children.

IT'S TIME FOR YOUR CHILD
TO CONSIDER THEIR FUTURE

I recently watched a 1997 video of the late Steve Jobs from Apple talking about rebranding Apple products. He spoke about many things, concepts, and ideas, but there was one thing that he said that resonated greatly for me: "People with passion can change the world for the better, and those crazy enough to think that they can, actually do."[1]

One additional thing that Steve Jobs said is that Nike became one of the best brands in the world by honoring great athletes and great athletics (not, in his words, by talking about "speeds and feeds," a manufacturing metaphor). **CHAMPION Now!** honors great manufacturers and great manufacturing—those who elevate the image of manufacturing, promote careers, and emphasize the importance of it in our culture and our lives. In this, we will find America's Greatest Champion!

Steve Jobs challenged us all to think differently.

As a young person, your child should take the initiative. The journey is entirely more productive with you by their side. After you are done with your half of this book, give it to your child to read their half. (Or maybe they have given it to you after they read theirs.) Ask their opinions, then tell them what you want to help them accomplish. Tell them you want them to have a career they are truly passionate about. In the center of this book are questions to start a conversation.

Some powerful and life-changing conversations are just up ahead. You can help make your child's path to success a great deal quicker, more effective, and efficient. Who knows where it can lead?

ONE LAST THOUGHT

This much I know: Your children are poised to sit in the driver's seat of their future. This can only happen with your support, but you might need to broaden your current perceptions and knowledge.

After running my company for many years, I have found that people want answers from me without having the diligence or patience to dig for the facts required to make a good decision. I defer an answer until I feel I have enough of the facts to decide. This practice has served me well. By doing this, you feel good about the direction you choose.

This also ties into the advice of one of my life mentors, John Comparini: "Terry, I never made a decision that I thought was wrong at the time that I made it."

John's words are only true if you have taken the time to gather all of the current and relevant information.

My words in closing are: Both you and your child are a team. Do your research. Get all the facts. Make your decision and feel confident that you made the best decision at the time. Good luck. Inspire your child to manufacture their future and be their own **CHAMPION Now!**

CONVERSATION STARTERS TO CONNECT CHILDREN WITH THEIR PARENTS

T ime to meet in the middle (literally, starting with the questions in this book). Below are questions for parents and children to ask each other.

The earlier you have candid conversations on life after high school, the better. Parents, explore your child's passions, talents, and vision for life beyond high school. Kids, ask your parents about their life—you might have a lot more in common than you might think.

PARENTS, ASK YOUR CHILDREN:

What was your favorite game growing up and why?

What was your favorite class in high school?

Do you feel pressure from other students or friends to attend a four-year school?

Do you like taking things apart and putting them back together?

Is there something that you are extremely passionate about?

With technology playing such a big role in manufacturing, can you see yourself working with technology?

What would it mean to you to make components, parts, products, or machines that make a difference in this world?

Where do you see yourself in five years?

Does the idea of using both your hands and your intelligence light you up inside?

Was there a particular topic that spoke to you in this book?

INTERVIEWS IN BOTH BOOKS

Tony Schumacher	Eight-time NHRA Top Fuel Drag Racing Champion
Rand Haas	MCIP Program Manager, Business and Career Services, Inc.
Titan Gilroy	CEO, TITANS of CNC Inc.; Creator of the TV series "TITANS of CNC" and TITANS of CNC Academy
Mark Hibner	Applied Technology Teacher, Palatine-Illinois High School
Andrew Crowe	Founder, the New American Manufacturing Renaissance
Dr. Laz Lopez	Associate Superintendent, Township High School District 214
Sheyenne Kreamer	Triangle Solutions Alliance
Leigh Coglianese McConnell	TMA Director of Training and Workforce Development
Harry Moser	Founder, the Reshoring Initiative®
Craig Rabin	Entrepreneur; Inventor of The Airhook
Dana Ward	Inventor of PreHeels; Founder and President of Barefoot Scientist

Frank Frangie	Radio play-by-play voice of the Jacksonville Jaguars
Tom McSheehy	Teaching Heart Institute (Social Emotional Learning)
Carrie J. Kurczynski	Technical Project Manager/ Operations, GE Power
Mike Rounds	President of Williamson College of the Trades
Vondale Singleton	Founder, CHAMPS Male Mentoring Program
Kathleen Burley	Former Executive Director, Greater Chicago Advanced Manufacturing Partnership

INTERVIEWS UNIQUE TO STUDENT EDITION

Tim Fara	Sr. Executive Vice President, Sales & Marketing at Accutek Inc.
Jossimar Mendez	Plant Manager, ITW Shakeproof Industrial

INTERVIEWS UNIQUE TO PARENT EDITION

Gary Skoog	Makerspace Advocate
Tim Tumanic	CEO, JR Machine
Virginia Rounds	Director, Apprenticeship Networks for the German American Chamber of Commerce
Ryan Pohl	Founder, Praeco Skills

Nicole Wolter	President and CEO, HM Manufacturing
Cathy Hurst	Vice President, Hayden Hurst Family Foundation
Ed Dernulc	Director, Foundation at the Fabricators and Manufacturers

ENDNOTES

CHAPTER ONE

1. Makerspaces, "What Is a Makerspace?" 2022, www.makerspaces.com/what-is-a-makerspace/.

2. Meghan Keneally, "What to Know about William 'Rick' Singer, the Lynchpin of the College Scam Case Who Claimed to Help Nearly 800 Families," ABC News, March 14, 2019, https://abcnews.go.com/US/william-rick-singer-lynchpin-college-scam-case-claimed/story?id=61653747.

CHAPTER TWO

1. Tony Uphoff, "3 Underreported Trends That Will Accelerate Reshoring," *Forbes*, August 24, 2020. https://www.forbes.com/sites/tonyuphoff/2020/08/24/3-underreported-trends-that-will-accelerate-reshoring/?sh=7f6cdf30668e.

2. Gabriel Evans and Rosemary Coates, "SURVEY SAYS: Americans Prefer 'MADE IN USA,'" 2020. https://reshoringinstitute.org/wp-content/uploads/2020/09/made-in-usa-survey.pdf.

3. Richard Frye, "Baby Boomers Are Staying in the Labor Force at Rates Not Seen in Generations for People Their Age," PEW Research, July 24, 2019, https://www.pewresearch.org/fact-tank/2019/07/24/baby-boomers-us-labor-force/.

4. The Manufacturing Institute/Deloitte, *Creating Pathways for Tomorrow's Workforce Today: Beyond Reskilling in Manufacturing* (Deloitte/The Manufacturing Institute, 2021). https://www.themanufacturinginstitute.org/research/creating-pathways-for-tomorrows-workforce-today-beyond-reskilling-in-manufacturing/

5. US Bureau of Labor Statistics, "News Release: Bureau of Labor and Statistics," August 2022, US Department of Labor, https://www.bls.gov/news.release/pdf/empsit.pdf.

6. Sam McEachern, "GM Dropping Four-Year Degree Requirement for Employment," GM Authority, June 13, 2022, https://gmauthority .com/blog/2022/06/gm-dropping-four-year-degree-requirement -for-employment/#:~:text=GM%20has%20dropped%20the%20 four,News%20in%20a%20recent%20interview.

7. Jim Peltz, "Tony Schumacher Wraps up His Eighth NHRA Season Title in Top Fuel," LA Times, November 16, 2014, https://www .latimes.com/sports/la-sp-nhra-finals-20141116-story.html

8. Associated Press, "Tony Schumacher breaks NHRA Top Fuel Speed Record," USA Today, February 23, 2018, https://www.usatoday .com/story/sports/motor/nhra/2018/02/23/schumacher-breaks-nhra -top-fuel-speed-record-force-returns/110766914.

9. US Bureau of Labor Statistics, "Employed Persons by Detailed Industry and Age," US Department of Labor, 2022, https://www.bls .gov/cps/cpsaat18b.htm.

10. Richard Frye, "Baby Boomers Are Staying in the Labor Force at Rates Not Seen in Generations for People Their Age," PEW Research, July 24, 2019, https://www.pewresearch.org/fact-tank/2019/07/24 /baby-boomers-us-labor-force/.

CHAPTER THREE

1. NAM News Room, "2.1 Million Manufacturing Jobs Could Go Unfilled by 2030," National Association of Manufacturers, May 4, 2021, https://www.nam.org/2-1-million-manufacturing-jobs-could-go -unfilled-by-2030-13743/?stream=workforce.

2. National Association of Manufacturers, "Facts About Manufacturing: The Top 18 Facts You Need to Know," The Manufacturing Institute/NAM, 2022, https://www.nam.org/facts-about-manufacturing/.

3. Marketing for Manufacturers, https://marketing4manufacturers .com.

CHAPTER FOUR

1. Victor Yanev, "Video Game Demographics - Who Plays Games in 2022?," January 26, 2022, https://techjury.net/blog/video-game -demographics.

2. Indeed Editorial Staff, "Are Game Developers in Demand? A Look at Video Game Jobs," January 10, 2017, https://www.indeed.com /lead/video-game-labor-snapshot.

3. Statista Research Department, "Percentage of People Aged 65 Years and Older among Total Population in Ja-pan from 1960 to 2020," Statista, February 15, 2023, https://www.statista.com/statistics/1149301 /japan-share-of-population-aged-65-and-above.

4. International Federation of Robotics, "Robot Density Nearly Doubled Globally," December 21, 2021, https://robotics.ee/2021/12/21 /robot-density-nearly-doubled-globally/.

5. Rick Romell, "Automation Will Prompt More Employers to Add Jobs Than to Cut, Manpower Says," *Milwaukee Journal*, January 19, 2018, https://www.jsonline.com/story/money/business/2018/01/19 /automation-prompt-more-employers-add-jobs-than-cut-manpower -says/1048467001/.

CHAPTER FIVE

1. Charles Sykes, *Fail U: The False Promise of Higher Education* (New York: St. Martin's Press, 2016).

2. Richard Vedder And Christopher Denhart, "How the College Bubble Will Pop," *Wall Street Journal*, January 8, 2014, https://www .wsj.com/articles/SB10001424052702303933104579302951214561682.

3. Advisor Magazine, "The Burden of Debt - A Student Debt Snapshot," Lifehealth.com, February 23, 2018, https://www.lifehealth .com/student-debt-snapshot/.

4. Thomas Snyder, *The Community College Career Track: How to Achieve the American Dream Without a Moun-tain of Debt* (Hoboken, NJ: John Wiley & Sons, 2012).

CHAPTER SEVEN

1. Illinois Manufacturing Excellence Center, Made in Illinois: *A Modern Playbook for Manufacturers to Compete and Win*, ed. David Boulay (Fig Factor Media Publishing, 2021).

2. Monte Whaley, "Colorado Families Struggle to Pay Skyrocketing Back-to-school Costs," *The Denver Post*, August 14, 2017, https://www .denverpost.com/2017/08/14/back-to-school-costs-colorado.

3. Nicole Ausherman, "How Automation and AI May Help Level the Playing Field for Women in Manufacturing," www.nist.gov, NIST Blog, July 30, 2020, https://www.nist.gov/blogs/manufacturing-innovation-blog /how-automation-and-ai-may-help-level-playing-field-women.

4. Jennifer Callaway and Yubing Shi, "Ignorance Isn't Bliss. The Impact of Opioids on Manufacturing," Manufacturers Alliance, https://www.manufacturersalliance.org/research-insights /ignorance-isnt-bliss-impact-opioids-manufacturing.

CHAPTER EIGHT

1. Steve Jobs, About Apple's Core Value (1997), YouTube, https:// www.youtube.com/watch?v=dR-ZT8mhfJ4.

ABOUT THE AUTHOR

Terry M. Iverson is President/CEO of Iverson & Company, a machine tool distributorship and rebuilder in Des Plaines, Illinois. Terry has been calling on machine shops and manufacturing companies for decades. His family owns businesses in manufacturing-related areas. His brother, Erik, runs a company that manufactures dial indicators (mechanical and electronic). Terry's uncles have had sub-contract machine shops, while his father ran the company during his tenure after his grandfather founded it.

Terry has spent thousands of hours speaking at schools, **on podcast interviews and writing** about manufacturing in America and has participated on advisory boards. He has served on the TMA Education Foundation, the CTE Education Foundation, and chaired the National Visiting Committee for FLATE (Florida Advanced Technological Education Center).

Terry married his wife Kathy after meeting in their junior year in high school, and they now have 3 adult children and 7 grandchildren. Terry studied mechanical engineering at the University of Wisconsin-Madison and Marquette University.

Terry founded **CHAMPION Now!** with the vision of changing perceptions of manufacturing careers, in hopes of assisting to solve the skills gap crisis in this country.

Hire Terry as a speaker, and purchase autographed books at www.terrymiverson.com

We invite you to join the **CHAMPION Now!** organization, sign up for our CNC Rocks camps, or have your student apply for the Jerry R. Iverson Manufacturing Memorial Scholarship at www.championnow.org.

Inspiring Champions
Student Edition Descripton

Growing up, we are often taught never to question the value of a good education. From the moment they "graduate," young adolescents are measured by how enticing they will appear on the almighty "college application."

But if you stop to consider that the total student debt in the United States is estimated to be $1.3 trillion (*more than credit card and auto loan debt combined*), you may begin to wonder the true value of a college education.

In *Inspiring Champions in Advanced Manufacturing*, Terry Iverson challenges the assumption that sustainable careers may only be achieved through a college education. Through his own love and mastery of the fine art of manufacturing, Iverson contends that careers in manufacturing offer stability, security, and prosperity for our entire nation.

Iverson illustrates the power of manufacturing through in-depth research, personal stories, and over 40 interviews with some of the most remarkable authors, CEOs, sports figures, and influencers.

While half of the book speaks directly to parents, the other half helps inquisitive students know about the options available to them.

With practical application questions and video resources online, *Inspiring Champions in Advanced Manufacturing* teaches parents and students:

- Why cultural pressure steers parents and high school students toward college
- How college pathways leave even the brightest students in debt

- The untold potential of a career in manufacturing
- How the US has a skills shortage that rewards fulfillment with impressive salaries
- How technological advances have made manufacturing into a digital ecosystem
- Action plans for both parents and youth to get involved in manufacturing

Inspiring Champions in Advanced Manufacturing provides parents and students a roadmap for career success and a zero-debt foundation. Reading this book will help you envision the potential that awaits in a lucrative manufacturing career.

Student Edition of Inspiring Champions in Advanced Manufacturing

TERRY M. IVERSON

CONTENTS

Family is everything. I was taught this by my parents.
Despite growing up in a broken family, both my parents
did their best, and I am a product of them both.
My father passed away at the age of 84 years old.
He was a guiding light in my life. The lifelong lessons
he taught me are too numerous to mention,
and many are in this book. All during my mom's
life and up until when she passed,
she taught me how to enjoy people
and life in general.

The Jerry R. Iverson Manufacturing Memorial Scholarship
was established in my father's honor. Both my Uncles
Ed and John Iverson led so many into manufacturing
greatness, and I thank them for helping me
find the champion within myself.

This book is for each of them.

A NOTE FROM TERRY

When I first started in manufacturing, I was totally enamored with recognizing things in everyday life and correlating them to where they were made, whether it was a water meter on the side of my house, a pen, a snow blower, or a lawn mower.

From an early age, buying something made in America was important to me. I always felt that supporting someone in the United States who made the product should be a priority. To this day, every car I have owned, both personally and for my manufacturing company, Iverson & Company, has been an American-made car. As you travel through the pages of my book, I invite you to share my passion. Join in my curiosity and love for this country in a way that gives back to our American manufacturers and American workers.

Our ability to make products ties to our national defense and our security, as well as our standard of living. Making things is in our country's DNA and assures the quality of life and choices that we have grown so accustomed to. At the same time, there is a sleeping giant among us—an opportunity for you, the future generation of leaders, thinkers, technologists, and makers. There is a great sense of accomplishment that comes from working with your hands, solving problems, and bringing new products to life, all while earning good money. Following your passions and interests is important, as well as making sure you're investing your money in a career that makes sense. The huge student debt crisis that many young people find themselves trapped in holds us all back.

There are many reasons to consider manufacturing as a path that will take our country to greatness. However, this book is not meant to convince you that manufacturing is the career for you. Rather, this book is meant to get you thinking that it is one great option to consider.

Why? Because thousands of young adults miss out on a satisfying, fun, and well-paying career for all the wrong reasons.

American culture has become blind to the importance of manufacturing, as evidenced by the awakening during the COVID-19 pandemic. Many Americans were unaware of how vulnerable we are as a country to supply chain connections outside the United States. We saw shortages well beyond the protective gear and medications needed in the first year of the pandemic.

My big lesson from those years was this: I had to market my profession. So many in our craft continue to do what I did—assume that young people are not interested or will not find our trade intriguing.

That's one big reason you're holding this book right now: to gain a quick overview of manufacturing as a career choice—something very few high school counselors and parents talk about.

Here's a look at what's ahead:

- In Chapter 1, you'll look behind the curtain of manufacturing—and learn what it is and what it isn't.
- Chapter 2 will take you a step further as you explore the many career opportunities for young people and why American-made products are on the rise.
- In Chapter 3, you will learn about internships and one person's extraordinary path to manufacturing.

- Chapter 4 will talk about technology in manufacturing and another individual's path to manufacturing (this one will blow your mind).
- In Chapter 5, get ready to have your eyes opened as I give you a startling look at time, money, and your future career.
- You'll love Chapter 6, as it shows you just how much control you have over your future.
- Dive into Chapter 7, and you'll be welcomed into a career in manufacturing with open arms and cash.
- Finally, in Chapter 8, we will get going on your shortcut to success!

The skilled workforce needs problem-solvers and innovators like you! Salaries are going up as opportunities abound—that is, for those perceptive enough to recognize them. The biggest challenge to the opportunities around you is the negative perception of manufacturing in the U.S. Our culture looks down on it sometimes, while our European counterparts—Volkswagen in Germany, Nestlé in Switzerland, and Fiat Chrysler in Italy, for example—hold a career in manufacturing in high regard.

I ask you to start a journey with me in this book. Whether you find the Champion in yourself, a relative, or friend—*I know this time will be memorable, enlightening, and inspiring.* As you move through these pages, I will give you the tools, resources, and insight to help inspire you all—our next generation—to become Champions in manufacturing. My hope is to take you on a journey about your current perceptions and then consider what your career could be. Throughout the book, you will find QR codes to provide a digital experience by simply using your cell phone.

When you are done, you will open up opportunities by, well, opening up. Smack in the middle of this book are "conversation

starters" or questions that you and your parents or other mentors in your life might discuss.

First, though, there are many exciting things I want to show you. Let's get going.

THE MAKER'S LIFE

Makers make things. The Iverson family
certainly has fit the moniker of 'makers.'
There is an entire movement in the U.S.
called 'the maker movement,' and I am asking
you to consider it as a career option.
It all starts in Norway . . .

This country has been shaped by a long history of crafts-men, artisans, and fishermen who have immigrated from countries near and far. In fact, my father's family originated in Norway. My great-grandfather came over on a ship and never got back on when it returned home. For decades, I had heard that he had "jumped ship" when he traveled over from Norway to the U.S. I took it to mean that he literally jumped off the ship, until, of course, I found out Dad meant it figuratively. Communication and storylines from families are incredibly important, and I have always felt a need to know our beginnings.

Like many immigrants coming to the United States, my grandfather started a family and hoped for a better life. The manufacturing sector has reaped the benefits of many talented and skilled tradesmen coming from lands far away. Our forefathers lived life with a code of honesty that led to success and happiness.

Think about this: Where did the people who came before you live and work? What were their ambitions? What did they sacrifice to make a better life for you? This is part of your story, too.

Let me share the legacy that manufacturing has left for me.

I believe in manufacturing. It has been good to my family, and it has been good to this great country. So many company owners and managers are struggling to find skilled workers to grow their businesses and replace Baby Boomer generation retirees.

My family has been in manufacturing for nearly a century due to the great careers it offers. My grandfather, Edward Iverson, worked for a small machine tool builder in Chicago back in 1925. Keep in mind that this was shortly before the Great Depression of 1929. When his father died at a young age, he had to quit school at 16 years old. He worked full-time to support his five siblings and mother.

He started at the shop by sweeping the floors. I know this "humble beginnings" story may seem cliché, but it is true. His

supervisor soon realized that he possessed talents, not only in math and science, but also in drafting. Grandpa quickly became a vital part of the company and rose in importance in his department. In fact, when the company was bought out in 1931, only three people were offered a position in the plans to move east to New York State. He was, in fact, the only one to decline and, as a result, stayed back to represent the manufacturer.

I have thought many times about this bit of family history. Here my grandfather was, in the middle of the Great Depression (1929-1932) in Chicago, and the company he worked for was purchased. He had to make a decision to move to New York or to stay. He made the tough decision to stay and not uproot the entire family. This bold move, and him being the major bread-winner at such a young age, were the first indicators I can remember of how important a sense of family is and how manufacturing is a difference-maker.

Grandpa was good at what he did and grew to know many industry leaders in the manufacturing sector. My father, Jerry, started working for my grandfather in machine tools in 1958. My uncle John joined Iverson & Company a few years after. In 1957, my uncle Ed started his own subcontract machine shop called Chucking Machine Products, which initially machined parts for Bell & Howell. It has now been in business more than 60 years and specializes in high-precision aerospace, defense, and military subcontract machine work. Uncle John bought a small job shop named Custom Products, which became a 700+ person shop under his ownership and vision by the time he sold the company in the late 1990's. My father stayed with the company and perfected the craft of machine tool sales and rebuilding. My

father was very detail-oriented, analytical, and financially astute. He has been my greatest mentor to this day, and I thank him for teaching me so much about life and work. His greatest words of advice were: "Terry, you have everything if you have family and your health. Everything else is secondary."

MY JOURNEY INTO THE FAMILY BUSINESS

My father wanted me to go to college. In one sense, I disappointed him, but I ended up making him very proud in other ways. Here's the story.

During the summers of the early '70s, around the start of my high school career, I started packing collets, cleaning machines, taking apart spindle motors, cleaning the shop, and mowing the lawn. We were in Chicago, where we had been for several decades. When we painted machines, the smell of fresh Sherwin Williams 7B paint would permeate throughout the shop. To this day, when we paint machines, the smell brings back memories of when I was 14, starting in the family business.

I had a knack for academics, especially math, so I went to college. I was told it was what I was supposed to do if I wanted a great career. College would open doors, they said. And they were right. I gave the same advice to my children. They were also wrong. Because for some people, learning needs to be hands-on. You need to see the impact of your work closer to the point where you are doing it. And you need to see the paycheck and the promotions and, well, your future.

I was in my second year of college when I realized I loved manufacturing and could accomplish more by starting my career than sitting in a classroom. I entered into the sales side of the business in Wisconsin. I would leave the house every day bright

and early to make sales calls. I found it fascinating seeing locks, water meters, motorcycles, and guidance systems being made from the ground up. Each machine shop I entered was either a screw machine shop with a very strong cutting oil "aroma," or a CNC (computer numerical control) shop with a differing water-soluble coolant smell.

At the end of the day, I made the drive home. I learned that my suit would absorb these industrial olfactory identifiers, not necessarily appreciated by my better half upon my arrival at home. "You smell like a machine shop," she would say. To me, it was the smell of money and opportunity, and the pride of helping customers make something useful to the world at large. Today's shops feature a great deal more mist collection equipment and are cleaner. They no longer have the strong oil smell throughout. But the opportunities for success are just as great.

My (much) younger brother Erik also worked for us from 1995 to 2002. Erik left our company to go to Chicago Dial, which he now owns and runs as president. Everyone in our family is proud of the "Made in America" moniker. We believed in the ingenious and productive means of making things here in the U.S.

MAKING A LIFE IN MANUFACTURING

For years, I had a tough time as the only sibling "going the distance" in the family business. There were ample chances to move on to other opportunities. As one who always finishes the job and is loyal to the family, I stayed through the years. Then, in 1999, came a week at the Harvard Business School. It was a week-long strategic finance seminar my father asked me to attend. I found that people were interested in what I had to say, from the

perspective of running our small family machine tool business. The thing that impacted me the most was a young lady from South America. I mentioned being the only child in the family business. She commented, "Oh, so YOU are the chosen one!"

What? I thought.

"In our country, it is an honor to be the chosen one—to run the family business," she said.

I thought long and hard about this. That one encounter was like signing my own permission slip to continue down the path of what is now my fourth decade in manufacturing. My wife Kathy works with me. I am very proud of her and have confidence in the fact that she can accomplish great things in anything she does. I also feel that way about our three adult children. God has blessed us with seven grandchildren at the time of this writing, and I cannot wait to see what endeavors each chooses to follow in life.

I HEAR YOU LOUD AND CLEAR

I began coaching and mentoring young people when our children were young. I retired from being a soccer coach when my youngest son turned 18, and several of his teammates went on to play Division III soccer. Yet, I still felt compelled to mentor youth. I was fortunate to have mentors when I was young, and I felt a great obligation to pay it forward.

The parallels between playing sports and succeeding in life and business are too numerous to count. If you find success in one area as a young person, your ability to find success in the other increases exponentially.

You have career options beyond what "everybody else is doing." In fact, "what everybody else is doing" has little to do with you.

I don't blame you if you are saying any of the following as you read this book:

- Your generation doesn't "get" me.
- How can you know the pressure of choosing a lifelong career at this age?
- All my classmates will have their colleges announced at graduation.
- My parents want me to go into (fill in the blank here).
- What if I fail?

Well, I *was* your age once. But even that doesn't give me the knowledge of what it's like to walk in your shoes. However, through the nonprofit I started called **CHAMPION Now!**, I talk with hundreds of young adults each year. Your voices, concerns, and questions stay with me because you are the next generation of leaders and makers—*you* will turn ideas into products used by millions of people around the world. For you to do that, though, you must see the truth about manufacturing and why, perhaps, it's a field you could be really good at. You are the reason I wrote this book and why I started a nonprofit to connect youth with manufacturing.

I have given presentations at annual conferences across the country in front of many young people. I also got involved in a Leadership Forum in Washington. On my way to one of these meetings, I myself became inspired.

I thought, *How do I coin a slogan or an organization to change people's perceptions?* I already had pitched a television idea, but that alone did not seem to be enough. There had to be a message alongside anything that talked about manufacturing. I struggled with the terms "changing," "perceptions," and "manufacturing."

While scribbling on a napkin on a plane, I toyed with the words CHANGE – MANUFACTURING – PERCEPTIONS. Somehow, I came up with C-H-M-P. I then found my way to the word C-H-A-M-P-I-O-N. It stands for Change How American Manufacturing's Perceived In Our Nation.

I added the "Now" to initiate action to move—immediately. In other words, there is a crisis in our country, which is that no one thinks about, is exposed to, or is encouraged to pursue careers in manufacturing. As a result, our workers, managers, and owners are getting older. There is no succession plan.

Come on in! Take a tour of **CHAMPION Now!** by visiting www.championnow.org.

THE WAY YOU SEE THE WORLD MAKES THE BIGGEST DIFFERENCE

How you see the world determines your path in life.

For example, what if you chose a career in manufacturing and then were asked to participate in a signing day with notable media recognition? Would you be more excited about the road ahead?

I would. I think most people would say "yes."

Well, in Henrico County Public Schools in Virginia, that's exactly what Director of Career and Technical Education (CTE) Mac Beaton did. He honored technical education graduates by having them sign letters of intent for employment. This is similar to high school athletes committing to their chosen college on National Signing Day.[1]

When I spoke as a keynote speaker for NC3 (National Coalition of Community Colleges) in 2019, I also learned of

the National CTE Letter of Intent Signing Day to celebrate high school graduates' intent to further their education in the skilled trade professions. Clark Coco, Tina Blair, and Clayton Tatro Washburn Tech in Topeka, Kansas, held the first CTE Letter of Intent Signing Day in 2014.[2] The event has grown exponentially ever since. Last year, 62 schools participated, with over 5,000 students signing letters of intent at ceremonies tied together by live, nationwide simulcasts.

It should also be noted that SKILLSUSA is an organization that also acknowledges National Signing Day each year and is one of the organizations leading the way nationally, not only in competitions but also in elevating the careers for these young people.[3]

Manufacturing is the best-kept secret that young people are often simply not aware of. Yet, it *is* one of America's greatest opportunities—one of her greatest Champions. Next up, we'll take a look at the surprising facts, highlights, and myths of manufacturing, why it is so crucial to our country's future, and our culture's profound—and surprising—influence on manufacturing.

MANUFACTURING AS A CAREER CHOICE

*"...so when I hear people go, 'You guys make
your product outside the U.S.' Really?
You buy products (made) outside the U.S.?
Stop buying it outside the U.S.
And we can start making it in the U.S."*

—Tony Schumacher,
NHRA Top Fuel Champion

The US manufactures just under 20 percent of the world's goods. Yet, our culture often gives the impression we aren't a manufacturing populace, and that manufacturing is not important. Time to *wake up*. Our culture needs to be engaged in *where* things are made, *how* things are made, and *why* it is important for us to care.

So, what exactly is manufacturing? Here's the definition according to Merriam-Webster.

MANUFACTURE:

1. *Something made from raw materials by hand or by machinery*
2. *The process of making wares by hand or by machinery especially when carried on systematically with division of labor. b: a productive industry using mechanical power and machinery*
3. *The act or process of producing something*

You might say, "Isn't that obvious? Of course, manufacturing creates things." But my explanation goes further than making products. It includes components like:

Manufacturing create$ Opportunities
Manufacturing create$ Jobs
Manufacturing create$ Careers
Manufacturing create$ Wealth
Manufacturing create$ Stability

Maybe we have gotten away from a basic understanding of what has made this country great. Much of the media likes to say that we have become a service-based country. I disagree. The U.S. manufacturing economic engine is the eighth largest economy

in the world. We manufacture approximately one-fifth of the world's goods. Does that sound like manufacturing is dead?

The biggest challenge for U.S. manufacturers is an inadequate supply of talent to make it happen. However, their challenge becomes one of your great opportunities.

MANUFACTURING CREATE$ OPPORTUNITIES

Here's a story about the day I went on TV and was put on the spot by a well-known personality. My response to her is the best way I can show you the opportunities in manufacturing.

In March 2009, I was invited to talk on the "Monster and Money" television show in Chicago. My high school buddy Don Dupree was the producer and knew of my manufacturing expertise. It was a live broadcast on Channel 2 Chicago local TV—at a very early time in the morning, somewhere around 5:40 a.m. I talked about the **CHAMPION Now!** organization that I founded to promote manufacturing careers and I said that manufacturing was still in need of young talent. They gave us five minutes to talk and answer questions on live television.

Of course, I was nervous… and a bit half asleep, as well. I doubt I had adequate coffee that morning. There were four hosts on the show: ex-Chicago Bear and sportscaster Dan Jiggetts, radio personality Mike North, Mike Hegedus of Hegedus World, and financial expert Terry Savage.

I wasn't cued into what questions were going to be asked or how the interview was going to go. So I simply mentioned my organization and how I had become a self-proclaimed advocate for manufacturing jobs. Mike North talked about how manufacturing companies had moved to the suburbs, and Dan Jiggetts

said that growing up, he had heard that manufacturing jobs paid well.

Then came the comment I never saw coming from nationally known financial guru Terry Savage. She said: "I find it very counterintuitive that you are sitting here saying that today there are jobs available and that we should tell young people to pursue careers in manufacturing!"

Needless to say, I was floored. Talk about being put on the spot! The answer I gave was simple: "Terry, there are some manufacturing jobs that cannot leave American soil—defense and medical, to name a few. We will always have to make the most complex, advanced, and most proprietary products in our country."

The component of the response that I left out was how the aging population in manufacturing exceeds the number of products and jobs leaving for China. Although it is true that a great deal of low-cost products and processes are going to China, with automation and advanced production techniques and equipment, we can compete globally.

The average age in manufacturing is over 50. With each recession, many of the Baby Boomers working in manufacturing postponed their retirement, but the catastrophic flow of retirees out of manufacturing is inevitable. During 2020 and the height of the COVID-19 pandemic, we learned of our dependence on products manufactured by other countries around the world. When we needed PPE equipment (masks and shields, for example), we learned that most of it came from China. As a country, we were all scrambling for PPE equipment to protect those who were on the frontlines taking care of our infected population.

Making products in our country creates opportunities.

MANUFACTURING CREATE$ JOBS

"The Boomer labor force has been declining by 2.2 million on average each year since 2010, or about 5,900 daily."[1] The average age of a manufacturing employee is well into their mid-40s. According to the Manufacturing Institute, by 2030 nearly 4 million manufacturing jobs likely need to be filled. The skills gap is expected to result in 2.1 million of those jobs going unfilled.[2] This is at a time when unemployment has hovered around 3.7 percent.[3] At the same time, the media preaches to not go into manufacturing-related fields.

Something doesn't add up. Those of us in the industry have an obligation to correct the course that seems to be set. To drive the financial stability of our country and all those employed by it, we need to encourage the brightest, most energetic, and most passionate to go into the manufacturing field. Boeing is blatant about how many engineers it needs to produce planes. Many companies have no idea how they are going to staff their production needs in the upcoming years. One ThomasNet article claims that Boeing has a backlog of 5,864 airplanes; those orders are worth $135 billion and amount to about 7 years of production work.[4]

It is no secret that many American manufacturers got complacent and fell asleep at the switch. My dad told me that deliveries in the machine tool business got to the point where it took 12 to 24 months to get a very basic standard machine tool in the 1960s and 1970s. This opened the door to aggressive machine tool builders from Japan and Taiwan to have more competitively priced products, as well as in-stock deliveries. Machine tool builders in these countries saw an awesome opportunity and seized the moment. As a result, the machine tool business was never the same in the U.S.

Many would say that the weak manufacturing sector is now to the point of posing extreme risk to our national defense. What would happen if we went to war with some of the countries that we now consider our allies? Many of these could be the same countries that supply machine tools to make our defense mechanisms. We could possibly be unable to keep these machine tools operational in order to supply an arsenal to our military. A strong machine tool foundation in our country is vital. With all the problems we have experienced through the pandemic, our culture is starting to realize that we need to manufacture more in the U.S. The supply chain deficiencies have become scarily apparent and have exposed our country's vulnerabilities in the global marketplace.

The automotive industry also became apathetic from the standpoint of quality. We made inferior products and expected U.S. consumers to not only accept them, but also to pay more for them. We did not listen to what the consumer wanted, expected, and needed. Japanese car companies came in with reasonably priced, economical automobiles that featured a great deal more miles to the gallon. The American automotive executive allowed products to be designed, built, and manufactured that were primarily status-defining, luxury cars that cost more and were inefficient.

Car manufacturers got what they deserved when sales declined. They didn't listen to consumers in both cases. What would be worse yet is if manufacturers didn't learn from our mistakes as a culture and stayed less competitive and less responsive to market demands. We also need to be more responsible in attracting, creating, and developing the next generation of manufacturing workers, employees, and leaders. Now we have executives like Mary Barra at General Motors (GM) who think

differently. Not only has she shown that the glass ceiling can be shattered for her gender, but she is also leading the automotive giant into new, more responsible, and responsive designs to build cars in the future.

I find the success of Tesla exciting, as well as the technological gains demonstrated in their electric cars and autonomous driving. I think of the freedom that my father would have had if he had lived another five years or so. My father had macular degeneration to the point that he gave up driving for good during the last five to eight years of his life. He loved cars and driving, not to mention the independence it gave him. While the trend is a long time coming, I find Tesla's innovations to be a welcome wake-up call for the U.S. auto industry. All the major automotive brands are playing catch-up at this point, but it will pay dividends for the earth as we try to reduce emissions and address climate change. Being less dependent on fossil fuels will certainly help our world.

TONY SCHUMACHER ON WHICH COMES FIRST: MADE IN AMERICA OR BUY IN AMERICA?

One day, I was at a Mother's Day brunch with my extended family when my sister Amy mentioned that a friend from work was moving into our subdivision. She thought the husband did something with racing but wasn't totally sure. I mentioned that I would stop in and say hello. Not long after the family moved in, I knocked on the door and introduced myself. As it turns out, they were a young couple with the last name Schumacher, and Tony was a drag racer. Over the years, we became good friends, and it was awesome to see Tony grow and become so accomplished. At the time of this writing, he is an eight-time NHRA

(National Hot Rod Association) champion.[5] At one point, Tony held the speed record of 336 MPH.[6]

Besides owning Don Schumacher Racing (DSR), his father also owns Schumacher Electric. Schumacher Electric is known as a first-class battery charger manufacturer. Tony became the winningest Top Fuel driver in NHRA history. He has the following to share with us:

Tony Schumacher's thoughts:

Now, if Americans, as buyers, would walk into a store and only buy the stuff made in America, we'd be great. We would be wonderful. But they go in and they want the cheapest price too.

I hear people go, 'You guys make your product outside the U.S.' Really, you buy products made outside the U.S.? Stop buying it from outside the U.S., and we can start making it in the U.S. It costs more to hire an American than it does to hire someone in China. We still save a ton of money, even with the shipping and all the containers, the taxes, everything coming in.

As buyers, we need to make the conscious choice that it's here that we want to be part of. Stop being so, *We're trying to save money*. It comes full circle. If we spend the money in the U.S., we all get paid more, everything goes up. The value of everything we do is good. I'm not making anything up. We can make America great again,

we just get to do it right. We have got to start being responsible as buyers, buying a product right here, so people who own companies can start making stuff here, because we want to. Guess what? If I want to go overseas and make stuff, don't buy it. Maybe you'll force me to do it. I think it's important that we take a little responsibility as the buyer.

While speaking to engineers at Boeing, I told this story. If I was going to get in my race car that goes 330 miles per hour, and I'm about to start it, and my crew chief leans over and goes, 'I've got great news for you: This car's built in China and Mexico, I just saved your dad a ton of money,' my response would be, 'I have great news for you. You can drive. I'm not getting in that car.' The place went nuts.

On a very bright note, there are some things that are starting to make a difference in the U.S. The Science, Technology, Engineering, and Math (STEM) and Project Lead the Way initiatives are making their way into high schools. Project Lead the Way allows high school youth to learn with their hands and makes the connection between book knowledge and project-based learning.

For Inspiration and Recognition of Science and Technology (FIRST) robotics and other robotic team competitions teach young people the troubleshooting tasks needed in any manufacturing field or career. Around 1994, I followed the lead by fellow machine tool sales professional Tim Doran to do presentations at local high schools. In our presentations, we encouraged students to attend our trade show, the International Manufacturing

Technology Show (IMTS), which is held every two years in downtown Chicago. This event opens an entire new world to the youth of this country. IMTS is like the Disney World of the machine tool and manufacturing industries. For many years, attendees had to be over 18, which did very little to attract the next generation of workers.

The biggest threat to manufacturing is the lack of skilled workers. This is one reason manufacturing creates jobs.

As the Reshoring Movement progresses, the new administration removes the regulations, taxes, and other hindrances that impede manufacturing companies from competing in the world market. We *must* address the lack of employees to allow the manufacturing renaissance to bring prosperity back to the U.S. and the middle class of America. This means more training, opportunities, and programs.

MANUFACTURING CREATE$ CAREERS

As we went into late 2021 and early 2022, the supply chain system became a disaster. Shipments of products from Eastern Asia were taking much more time than previously anticipated. We found ourselves unable to purchase our favorite products, food items, Christmas presents, and more. Cars could not be built because of the lack of computer microchips. Deliveries for everything were pushed back longer than anything I had ever experienced in my lifetime. The fact that 75 percent of the microchips are made outside the U.S. could be an omen for trouble for our manufacturing and our standard of living.

If that wasn't enough of a challenge, then came the "Great Resignation." In December of 2021, 308,000 workers left manufacturing employment, while in that month, there were

433,000 hires. The previous months saw 294,000 (November), 298,000 (October), and 324,000 (September) workers leave manufacturing employment when three years prior to the pandemic attrition each month averaged between 225,000 and 300,000.[7] In 2000, the average age of a manufacturing worker was 40.5 years of age. Twenty-two years later, that number has risen now to 44.2, compared to retail, where the average age is 37.7 years of age.[8]

We have been preaching that the baby boomers were near retirement in droves and that the "Silver Tsunami" of retirements was coming. As mentioned earlier, the boomer labor force has been declining by 2.2 million on average each year.[9]

Additionally, we had a collective epiphany about millennials who were fed up with the work-life balance, or lack thereof. In Europe, there seems to be a better understanding of how to balance things. Travel in Europe in August, and you will find that plants are shut down for an entire month while the rest of the world waits for their return.

The truth is that manufacturing isn't just a job. Manufacturing is a great career where you can experience steady career growth if you want: a leadership path, a learning path to expand your skills and make more money, and a technology path to be a programmer or work with robotics or do data analysis if you want to.

TIM FARA: MANUFACTURING HAS COME A LONG WAY

I met a person in the machine tool industry with a similar vision about addressing the vast need in skilled labor. He, like me, had way too many customers asking for an operator/programmer with every machine tool sold. His name is Tim Fara, and he is the Senior Executive Vice President of Sales & Marketing at Accutek

Inc. Using his words below, Tim speaks to the many opportunities that await you in the manufacturing sector.

Tim Fara's thoughts:

Over the last two or three decades, we've lost a generation of skilled workers—young adults, male, females—coming into the manufacturing world.

When I was young and starting out, machine shops were not the safest. They weren't unsafe, but they weren't as safe as they are today. They weren't as clean as they are today. A lot of the machines were open… they didn't have sheet metal shrouds around them. They were open, and that's because we didn't have the high RPMs that we have today.

The CNC machines that we have today are highly technical, and well-enclosed. You walk into the machine shops, the production shops, many of them are very, very clean. They're very, very safe. They're very well-lit. They're not dark, dirty, and dangerous, as we used to refer to them.

There are so many different things that you can do with the skills trades: mechanics, plumbers, carpentry, machinists, electricians, robotics, lab tech; you name it. There are so many different avenues you can go to. I myself am a product of that; I have a complete manufacturing background, can operate most machines, and can program most machines, but I'm not working in the shop. I am part owner of the tooling company that manufactures tooling and sells it for those machines that

we're talking about. And so there are many opportunities for young adults to do that, to let them know that there are great careers beyond being a doctor, a lawyer, or a scientist, and that there are other avenues out there.

To define what our children should be doing based on our perceptions, to me, is very wrong. We need to guide and encourage them. We need to let them know what opportunities are out there, and this is something that has to be done during the high school years because those are the formative years that teenagers are discovering who they are, what they like and don't like, who they like and who they don't like, and what they're going to do for the rest of their lives.

If students were really smart and went to a community college or vocational tech school, where they could take a little bit more time to decide what they like and don't like, you do it at far less expense, but it's still a very good education. Then from there, you could move on to a four-year university and finish up the two years remaining and have a very successful time and a very successful career.

Europe, I think, is a great place for the United States to learn from because, back in the '50s and the '60s, and even in the '70s, we had what Europe has today, but we let our culture in the United States evolve and change that. To a certain degree, we destroyed the strength that we had.

The manufacturer in the United States needs to have that pool of people that are capable out there. Not everybody wants to be a doctor. Not everybody *can* be a doctor. Not everybody wants to be a lawyer or can be a

lawyer. Not everybody wants to be a teacher or can be a teacher. But there are so many other areas, especially in manufacturing, that you can aspire to that. And Europe continues to educate and respect those people that go into the trades.

Be it plumbing, electrical, electrician, engineering, manufacturing, they (Europeans) treat them as professionals, as they do their doctors and their teachers and their nurses. So we have lost that here in the United States.

Without manufacturing, we become a service country. And then through this last pandemic, we saw what happens when so many of our products are supplied from the rest of the world. We are very susceptible to long delivery delays and things like that. We have to be ready at all times. And that means that manufacturing here in the United States has got to be strong and sustainable. And the only way we can do that is by continuing to build the careers and capabilities of our young adults going into manufacturing.

MANUFACTURING CREATE$ WEALTH

Historically, if you look at any leading nation in the world, you will find that they have economic success. Manufacturing is at the core of their sustained prosperity.

My immediate and extended family has done well in the manufacturing sector. We have all owned nice homes, driven nice cars, provided for our families, and saved money for that

"rainy day." This is all possible with hard work, determination, and taking advantage of great opportunities. Starting with my grandfather, many have taken this path. Some took a more direct route, while others had to find it in a more cumbersome fashion (that was me). However, despite that, I was in the groove by age 22! I look back at my 42-year career, and I am thankful, grateful, and proud. Going forward, my goal is to yell this from the mountaintops so that others can accomplish the same.

MANUFACTURING CREATE$ STABILITY

Manufacturing creates wealth, and wealth leads to stability. There is no doubt that manufacturing has ebbs and flows, peaks and valleys. Leaders and owners know this and plan accordingly. Many pay off their debts with profits earned when times are good.

Workers that have been successful learn their trade each and every day to the best of their ability. The more they learn, the more value they add for their employer and themselves. There is no job that is guaranteed for life. The market changes dramatically each and every year. Technology has prompted such changes. In today's job market, young have to compete with many other applicants for the same job openings in the same sector. We are producing more lawyers, accountants, and other traditional careers. Meanwhile, all things technical are getting fewer and fewer applicants.

Companies are realizing that they don't necessarily need a new employee to have a degree; they need a skillset. So, yes, manufacturing creates stability. Simple supply-and-demand proves it to be the case.

I hope that this chapter has enlightened you in many ways and that you have a newfound appreciation for the significance of

manufacturing and our country's place using a global perspective. Automation is a means to build our economy that needs even more skilled workers, not less. Chapter 3 will present stories from those who hope to reinforce the **CHAMPION Now!** messaging by changing perceptions through plant tours, podcasts, talk radio, and TV programs. They are my heroes. Collectively, we can be the key to building tomorrow's skilled workforce in the U.S.

THE BRIDGE TO MANUFACTURING, CONSTRUCTION, AND OTHER PATHS

"They keep going down this road like sheep to a slaughter, man. Everybody told me I couldn't have a shop and that American manufacturing was dead and I was like, 'I'm different.'"

—Titan Gilroy,
CEO, TITANS of CNC

The U.S. manufacturing industry is thriving and enjoys the promise of even greater growth and prosperity ahead. In fact, 90% of manufacturing companies recently surveyed feel positive about their own company outlook. The statistics hold the promise of new prosperity, benefiting our global competitiveness, economic growth, and communities across the country. But there is one huge threat to the future of U.S. manufacturing: "The manufacturing skills gap in the U.S. could result in 2.1 million unfilled jobs by 2030."[1]

Not only are there great opportunities in manufacturing, but there are other industries closely connected with manufacturing to consider. Consider these career options and salaries. These are the 2021 median salaries from the U.S. Bureau of Labor and Statistics website:

CNC Operator	$46,240.00
Welder	$47,010.00
Precision Machinist	$47,730.00
Carpenter	$48,260.00
Sheet Metal Workers	$53,440.00
Tool & Die Worker	$57,000.00
Plumbers	$59,880.00
Electrician	$60,040.00
CNC Programmer	$62,360.00
Production Supervisor	$67,330.00

You might wonder: Why didn't I know about these career options? I have a story about that.

There is a TV commercial from MB Financial Bank in which the lead character is walking through his machine shop, stopping to explain various aspects of his company to the banker. While

the shop owner is rattling off various aspects of his machinery—the CNC (computerized numerically controlled) lathe, his coordinate measuring machine, and his press brakes—the banker stays quiet during the entire 30-second spot.

 This type of commercial speaks volumes about our culture, one where few in the general populace understand the full potential of manufacturing.

When people ask me what I do, it's hard to come up with a response sometimes. Will they have a clue as to what I am talking about? Or will they seem politely interested with a *deer in the headlights* stare while thinking to themselves about how unglamorous it all sounds?

Companies like Gillette and Harley-Davidson are changing the game by starting to share the pride of making quality products in America. Some of their commercials talk about their companies competing globally, with American workers making a quality product.

WHY CNC ROCKS!

We have already covered how important manufacturing is to this country. What we haven't covered is how absolutely awesome today's manufacturing technology is! CNC operators are one reason why.

I sincerely believe that given exposure to CNC (Computer Numerically Controlled) machine tools, today's youth will find manufacturing to be exciting and fascinating. CNC is where it's

at. The next generation has been brought up in a digital environment. You text rather than pick up a phone. You play computer games rather than go outside and play a pick-up game of soccer, football, baseball, or hockey (unless, of course, it is organized ball). You start using your iPhone around the age of eight or nine. My question is: Given our digital culture, why aren't kids lining up for careers in manufacturing? You have all the innate capabilities from a very young age.

The answer is back to the **CHAMPION Now!** message. Young people perceive that they can't make good money in these fields, or that it is not a safe or clean environment. That manufacturing is not for smart students or that it is not an honorable profession.

The facts disprove these perceptions. According to the National Association of Manufacturing (NAM), in 2021, manufacturing workers in the U.S. earned $95,990 on average, including pay and benefits. Workers in all private nonfarm industries earned $81,308 on average.[2]

We need to change these perceptions among young people, but also among parents, grandparents, the media, and guidance counselors. That is the difficult task, it will take time, and it will not come without a price.

More TV shows, commercials, news reports, an active approach to plant tours, and programs to educate guidance counselors will make you more aware of your choices.

The term CNC Rocks is a slogan I came up with through **CHAMPION Now!** to convey that manufacturing is an exciting place to be. The CNC portion of the industry is especially pertinent to youth. I thought of a lot of other slogans, but this one spoke to me because it speaks the language of young people.

DO YOUR HOMEWORK
ABOUT YOUR CAREER OPTIONS

Whether you go into manufacturing or some related field, doing your homework pays off. Making assumptions doesn't. The following are myths about manufacturing you might find helpful. Both the websites for Marketing4Manufacturers[3] & The Manufacturing Institute (NAM) say it best:

Myth: Manufacturing jobs are disappearing, and the ones that exist don't require many skills.
Fact: There are an estimated 350,000 manufacturing jobs unfilled today. More than 80 percent of manufacturing companies have reported shortages in skilled production workers from entry level on up. Since machines are increasingly computer controlled, the jobs that need to be filled are for programmers, operators, and maintenance workers. Highly skilled maintenance workers can earn more than $100k per year.

Myth: Free trade agreements hurt U.S. manufacturing.
Fact: About half of all manufactured goods exported from the U.S. went to countries with which we had free trade agreements. U.S. manufacturers in 2015 had a $412.7 billion surplus with countries with which we had free trade agreements, versus the $639.6 billion deficit they had with countries without agreements.

Myth: U.S. manufacturers can't compete with cheap, overseas labor.
Fact: Over the past 25 years, the export of U.S.-manufactured products has quadrupled. Also, manufacturers fund more

than 75 percent of all private sector research and development in the country, creating more innovation than any other sector. With the large amount of growth in the manufacturing industry and its focus on innovation, U.S. manufacturers have become more "lean" and automated, which is helping them become more competitive in the global market.

Myth: Manufacturing jobs in the U.S. are disappearing, and they don't pay well.
Fact: In 2020, millions of manufacturing employees made, on average $92,832/year, including benefits. In addition, nearly 4.0 million more manufacturing jobs are expected to become available by 2030.[4]

Myth: There aren't many "small" manufacturing firms in the U.S. anymore.
Fact: The vast majority of manufacturing firms in the U.S. are small. In other words, there are 239,651 manufacturing firms in the U.S. with fewer than 500 employees. Furthermore, 74.3 percent of these small manufacturing firms have less than 20 employees. It's also interesting to note that manufacturers have one of the highest percentages of workers who are eligible for employer-provided health benefits—95 percent!

Myth: Manufacturing isn't a big part of the U.S. economy anymore.
Fact: In 2021, U.S. manufacturing contributed $2.77 trillion to the economy and accounted for approximately 8-10 percent of the total workforce. Additionally, in 2020 manufacturing accounted for over 10.8 percent of GDP in the economy. For every $1 spent in manufacturing, another

$2.68 is added to the economy. That is the highest multiplier effect of any economic sector. In addition, for every one worker in manufacturing, there are another four employees hired elsewhere.

MANUFACTURING INTERNSHIPS ARE MAKING A DIFFERENCE

Next up, meet Rand Haas. He'll talk to you about his Manufacturing Careers Internship Program (MCIP) program. In Rand's first internship group, I took two of the ten interns and hired both full-time. One still remains with Iverson & Company. The internship program is vital in bringing along young people towards manufacturing careers, and in some ways, can be combined with an apprenticeship program that I call an "ApprInternship." Rand's program is by far one of the best that I've seen.

Rand Haas's thoughts:

The Manufacturing Careers Internship Program (MCIP), developed by Business and Career Services (BCS) in 2011, has been recognized as one of the most effective and innovative workforce development programs in the United States. It received the innovation award from the State of Illinois as one of the most innovative workforce programs in the state, with more than 70 percent of the participants who completed the program now successfully employed. It also has been cited by the Brookings Institute and the Aspen Institute out of Washington, DC, as a 'best practice' workforce development program.

Designed to address the critical need for younger workers in the manufacturing sector, the MCIP has three major goals:

Help employers identify, vet, and hire motivated, out-of-school youths ages 18–24.
Help young adults learn about manufacturing careers and start a successful career path.
Change the perception of manufacturing and promote it as a highly desirable career.

The MCIP is funded through the Illinois Department of Commerce and Economic Opportunity (DCEO) and a federal WIOA grant from the US Department of Labor. It starts with a Career Exploration Camp that leads directly to an internship. BCS serves as the employer of record during the internship and covers wages and liability and worker's comp insurance. Participating employers interview and select interns prior to the internship and can hire them at no charge upon completion.

The Career Exploration Camp is one of the reasons for the success of this program. One issue that was identified early in the program's development was that many young adults entering the program had no clear career goals and lacked training and skills to start a career in manufacturing. We found many young adults finished their high school with no clear career direction or didn't know what was expected of them in their workplace. Before the internships, BCS brings all the participants together in a classroom setting on

work readiness training during the Career Exploration Camp, which includes:

- Tours of local area manufacturers to learn about careers and skills required.
- The opportunity to earn 10-hour OSHA and forklift driving safety certifications.
- An emphasis on work-readiness, including attendance, accountability, and problem-solving.
- An emphasis on learning shop, math, and communication skills.
- Resume preparation and interviewing skills.

There was a group out of Denver, Colorado, that did a study of over 1,500 companies. They asked the HR departments, 'What are the soft skills you look for when you hire and promote?'

The seven attributes they found to be almost universally desired by HR departments are: Attitude, Attendance, Ambition, Accountability, Acceptance, Appreciation, and Appearance. In addition, the eighth A is "Ask." Those eight As have become the basis of our boot camp.

These soft skills are covered in-depth during the work-readiness camp. The same soft skills are reinforced when we go out and visit several different manufacturing companies in the area. During the tours, the participants will ask the owner or the general manager, 'What do you look for when you hire or when you promote?' or

'Is attendance important? Is attitude important?' These young adults hear the same message repeatedly from different sources during the boot camp. At the end of the training, we see a changed attitude and improved attendance.

The program can also provide a forklift driving certification and a 10-hour OSHA (safety) certification. The importance of these certifications is to make them safer, as well as give them a nominal skill in forklift driving. It also helps their self-esteem. Many young adults don't have these certifications when they're just out of school and looking for a job. This gives the interns an edge to start a career path.

The young adults are quick to realize the value of a strong work ethic and industry certifications. It helps build their self-confidence that they can achieve something. Other parts of the program include shop math, conflict resolution, financial literacy, and business communication skills.

At the end of boot camp, candidates interview with participating employers. We call it Internship Selection Day. The purpose of this is to help the interns learn how to do a job interview prior to the internship selection day; we do mock interviews. We videotape them. We help write their résumé and prepare them for the all-important question, 'Tell me about yourself...' After intensive preparation, the employers come in and interview all the interns.

The intern selection process is similar to a job fair. It's a private job fair for just the employers and the interns in the program. Every intern has about 15 minutes

with each employer. At the end of selection day, each employer writes down their top three or four interns that they would consider hiring. The interns write down their top three or four employers. This creates buy-in. After the interviews, the staff sits down and places interns at the location that best suits them.

What are the results?
- More than 300 companies have participated.
- Over 900 interns have completed the program.
- More than 75 percent of the interns completing the MCIP are now employed or pursuing post-secondary education and training.
- More than 85 percent of those hired after the internship have stayed with the company six months or more.

Employers play a huge role in the success of the MCIP. BCS has been doing this since 2011, and we are constantly surprised at the commitment manufacturers make to the success of the MCIP. It's amazing. Their goal is to design and/or build quality products for their customers. And yet, they also willingly accept the role of a corporate citizen. Even if the internship may not work out the first time, the manufacturers are willing to try it again.

The good news is that the perception of manufacturing is changing. Some high schools in the Chicagoland area are offering manufacturing classes as part of their Advanced Placement curriculum. Enrollment in these classes is up. It just takes time. Internship programs like the MCIP help turn potential into reality.

TITAN GILROY: TITAN TV, TITAN MANUFACTURING & ACADEMY

I have been fascinated by a significant new force in manufacturing: Titan Gilroy. He is bridging the gap between television and technical education in innovative ways. You will love his show! You can see from his remarks that there are many paths to success in manufacturing.

Titan Gilroy's thoughts:

My name is Titan Gilroy, and I am an American manufacturer. I started this company in 2005, after 10 years of working for different shops. I entered the industry without even knowing what a machine shop was. I started by working on parts for Siemens and NASA in a prototype custom-shop atmosphere in the Bay Area. I've always loved making things. Ever since I was a kid, I've been very creative. I didn't have money, so I built my own toys, I built my own surfboards in Hawaii, and I painted the beauty I saw around me.

I took to manufacturing naturally. It's a cool story. I owned a machine shop at 35 years old. Around the same time, I met with my grandmother for the first time. She showed me a picture of my grandfather, who had been a machine shop foreman at Boeing (I had no idea.) Later, I met my other grandfather for the first time—and he had been a machinist for Chrysler! I walked into the trade for nine bucks an hour and never knew the heritage of great machinists in my family before me.

I grew up in Hawaii fighting and being the only white kid in my neighborhood. I went from scrapping

on the streets and getting in hundreds of fights because I didn't back down when people picked on me to being one of the top fighters in the U.S. and fighting for Top Rank Boxing. Fast forward… and when the path toward a future in boxing ended, I took all of my aggression and my competitive nature and devoted myself to the CNC machines that I was working on.

Other people would sit there and push a button. I was more curious. *How fast can this thing go? How can we make the surface finishes better? How can we run more parts and compete?*

If you solve problems for the right people and make them money, you can be incredibly successful. It's about striving for perfection. You have to be proud of the quality that you are producing and blow people's minds and expectations out of the water. I want my customers to *love* the parts I make for them. I get comments all the time that the parts look like jewelry! That's what it's all about: having pride in your workmanship.

After solving huge problems in the industry and making a name for myself and the company, the global recession in 2008 took it all away. I almost lost the shop. Every day for a year, I sat on the edge of a massive local bridge, taking in the vastness of God's beauty and praying for the company to be saved. Ultimately, the shop was able to continue, but something was different. My perspective changed, and, after seeing 50,000 shops close, I had a fire in my heart for the industry like never before. That's when I knew I had to do something and developed the idea for a TV show (TITANS of CNC), which would be the only national television show

featuring CNC machining. I wanted to inspire people with the possibilities that manufacturing has to offer. I wanted to tell the stories of great companies and open the doors to an industry that no one knows anything about. I needed a way to start closing the 'awareness gap' for this great industry. It still plays on MAVTV, and is continually growing and bringing new people into our sphere of influence. Even with the TV show, I knew that more had to be done, and I dedicated myself to CNC education. In the third season of the TV show, the State of California asked me to develop a CNC program inside of San Quentin Prison. We documented the entire process by bringing cameras where they had never been allowed to go before. This led me to develop an advanced curriculum for CNC machining and create true change in the industry that has been desperately needed for decades. My focus has been education ever since. I haven't lost faith in the industry, but I've learned to harness my attention and focus it on creating things that truly matter.

After the third season of the TV show, I fully dedicated myself to creating a comprehensive curriculum for CAD, CAM, and CNC. This revolutionary platform is called 'The TITANS of CNC: Academy.' It is the most advanced CNC curriculum ever developed. The bottom line is this: There is a real problem in this trade right now. Everyone wants to talk about the 'skills gap,' but in reality... we are dealing with one of the greatest 'awareness gaps' ever seen. And even when awareness is achieved, there is no advanced curriculum to support the training that students need. Currently, students simply

aren't learning enough. They aren't learning through repetition. They only make a couple of parts as individuals and spend most of their time working in teams, which is not how the industry operates. I've looked at the problem, and they are simply not making enough parts to be successful. Not only that, they're not running the types of parts that matter to the industry that will hire them.

Teachers and instructors are not sufficiently resourced, so even the advanced classes are simply not even close to being truly advanced. They're still pushing the basic philosophies that were taught 20-30 years ago. That's why I put out so many videos and so much content because instead of just talking about it, we're doing it.

Why is our curriculum different? We make what was once complicated easy. We embrace technology and teach how to use it efficiently. Our tutorials take you from the first step of designing a part on the computer, to holding the same finished part in your hand. We've standardized materials and standardized tooling, and we do things in a way that progresses students rapidly. They learn through repetition. Everyone is picking it up. We have 6-year-old kids, 13-year-old kids, 40-year-old machinists, people of all ages entering or shifting positions within the trade. We have 160,000 students all over the world, in 170 countries, and over 2,500 schools. Even established shops are picking it up and advancing their capabilities and efficiency, making payroll easier, giving raises, hiring, and buying machines. It's all changing, but one of the reasons it's all changing is because I buckled down and started working and doing what I knew needed to be done.

One thing that I realized was, *Wait, there's no 'national curriculum.'* There are people trying to make money off of this type of training, and that is actually a big problem. Everybody 'talks the talk,' but who sees through all the platitudes and empty promises? If you're a principal or a dean of a school and you want to have a super elite CNC education program, what do you do? The truth is, you have to go find somebody who's great at manufacturing and is willing to teach for the money that you're willing to pay. Nobody is teaching the teachers. Nobody is saying, 'Hey, you're doing it wrong.' Everybody's too scared to say what needs to be said, but that fear is pushing us further and further behind on the global manufacturing stage, and we can't allow it any longer.

I did not build this platform out of selfish necessity. If I simply wanted to make money, I could have stayed at a shop producing parts for the largest aerospace companies in the world. I'm doing what I'm doing because I'm sick and tired of seeing what has happened to our country and what is currently happening to our kids. We're not competing. We're not teaching our kids to compete. I've been to all these schools. I haven't seen a single one where I thought, *Man, this is awesome!* and that is a tragedy. These are beautiful machines, but the educational programs are horrible.

Going to college is awesome, but not everybody has the same opportunity. There are people like myself who never had the resources, the time, or the opportunity. There are so many people like me who are creative and love to work with their

*hands. Manufacturing opens doors for those
people: 'If I can figure out and solve some of these
problems, I can actually make good money.'*

Our curriculum is free, and it's the most advanced.
We have millions of followers on our social media platforms hungry for the educational and entertaining content we put out.

The Academy has become the glue for in-house
training. Machine shops have created schools within
their facilities using our free education system. They
meet in their spare time: on a Monday night, on a Friday
evening, or on a Saturday morning. They teach the trade
to the people in their company and community, as 90
percent of them open their doors to the public. You can
learn this trade using our curriculum and it's an absolutely *free* education! These shops then turn around and
hire the very people they've trained when they need to
expand their teams. They're learning in weeks what previously would've taken years in a school environment.

We continue to develop new curriculum for aspects
of manufacturing in addition to CNC machining. We've
launched the Aerospace Academy, focused on high-end
difficult parts with real-world applications in rockets,
engines, and flight components. We have launched the
Grinding Academy, which intimately teaches the art
of high-precision CNC grinding to reach tolerances
measured in microns. We have curriculum for additive
production, 3D metal printing using extrusion and powder bed machines... We are showing the world of wire
and sinker EDM. Our passion for teaching all aspects

of manufacturing isn't slowing down, and, in fact, we're mashing the gas pedal to the floor because this country *needs* it.

We've even launched a new social site dedicated to manufacturing called CNC Expert. This is another revolutionary platform that allows individuals to achieve actual certification for each part they've designed, programmed, and CNC machined from our Academy series. It also gives users a visual home on the web to showcase their certifications, personal projects, pictures, info, and videos of work they've done. It allows users to connect with each other to solve problems, review job opportunities, and is effectively turning a disconnected global manufacturing community into a tight global manufacturing family.

Everybody else out there is stuck for months or even years trying to prepare students to be effective in their jobs. I'm saying this is actually pretty damn easy. I understand that it may be complicated to some people, but I'm not going to say that to your face. I've taken what was once difficult and simplified it. I leave you a little trail of crumbs. Follow the crumbs. Don't think about it… just repeat… and you're going to have success.

Everybody told me I couldn't have a shop, that American manufacturing was dead. But I'm different. I didn't learn from textbooks; I learned by doing and through putting in the work. Do I have a different way of doing things? Sure. Was it hard? Yeah, but look. Now I'm talking to you. We've had a national TV show. We've made crazy aerospace parts for the world's top rocket companies. But I look out into the world, and I see the current state of education…

As a leader in manufacturing, I'm bewildered at the fact that nobody's ever fixed it or solved it. They keep going down this road like sheep to the slaughter. Man! Nobody's changing. I'm like, *What the heck is going on?* I have dedicated myself to education to make a difference. If you want to step into this trade and do  something big, then surround yourself with talented people and put in the work. It is up to you to make it happen! To learn more about TITANS of CNC, head to www.titansofcnc.com.

ONE LAST THOUGHT

It is time to make manufacturing and the other "skilled trades" cool! By educating young people about what CNC is and by stating that it *rocks*, maybe your curiosity will pique, and you will start asking questions. I have told many young people like you that if you look into manufacturing and you decide it is not for you, that is OK. Those of us in the manufacturing community need to share these careers with you to begin with. I am here to share how many high-paying, exciting, challenging positions with computerized and automated equipment are out there; most of today's youth do not even know about these opportunities. That is my quest: to share that CNC ROCKS.

During the COVID-19 pandemic, I produced video content to explain some basic manufacturing concepts to those wanting to know more. My audience is industry members who want to use these videos for new potential employees or for their existing workforce not directly involved in making things. The audience

member could be an accountant, receptionist, shipping and receiving clerk, or any number of employees who really should know more about manufacturing in general. Educators can also use these videos to introduce or augment manufacturing programs to new or existing students. These contain great content for all to see! The name is CNC Rocks Virtual Manufacturing Camp.

Don't lose sight of following your passion and what you love to do most. If you enjoy making things, designing things, and working with your hands, then you are a natural for the manufacturing world. Many manufacturing companies pay their employees to go to school to further their degrees. They will pay for classes at night while employees work during the day. Manufacturing companies have gotten very good at mentoring young people as they enter into the workforce. Many of these mentors are over 50 years old, and they have a genuine concern for passing on their skill sets, talents, and knowledge to the next generation.

There is an alarming shortage in manufacturing and other related fields. Companies are not growing because they do not have the skilled workers needed. All this to say, you have a great opportunity to enter a stable, interesting, long-lasting career. One reason why this is the case is the latest technology, as you'll see in the next chapter.

TECHNOLOGY IN MANUFACTURING—WHAT ARE YOU WAITING FOR?

"...and then I saw the CNC machines, and then I saw them running, and I was like, they take this raw piece of aluminum. You put it into this machine, it cuts it down, it takes away from it. But now it's worth 10 to 1,000 times more than what you just bought it for. It blew my mind."

—Andrew Crowe,
Founder of the New American Manufacturing Renaissance

The advent of technology has changed our lives forever. Younger generations are practically born with cell phones in your hands. Just watch how intuitively a toddler knows in today's world to swipe a screen left or right. Today's iPads are yesterday's television sets with Sesame Street episodes or Tom & Jerry cartoons. With this degree of technological adoption at a young age, there needs to be a parallel made with how technology transfers over into the manufacturing arena and what implications that brings.

When I entered the manufacturing world in 1980, computerization was just beginning to emerge. Heck, when I entered college in 1977, computers were just being introduced to the student population. I remember taking a Fortran class at Florida State University that led me down the path of what would be known decades later as "coding."

Almost 50 years later, we find ourselves in what is called the Fourth Industrial Revolution. The digital transformation is modernizing manufacturing through robotics, programming, data analysis, cloud computing, edge computing, and sensor technology.

I even find myself programming a computerized lathe for customers who have never truly entered the technologically savvy age of manufacturing. It is gratifying to see their world open up with increased efficiencies and productivity they could never imagine. So, let's drift back to the comments above about young toddlers learning early on to swipe a smartphone to see photos. That circumstance then leads to them surfing the web and scrolling Facebook posts, immersed in social media mania. So, then why are the careers that feature computerized, highly technological CNC-controlled devices and automation in manufacturing so foreign to young people? I contend that

you are not making a conscious decision not to pursue these careers. Instead, you simply do not know what you do not know! The responsibility lies with us—the manufacturers, parents, teachers, and guidance counselors—to ready you for your future. Part of that is showing you the real story behind manufacturing.

MARK HIBNER OF PALATINE HIGH SCHOOL: THE MAGIC IS GOING TO HAPPEN

I invited Mark Hibner, one of the best applied technology teachers in Illinois, to highlight how technology is driving manufacturing.

> **Mark Hibner's thoughts:**
> I've been an educator for 20 years. In my fourth year of teaching, I was fortunate to be offered a leadership role as an Applied Technology Department Chair. The following year, I became the District Chair. It was a great opportunity to be in those leadership roles early in my career. A few years later, working with the Applied Technology Department Chairs, we successfully implemented the Project Lead the Way engineering pathway of study in all five high schools in our district. Soon after, I worked with educators, manufacturers, professional organizations, and the community college to implement the manufacturing pathway of study. It's hard to believe the Engineering and Manufacturing programs have been up and running for over 10 years.
>
> We've changed the face of what the Applied Technology Department looks like. We've introduced new career pathways and advanced technology into the

lab, which helped establish the persona and perception of what the Applied Technology Department is today.

I have a very diverse classroom. Several students come to class having a variety of home-life challenges. For instance, some students are being raised by single parents that work the night shift. As a result, those students are left at home taking care of their younger siblings. Other students work 40 hours or more to help support their families. These are a couple of obstacles students may face that challenge their social and emotional well-being.

In the past several years, I've heard a lot of debate on whether or not students should attend a four-year college. Manufacturers need highly trained and educated employees. Young adults need to be challenged with extending their learning so they can add value to a company. It's advantageous when manufacturing companies and the student work together to develop a plan on what education is best for both sides. Some companies provide in-house training, and others pay for students to complete an apprenticeship that leads to an associate degree. Other companies will pay for students to complete a bachelor's degree. In order to have the best workforce, some type of higher education and training must take place.

I think the mindset needs to be: 'Here you are in high school. You gained this interest in manufacturing, so what is your next step? What are you going to do to pursue a career in manufacturing? Are you interested in going straight into the workforce, attending college, or enlisting in the military? If you are interested in the

armed forces, are you aware the military has occupational jobs to become a machinist or a welder?'

Educators should take responsibility for informing students of the opportunities available post-graduation. Numerous approaches exist to obtain higher education and training in manufacturing. One option is to find employment with a company that sends their employees for training at a professional organization, such as the Technology & Manufacturing Association. A second option is to apply for an apprenticeship with a company or a community college, such as Harper College. A third option is to pursue a bachelor's degree at colleges that focus on manufacturing, such as Illinois State University, Bradley University, and Northern Illinois University. With numerous opportunities post-graduation, educators should be able to inform students of the path that is right for them. I feel it is the responsibility of the Applied Technology teacher to market, promote, and educate all stakeholders about the awesome opportunities that exist in taking Applied Technology classes. Marketing starts with selling a quality product and quality service to our students. It's just like a business. If you're not selling a quality product or service, you're not getting the business. On the flip side, when providing exciting and worthwhile education to students, they promote the classes. They recruit for you.

For parents, the Applied Technology teacher must promote all the benefits manufacturing companies are willing to offer their children. Parents need to be invited to attend events at manufacturing companies. They need to hear from industry professionals what it is

like to have a rewarding career in manufacturing. They need to see how safe, clean, and advanced manufacturing environments are. They need to see the opportunity for advancement.

In addition, it's important to educate counselors, administrators, and other teachers about your course offerings. You have to invite them to walk through your labs, see the projects students make, and observe the skills they develop. Also, you need to inform them about the awesome career opportunities and all the benefits companies are willing to offer. I believe when you accomplish that level of communication, magic is going to happen. Students will be provided with opportunities for growth in a rewarding career. Parents will trust their child pursuing a manufacturing career. Educators will support students going into manufacturing. Manufacturers will hire talented students. As a result, we will build a stronger workforce, community, and economy.

ANDREW CROWE: SECOND CHANCES

While Mark speaks from the perspective of someone working in high schools, Andrew Crowe explores an unconventional path to manufacturing. Second chances are not always given or earned easily. Andrew is one of the fortunate few who took full advantage of his second chance through superior attitude, effort, and determination. Be prepared to take note!

Andrew Crowe's thoughts:
I was raised in St. Louis. It's a typical inner-city youth story. Whether you're black, brown, white, or

other, it doesn't matter typically when you're in an inner city with a sector that has jobs that have been leaving. All American inner cities have been dying. I had a single-parent household. My mother raised me and my brothers and sisters. She was literally always working. That gave me two things. It gave me a lot of time to get into stuff. And it also gave me an outlook on life that I didn't want to be like her.

I love and admire my mother, but I knew that there had to be something better than just slaving every day at three different jobs to barely make ends meet. We'd have lights with no running water, or we'd have food in the refrigerator, but we wouldn't have lights. I saw how hard my mom worked and that the American dream wasn't really panning out for her.

My options, or so I thought at the time, were limited to my experiences and the things that I saw every day.

My school wasn't funded to the point where we had a STEM lab. We didn't have speakers who came in and told us about different career pathways. What I saw around me was that the people that were not struggling day to day were the people whose parents weren't struggling day to day.

I naturally gravitated towards the street. It was never to be diabolical. It was always with a mindset of helping my mom out and not becoming like her. That was the only avenue that I saw that could get me there. Because of that, I made some adverse decisions in my life. Before

I was 18, I was a two-time felon. I was a teenage father, and I didn't really have much of an outlook still.

The people on the streets were the only people that have hired me with a felony on my record. I was in that cycle of jail, I guess, worthless existence, meaningless, just going through the motions.

I got tired of going through the motions, and I got tired of not feeling like I was important. And I got tired of being the example that I was to my son. More importantly, I woke up one day and I said, 'I don't know what I want to be, but I know what I don't want to be anymore.'

I reached out to my network: 'I'm looking for a legal job that I can get as a felon. I will humble myself. I don't care if I'm shoveling shit at the zoo. I will be the best I can be.' I got a library card at the same time and started reading books. I started reading *Think and Grow Rich*. I started reading Wallace D. Wattles self-help books, and all these different books that help you shift your mindset. I still didn't have a career path or anything that I thought I was good at, but I just had a different mindset.

A lady that was close to the family reached out to me. She said, 'Hey, I got a job for you.'

I walk into this place, and I sit across from the gentleman. He hands me a machinist test. 'I got two job openings. One's for machinist, and one's for saw operator. A machinist pays this, saw operator pays this, and saw operator pays less.' So, I want to be a machinist, not knowing what it was, having no idea what it was at

all. This was also during the same time as the recession. There were no jobs really available for anybody. You know what I'm saying? (Let alone a two-time felon that had no experience in the fields.)

That's where manufacturing was different, where it weathered that storm and was still paying. At the time, it was $19 an hour, or $22 for the machining, and then $15 an hour for the saw job, which was almost 2 to 3 times the minimum wage at the time. It was still really appealing to me. I was like, 'Oh, I got to do this!'

I saw manual machines first when we went into the manual department, and I was like, Wow. My mind just exploded!

I saw the CNC machines. I saw them running. I was like, *You take this raw piece of aluminum. You put it into this machine, it cuts it down, it takes away from it. Now it's worth 10 to 1,000 times more than what you just bought it as.* It blew my mind!

I felt a fire light inside of me. Oh my God, I had never seen or even thought about where things were made. Now that I'm around it, I don't want to leave it. I just became the best saw man that I knew how to be. I'd make sure the cuts were proper. I would go drop off the material at all of the CNC machines, so first shift was set. I started seeing what their preference was, what their materials were. If they wanted it set up in a corner to the jobs that they had, I would go the extra mile.

After that, as I would leave, third shift going into first shift, I was looking in the parking lot. I'm like,

Damn. That was the first time I saw a Ducati motorcycle. Then in the locker room, as I'm changing out, and they're dressing in, I'm hearing the conversations are like, 'Oh yeah, I just closed on my lake house.' During the recession, this is crazy. Even before the recession, I had never been around conversations like this. *Damn, I got to get the first shift. I got to be a machinist.* Whatever these people were doing, I needed to be able to do it if they were doing it in a recession and making that type of money.

I started staying after. I would clock out and stay after four hours in the first shift, and just beg people to teach me. YouTube wasn't big. There was no Titan. There were no tutorials. There was nothing online. I bought an old machinist handbook. It was probably four or five versions back. I was buying coffee and doughnuts to have there in the morning for the old machinists when they came in for a shift.

It took maybe a month of them eating my doughnuts and coffee to where one person was like: 'Look, you can stand next to me. Don't ask any questions. When I talk, you write. That's it. When I tell you to do something, you do it. I'm not going to tell you twice.'

That's how I learned manual machines. By the time I had my year anniversary, I was a CNC machinist. I would go home. The notes that I would take, I would compare them to my machinist handbook, and then go through all of that, and try to reteach myself this stuff.

This was the first thing that I had to apply myself. I would go to sleep at night thinking about G-code. I'd wake up early in the morning before the sun, and be

excited, *I can't wait to be at work.* You know what I'm saying? I would not get tired at all.

As a black man in America, we live a different experience, you know what I'm saying? I didn't feel like an American. I felt like a second-class citizen. On top of that, throw in the felonies and stuff; I was really down. I didn't feel like I had a meaningful purpose in this country until I became a machinist. It's like, *Yo, if I don't show up to work today, and if I don't cut this stock right, if I don't give it my all, then the jet fighters that are protecting us aren't going to be as good.* You know what I'm saying? For once, I felt like the work that I was doing in my life when I woke up every day actually meant something, not just to me, but America, and my country. It made me feel good as a person for once.

At the end of the day, I knew what the alternative was if I didn't take the shot. If I didn't really give this my all. The only thing that was waiting for me on the other side was death or jail. That was the route that I was going. You know what I'm saying?

It's like, *Damn, this is my second life right here. I got to give it everything I have.*

Let's talk about another component of the current technological world we live in. Young people are totally infatuated with the gaming world. In 2011, an article claimed that 91 percent of kids between 2 and 17 were playing video games. This solution is staring at us in the face. Industry members should take notice and take advantage of a trend that is here to stay. One of the most difficult, most sought-after, and competitive careers that young people seek is being video game programmers. Why not

turn that aspiration into becoming a CNC Programmer on a shop floor? This connection is not at all far-fetched. It is just a matter of connecting the dots between a career set that is aligned with your interests and skill set, which has been honed since you were a toddler.

Here are some important facts to note about the video game industry[1]:

- The gaming industry is expected to reach $337 billion in revenue by 2027.
- There will be more than 3 billion video gamers around the world by 2023.
- The average gamer is 34 years old.
- 70 percent of gamers are age 18 or older.
- 60 percent of Americans play video games daily.
- 45 percent of U.S. gamers are women.
- 70 percent of parents believe video games have a positive influence on their children's lives.

Here is information from another article[2] about the interest many gamers have when they decide on careers:

Are game developers in demand? All signs point to yes—but it shocked us to learn that jobs for game developers and game designers have shown a strong decline since 2014 with a 65% drop in the number of postings. However, searches for gaming jobs have remained relatively constant since 2014. Searches for 'game developer' have even grown by 50%, which shows there is interest from job seekers. Our team examined the job market outlook related to the overall gaming industry

and found some interesting patterns to signal strong growth for jobs in gaming.

The next intriguing thought is the trend that the game developer career set is very highly sought after, but the number of postings for openings is actually freefalling. The number of postings is dropping 65 percent while the interest is increasing by 50 percent, leading to an army of disappointed coding-talented young adults. This is where the manufacturing community needs to step in and educate, inform, and inspire! There are many young people that are prime candidates for careers that feature some of the same skillsets and cutting-edge digital flavor required to be a video game developer.

WHEN PARENTS DON'T SEE
THE MANUFACTURING PATH

Sometimes parents don't understand or don't agree with the manufacturing path for their children. With the emergence of technology, many times, they do not understand it. Let's listen to a great parallel from Andrew Crowe, who spoke about how parents sometimes need to be open to new ideas and careers and maybe even reconsider their perceptions. Andrew shares this story about a student:

> **Andrew Crowe's thoughts:**
> I had a potential student that emailed me about a video of mine that he saw online. In the email, he was really excited to learn more about the trade and learn more about manufacturing because of what he saw me do and say in the video. I talked about how it could change

his life. I told him about how they are high paying, with over 2.8 million careers open at the time. How you can literally take anything that you can think of in your mind, turn it into a solid model, telling a machine how to make that out of metal. Then the machine will do it for you. It just really blew his mind.

So, we set up a tour. As we're going through the shop, he's looking at these CNC machines and seeing their capabilities and watching them run. I can just see the fireworks going off in his head. We were really creating a bond. He was a junior at the time. He stayed in touch via email and sent me machining videos. He asked all these questions. I was really fostering this relationship. I was fostering his mind and trying to channel him into becoming a machinist, and then a programmer. Showing him the different career paths that he could take to eventually become an engineer and work for DOD—Department of Defense (his main goal). Eventually, he just stopped. There wasn't a slowdown. There was a complete stop.

I reached back to the kid. I said, 'Hey man, it's coming up on graduation for your senior year. We've been working towards this thing. Are you still going to come? I haven't seen your application.'

He told me that he was considering it. He was really loving it. It was time to throw in for college scholarships. His mother told him it was not a good idea because he'd be staring at a screen all day pressing buttons. So, I told him, 'You already stare at a screen all day pressing buttons. You might as well get paid for it!'

> The future of manufacturing is going towards more CNC, more robotics, and more automated processes. This requires more programmers and tech-savvy young people with high-paying careers. Let's dive into what these careers are and what they look like now that we have indicated the people who can fill them: you!

AUTOMATION: JUMP ON BOARD BEFORE IT IS TOO LATE!

While we may have fewer people in the manufacturing workforce, we will have higher-paying jobs. Because we are competitive in global markets, our production in this country will expand and result in an increase in higher-paying, skill-based jobs.

Robot installations worldwide totaled 3,020,000 in 2020, which was double the level in 2014. Throughout the world, countries have embraced robotic automation to different levels. Those with an aging working population have done more so than others. In 2017, 14.5 percent of the United States population was over

the age of 65, while Japan conversely had 27 percent over 65. Both countries have been included in the "silver tsunami" metaphor, alluding to the tidal wave of pending retirements.[3] The following dataset will explain Japan's notably higher ratio when compared to the U.S.

The following scores represent the number of robot installations per 10,000 workers. Korea (932), Singapore (605), Japan (390), Germany (371), Sweden (289), Hong Kong (275), the

U.S. (255), and China (246). What is interesting about China's ranking is the extreme size of its workforce: Its rank is lower than one would think, but the country still employs the largest number of robot installations in the world due to the size of the population.[4]

Rick Romell from the Milwaukee *Journal Sentinel* writes:

> After overseeing a huge survey of employers worldwide on the impact of automation, Manpower Group has a calming message for workers worried about the digitized future: Don't fear the robot. Among the employers polled, only 10 percent told Manpower Group that automation would prompt headcount reductions over the next two years, the Milwaukee-based staffing company said. Twice that share—20 percent—said they expect to add workers because of the increased use of digital technology. Two-thirds of the employers, meanwhile, said automation would have no effect on their staffing levels over the next two years. The findings come from a survey conducted in October of 19,718 employers across 42 countries and 6 industry sectors. The results vary by country and occupational group. U.S. employers were among the most optimistic, with 25 percent saying automation will increase their headcount in the near term."[5]

One of the most noticeable technological gains has been the emergence and adoption of 3D printing, which has led to the term additive manufacturing; all other conventional manufacturing is now back-labeled as subtractive manufacturing.

Many schools are now employing 3D printing in the classroom, which, looking back, could be the single technological gain most responsible for bringing young people into

the manufacturing fold. Not only is 3D printing employed in industrial production and R&D rooms, but it is also gaining momentum among hobbyists and tinkerers alike. Maker spaces are popping up with CAD classes through local libraries with waiting lists to attend their classes. This is a significant movement that will have a positive impact for decades to come.

Due to tangible, relevant, and approachable (like 3D printing) technology gains, we are ready to dive into the next subject in Chapter 5. Now that you have a reason to be enamored with manufacturing, let's talk about the financial justifications for an alternative educational path into manufacturing employment.

Whether you can relate to Andrew Crowe, or in the next chapter with Sheyenne Kreamer or Leigh Coglianese McConnell, there are always examples of people like you who found success in manufacturing. Some may have found success in something almost by accident, while others may have searched for a balance between definitions of success and happiness for a lifetime. Just knowing manufacturing is an option is most of the battle. Whether it is right for you is your decision to make.

RETURN ON EDUCATION—LOOKING AT YOUR EDUCATION PATH AS AN INVESTMENT

"Right now, no one is really accountable for student outcomes. It's graduation rates."

—Vince Bertram,
Former President of Project Lead the Way

n business, we look at the return on investment (ROI). This is a basic concept. If I put $100 into an investment, I am looking to get more than $100 out of it. ROI is basic, simple, and practical.

This applies to education, too.

Ask: What is my return on education (ROE)? ROE is about more than money. It is about your time and your future. It takes into account what you have studied (with your time and money) and what you will get back in return in money, happiness, and satisfaction in your career.

In this chapter, I am not trying to dissuade anyone from going to college. Rather, I hope to open your eyes to compelling facts about attending college and how to assess the right choice for you. There are many factors, and each and every person's situation is different. Key factors in deciding what to do after high school include:

- The job market
- The institution's educational model
- Our culture
- The affordability of college
- Lifelong opportunities
- The market demand for your career choice

MORE OPTIONS, MORE SUCCESS

How many of you can afford the college of your choice? How many of your parents will put a second mortgage on the house in order to pay for your post-secondary education? What happens if you do not get accepted into the college of your choice? Are you taking out student loans that have put you in a hole you cannot get out of?

In these uncertain times, there are many financial reasons to investigate alternative educational paths that can lead to productive and financially rewarding careers.

Technical and community colleges offer two-year degrees that cost a fraction of many four-year university degrees. As a result, you can enter into the workforce making $50,000-$60,000 a year and have a very short payback on your educational costs.

The four-year degree student is finding him or herself in debt after having paid $160,000-$200,000 (or more) for their education. You will have a decade or more of trying to pay back these costs. You will also have a difficult time finding a job as you differentiate yourself from others with the same degree. Unemployment is now around 4 percent, and some individuals make $40,000 a year, with experienced individuals willing to work for less. These factors are creating a reverse competitive market for the employer.

The irony is that manufacturing companies many times have to bring in engineers from Europe, India, and other countries because of the lack of supply in the U.S. Some manufacturers cannot expand their business due to the lack of domestic talent. Clearly, there is a significant demand for talent.

MORE OPTIONS, MORE OPPORTUNITIES

In his book *Fail U: The False Promise of Higher Education*, author Charles Sykes brings out a number of good questions and challenges to help us all rethink the typical education advice we hear. Here are some of the highlights Sykes points out[1]:

- The cost of a college degree has increased by 1,125 percent since 1978 (four times the rate of inflation).

- Total student debt surpassed $1.3 trillion.
- Nearly two-thirds of all college students must borrow to study.
- The average student graduates with more than $30,000 in debt.

What, then, can we learn from these facts? Sykes describes a vision of higher education as "one that is affordable, more productive, and better suited to meet the needs of a diverse range of students and that will actually be useful in their future careers and lives."

Sykes points to private education as the equivalent of buying a BMW every year and driving it off of a cliff. He cites many private colleges like Duke University, Dartmouth College, Wesleyan University, Boston College, and Southern Methodist, which command more than $60,000 a year in tuition.

Student loan debts exceed both the nation's total credit card and auto loan debt. The delinquency rate on student loans is higher than the delinquency rate on credit cards, auto loans, and home mortgages. Here are a few other facts to consider:

- A survey of 30,000 alumni by the Gallup-Purdue index found that only 38 percent of recent college graduates strongly agree that their degree was worth the cost. Only a third of graduates with student debt think their education was worth the price tag. Their skepticism is understandable.
- A study by Rich Richard Vetter and Christopher Denhard found that there are more college graduates working in retail jobs than there are soldiers in the U.S. Army and more janitors with bachelor's degrees than chemists.[2]

- Only 34 percent of students entering four-year institutions earn a bachelor's degree in four years.
- Barely two-thirds or 64 percent finish within six years.

MY STORY ABOUT GOING TO COLLEGE

I witnessed the dubiously ineffective educational model first-hand. From 1977 to 1983, I attended five different universities. In each case, I decided that the educational model, at least from my youthful perspective, was ineffective. I found the approach to be extremely boring. I had trouble focusing in the classroom. The lack of challenge and effectiveness was not consistent with my learning style.

One late night while sitting in my thermal dynamics class at Marquette, I had an epiphany. Listening to the teacher lecture, I had the realization that Kathy and our two young children were at home alone again without me—why? Several times a week, I would arrive home after midnight. Why was I doing that to our family? At the time, I had a full-time job. I had more engineering background and education than my job would ultimately require. I was selling machine tools. I totally understood and was fascinated with making parts, not designing the machine tool itself. In retrospect, I would probably have been best served learning to program a CNC machine tool—but that technology was just emerging in the industry.

My young family was suffering from my absence more than the benefit (economic or otherwise) of me furthering my education. I decided, in that instant, to go home and quit college. I also came to the realization that maybe I was more concerned with what people thought than about the impact education would have on my life. The only person whose opinion I cared about was

Kathy. She agreed it was up to me whether I finished school or not. That was the last college class I took. The Bolles School, my prep high school in Jacksonville, was what set me up for success more than any college I attended.

CONSIDER THE NUMBERS: THEY DON'T LIE (SHOCKING REVELATIONS AHEAD)

Millions of young students come out of school with a mountain of debt from student loans. The website Comet estimates that there is a total of $1.419 trillion in student debt. Just to explain the gravity of this number, let me share some statistics from Lifehealth.[3]

Americans now owe more than $1.3 trillion in student loan debt, based on the most current figures available to Comet. That money is not only owed by young people fresh out of college but also by borrowers who have been out of school for a decade or more. The standard repayment timetable for federal loans is 10 years, but research suggests it actually takes four-year degree holders an average of 19.7 years to pay off their loans.

Here are some top statistics on the student loan debt landscape in 2018:

- Current U.S. student loan debt = est. $1.4 trillion
- 1 in 4 Americans have student loan debt, an estimated 44 million people
- Average student loan debt amount = $37,172
- Average student loan payment = $393/month

In the past decade, total U.S. student loan debt has surpassed credit card debt and auto loan debt. In the third quarter of 2017, Americans owed $810 billion on their credit cards and $1.21 trillion in auto loans. Currently, U.S. student loan obligations are larger than both, trailing only mortgages in scope and impact.

Student loan debt has ballooned in the past few decades, primarily because the costs associated with higher education—tuition, fees, housing, and books—have grown much faster than family incomes. The College Board has tracked costs at public and private universities since 1971.

When the organization first started monitoring prices, the average cost of one year at a public university was $1,410 ($8,450 in 2017 dollars). That was 15.6 percent of the median household income of $9,027 and manageable for many families without going into debt.

Fast forward to 2018, and the picture is different, when the average cost of one year at a public university is $20,770, which is 35.2 percent of the median household income of $59,039. That could be why more than 70 percent of bachelor's degree recipients emerge from college today with substantial student loan debt, and why many find themselves in need of loan consolidation and refinancing.

There is a lesson here. Maybe we need to stop and think about the ROE on a college education: the time it takes, the costs, and how soon a young person can be in the working world making money (rather than spending it on education). Starting out a career with a boulder of seemingly insurmountable financial responsibility is putting a huge strain on your future.

DR. LAZ LOPEZ: BEING RELEVANT IS THE KEY

Meet Laz Lopez. His comments speak to how high schools need to do a better job of meeting the needs of students and surrounding employers. His vision and development at Wheeling High School in Wheeling, Illinois, has gained him respect and admiration from parents, administrators, and industry members alike. Additionally, Wheeling High School was one of the very first PRIME High Schools as designated by Society of Manufacturing Engineering. Dr. Lopez currently serves as the Associate Superintendent of Township High School District 214.

Laz Lopez's thoughts:

As a school principal, my goal is to ensure that we are relevant. The value of a high school diploma is widely questioned. One of the strategies the high school leader can use is through the authentic and relevant experiences students can have that give the community insight into the school and into the value it's offering.

If you have an increased number of students being employed in the community as a result of the work that's happening in the high school—as well as those earning professional degrees or credentials in demand and returning to the community to work—that is a direct validation of the quality of the school.

A high school can serve as a lever for broader economic development. I think this is a unique perspective. As an engine for economic development, principals need to develop deep ties with employers and understand the business climate of their community. We did this at

Wheeling High School. We found that our community had the third-largest concentration of manufacturers in the entire country.

There was nothing the school was doing to help meet the needs of that particular employer group, or that industry. In my meetings with employers, they stated, 'We have a shortage of qualified individuals applying for and even considering this as a well-paying career.' There seemed to be a mismatch between these local opportunities and the fact that many of our residents were living in poverty. The school could play a role in making the connection to local employment more directly.

The initial efforts were to respond to the immediate need. Keep in mind that, at that time, we were still in the midst of the Great Recession. A lot of people thought I was crazy for trying to create a manufacturing lab at a time when everyone was saying, 'We're supposed to be only about college-ready or college-bound students. Why are you going backward instead of forward?' Where I did get support was from the Economic Development Office in the Village of Wheeling. They have all of these manufacturers they're trying to serve and support, and they understood if they could not deliver on a talent pipeline locally, they could consider relocating. Their encouragement and validation helped me move forward.

Our entire public education system, from a lens of accountability, focuses on trying to ensure that our schools are graduating students who are ready for college. This was a result of a loss in our belief that earning a high school diploma actually meant something.

A multitude of assessments were introduced, and the focus of the entire K-12 system narrowed for over a decade on testing and test scores. And while that is one valid measure, it is not the only measure of student potential for success. In that process, we got rid of everything and anything not directly contributing to test scores, and the central focus of school leaders has been on, *Can my kids score a certain number on a standardized test?* So, you're correct in the sense that the end goal is an assumption that if we can get all the students high enough test scores, all of them are going to college, and that is the right path. However, as any parent knows, students are more than just a single test score given on a single day. 'Redefining Ready,' adopted by the National Superintendents Association, attempts to counter this assumption by redefining the way we should be holding schools accountable. Utilizing multiple measures, students can show readiness for both college and career.

We've structured the comprehensive high school academic program, and all coursework, around each of the 16 national career clusters along representative career pathways that encourages all students to engage in work-based learning experiences prior to graduation.

The apprenticeship program at District 214 was started to provide a high-quality work-based learning experience for students. The program provides opportunities in over a dozen occupations that allows students to have paid employment while gaining employment experience in their area of interest, as well as beginning to build a professional network for themselves.

One of these apprentice-able occupations is Construction and Building Systems, where students gain experience on both commercial and residential projects under a general contractor. Apprentices are involved in all aspects of architectural design to do hands-on work in the trades.

Another is Industrial Manufacturing Technician. Students are employed with local manufacturing employers, learning about workplace safety, set-up for production run, operating equipment according to the production schedule, and producing products that contribute to business goals.

Whether it's the students who are tearing down the walls or operating equipment, each experience affirms their career choice. Is this what they want to do with their life? We should make sure that high school is the place where students are able to discover that future.

The application of manufacturing challenges students in math and science beyond the theoretical to real-world projects. Wheeling High School was selected as one of 15 schools in the nation that prepared components for the International Space Station in partnership with NASA. The tolerance for manufacturing the parts was less than a human hair. There is no room for error when you're working with NASA. The application of skills, technical and interpersonal, to actually produce these brackets and handles with real-world consequences was incredible. That project, which will impact the students and teachers involved for a lifetime and provide

education to them, is applicable to other teams and industries.

The process of developing a product is also replicated through our 'Robot Rumble.' Students begin with a hunk of metal. They design and build remote-controlled robots that are going to combat other student-built robots at a regional competition. The result is that bringing all these experiences to scale gives students a real opportunity to authentically discover their future.

THE COMMUNITY COLLEGE CAREER TRACK

In reading about Thomas Snyder and his career at Ivy Tech, an Indiana institute known for technical education excellence, I learned of his passion about the community college's alternative path to help students succeed.

Over the decades, I have found Snyder's comment about employers being willing to pay for night-class training for their employees to be spot-on. This is a win-win for both parties.

This is what Synder has to say about community college: "Nothing can hide the fact that community college is the smart higher education choice for an increasing number of students. Professional certificates and associate degrees have become the favorite gateways to many of today's and tomorrow's best jobs."[4]

Snyder adds that going to community college in lieu of the first two years of a four-year university is a viable alternate path. He goes on to say that a degree from an elite college may not hold the same mystique and impact it once had, adding: "Conversely, there is strong evidence that community college can accelerate your bachelor's degree attainment and/or quickly put you on a

desirable career path. Not for the first time in the nation's history, the American dream stands in need of reinvention and renewal. The process of reinventing and renewing the American dream will be a complicated one with many elements, but there is no doubt [that] community colleges will remain at the center of the story over the years ahead."

SHEYENNE KREAMER: SMART KIDS GO INTO THE TRADES

When I was in high school, I was often bored. (Keep in mind this was before computers.) Nonetheless, I was capable of Advanced Placement coursework. There are young people who, despite their intellect, do not learn in a conventional manner. That was me.

Next up is a story of someone who also fits this same storyline. Sheyenne Kreamer was introduced to me by my friend Eileen Bild from OTEL Network, who handles the **CHAMPION Now!** ROKU Channel. Manufacturing is not just for those deemed unsuccessful in conventional careers. Manufacturing is for those who can find success in anything they choose.

> **Sheyenne Kreamer's thoughts:**
> I was valedictorian of my high school class. And as I was kind of struggling through the process of trying to determine what I wanted to do after high school. There were a lot of well-meaning people who I kept saying, 'Oh, you're going to be eligible for scholarships. You need to go on to college.' And I had a well-meaning parent who was sure that I needed to go to college and learn electrical engineering. That's where all the money

was going to be. Somehow, that didn't feel right to me. It did not make me happy.

I was extremely happy the day that our high school brought in a recruiter from a major manufacturing company. She actually showed up with a video talking about career opportunities for women in manufacturing.

They were trying to bring more women into manufacturing. They were trying to diversify the workforce. I watched that video, and I talked to the recruiter afterward. I just said, 'You know what? What a cool way to be able to get hands-on doing something where you're actually creating stuff.' It was a three-year apprenticeship program that would allow me to work in all these different departments, on the manufacturing floor, and in different office departments as well.

[Internships] just make so much sense because our young people are confused, especially today. I saw an article on LinkedIn recently that said that we are living in a generation of the most depressed young people that we've ever seen since people started recording this kind of information. Of course, a lot of it has to do with the pandemic we've all come through and all of that. If we're not spending a little bit more time earlier on in the high school years… Really, I mean, I swear, guidance counselors are pushed to the wall. I'm not blaming them for any of this whatsoever because some of the problem does exist with our trades organizations. If they're not coming out to the career fairs to shake hands with and

explain about the opportunities that exist to these students, they're as much to blame as anybody.

The guidance counselors are getting measured by how many kids go to college. That is just a fact. There's not as much internal incentive to be exposing them to things like manufacturing. I think it's a crime because more kids would go there if they knew what the opportunity looks like.

I am a big advocate for alternative career paths. Pursuing those alternative career paths earlier can end up saving a lot of frustration later on. They say that 76 percent of all college students this year have thought about dropping out. That's just because they're all stressed out and anxious these days. So, it's like, Okay, so why do we think that the only lucrative career paths are by going directly into a four-year college?

For a young person who's struggling with all these things, I say, 'Oh my goodness, ask somebody in your school to try to find some tradespeople, whether it's in manufacturing, automotive, construction, whatever. Ask them to hook you up directly with some of these people, even if it's just a site visit where some of these people are working. You can actually see what they do and how they do it. That is one of the best ways that you can explore for yourself instead of just letting everybody else make the decisions for you.'

DO THE MATH...

This is a sample of two students. One goes to college for four to five years, taking loans or using money other than a gift from Mom and Dad. The other goes to a two-year school for a fraction of the cost and goes out into the working world two to three years sooner, making good money!

What this shows is that, in year 12 (7 years after graduation), a person with a four-year degree is still $130,000 in debt. The two-year vocational student in year 12 has a surplus of $90,000. This is almost a quarter-of-a-million-dollar difference between the two. This assumes that only 20 percent of a person's wage can be used to pay back principal, while the vocational graduate makes 25 percent less per year, which may not be the case at all.

	4-5 year college degree			2 year vocational degree	
	Tuition/Income	cost/paycheck		Tuition/Income	cost/paycheck
Year 1	$(50,000.00)		Year 1	$(20,000.00)	
Year 2	$(50,000.00)		Year 2	$(20,000.00)	$(40,000.00)
Year 3	$(50,000.00)		Year 3	$50,000.00	$10,000.00
Year 4	$(50,000.00)		Year 4	$50,000.00	$10,000.00
Year 5	$(50,000.00)	$(250,000.00)	Year 5	$50,000.00	$10,000.00
Year 6	$75,000.00	$15,000.00	Year 6	$50,000.00	$10,000.00
Year 7	$75,000.00	$15,000.00	Year 7	$75,000.00	$15,000.00
Year 8	$75,000.00	$15,000.00	Year 8	$75,000.00	$15,000.00
Year 9	$75,000.00	$15,000.00	Year 9	$75,000.00	$15,000.00
Year 10	$100,000.00	$20,000.00	Year 10	$75,000.00	$15,000.00
Year 11	$100,000.00	$20,000.00	Year 11	$75,000.00	$15,000.00
Year 12	$100,000.00	$20,000.00	Year 12	$75,000.00	$15,000.00

$(130,000.00) NET $90,000.00 NET

**Assuming that only 20% of a person's
wage can be used to pay back principal**

If you include the financial model to take the $250,000 gift, deduct the $40,000 and instead invest the balance of $210,000 in a conservative investment, then the justification goes to an entirely different level. Now the two-year student has enough money to start his or her own business. At a rate of return of 5 percent re-invested, the two-year student would have $325,800.00 to fund a start-up, pay cash for a house, or re-invest in stocks. Add the $90,000 to that, and you are approaching a half-a-million-dollar nest egg for someone who is quite young and only went to a trade school for two years.

LEIGH COGLIANESE McCONNELL: GIRLS, YOU GOT THIS!

With my educational ties, I often get asked to speak to high school and college students. Twice I ended up on the same panel with Leigh Coglianese McConnell, Director of Training and Workforce Development for the Technology & Manufacturing Association. After hearing her powerful story on these panels, I asked her to share it in the book. Here is a young woman who was a great student and had the foresight to forego the college route. She, like me, also found it difficult to learn in the conventional class environment and thought there had to be something better. Thankfully, Leigh found her way into a manufacturing career path. Here are some of her comments about the path that she took.

> **Leigh Coglianese McConnell's thoughts:**
> I just really didn't want to go to school. I was kind of done with school after high school, and I didn't want to pay for college. I work at the Technology and Manufacturing Association, or TMA. And I am the Manager of Training and Education there. I also work

on the Education Foundation. I initially started in the Education and Training department. Since then, my responsibilities have evolved while I've worked on the Education Foundation. I work closely with high schools in supporting their machining programs.

I had the grades, and I probably could've gotten a scholarship, but I just didn't want to go to school to figure it out. I kind of wanted to know first, before heading into college. So, I entered the workforce, and I did a lot of random jobs: retail, worked in a locker room, I was a nanny, and I cleaned houses. I was really fortunate enough to have someone ask me if I'd ever considered manufacturing as a career. Prior to that, I really didn't know what I was doing in the world, or what my purpose here was.

I think there are a lot of women in manufacturing. The first thing everybody's mind probably goes to is the individuals running the machines. But on the production side, where I worked with plastic products, they were almost all female. There weren't very many men in that type of manufacturing. Quality control usually has a lot of women as well. So, I have a hard time thinking or agreeing that it is a heavily male-dominated industry because there are a lot of women.

On the machining side of it, of course, there are not as many females. However, I do believe that's changing, especially to see the work I do with high school students and our precision machining competition. There are a lot of girls that are competing in there, and they're also placing. They're accepting their awards in dresses and with their long nails; I just think that's super cool. Super

empowering, and I think they end up empowering one another as well.

When I was in high school, I took a dual credit class on Intro to Engineering. I took it for one day because I was the only woman in the class and probably the only individual under the age of 30. My first day in class, the instructor picked on me the whole time and wanted me to know all the answers; I didn't know one.

There are a lot of company owners and individuals like yourself who are supportive of women in manufacturing because I had at one time experienced the opposite. I would tell an individual who's not sure what they want to do, I would encourage them to do their own thing. *Don't worry about the outside world and what they're telling you; there's nothing wrong with not going to college immediately after high school. There's no expiration date on when an individual can go to college, so put that completely out of your thought process.* I would strongly encourage them to enter the workforce and figure out what they want to do and what they enjoy prior to making a decision to go to school. And then, of course, after that I would recommend they consider manufacturing.

It's really hard to explain manufacturing, just using your hand or words that people don't fully understand, or they can't picture it. So, to be able to show them something or offer them an opportunity to go to a manufacturer for a tour, I think that's a real game changer. But don't be afraid to do what everybody else isn't doing. And don't feel like you have to fit inside a box because nobody does, and usually, the ones that are more successful are the ones that venture outside

the box. I guess the first thing I would recommend is to go on YouTube.

I hated school since first grade. I don't know what it was, but I never liked it. I always gave it my all, I was on honor roll every semester, but I just wasn't a fan of school. So, I think even if my mom and dad did save money, it wouldn't have been my first option. I didn't understand why my generation was pushed so hard into college. I guess I was very fortunate enough to see other people—I don't want to call it mistakes—but I kind of caught on to the fact that a lot of people were going to college, and they weren't necessarily getting the jobs that they had gone to get the degree for.

So, I've never once wondered: *What would have happened if I did go to college?* Maybe that's just because I feel like I'm just as successful as my siblings who did go to college. So, I don't believe there would have been a difference in my life except that I would not be happy as I am today.

I'm a huge science and math nerd, and I felt like every year, we learned the same thing in science: the structure of an animal cell and the structure of a plant cell. I just felt like there was so much they weren't teaching us. We just kept learning the same material over and over again. I wouldn't say it was the way I was taught but I just felt like there was so much out there that they weren't teaching us. Loving science and loving math, I honestly thought the only things I could do with those two was teaching math or science. I was not aware of any other careers at that time of my life associated with the two.

I know you mention this in your book, actually, just being proud to be made in America. I don't know if it was a little bit because of my dad, he was always very proud to be American and he didn't claim to be anything other than that. But I remember at a young age trying to always buy things that were made in America at the grocery store. For whatever reason, I always paid attention to that label. I wanted to be a positive impact in America's economy to continue to allow this country to be great.

I look forward to continuing reading your book, and a lot of stuff that you've heard me say kind of resonates with you and vice versa. I appreciate you doing it because there are a lot of people that probably should have gone into manufacturing and never considered it because they don't know what's out there. Nobody tells them about it. I tell everyone.

CHAMPION YOURSELF

Enough about the financial side of life. The fact is that *you* are the true Champion. You are young and have your whole life ahead of you. In the next chapter, you'll find ideas on how to "own" the awesome responsibility of finding your passion and really making a path toward achieving it. Find what makes you happy and follow that path. If you work hard enough, eventually, you will make the money necessary to sustain a career. The financial rewards are the icing on the cake; ultimately, it is your satisfaction and self-worth that will carry you the distance through life. Choosing the best fit will give you just that.

OWN THE AWESOME RESPONSIBILTY OF FINDING YOUR PASSION!

"Why did the 11th one work? Well, I learned from those 10. I don't want to be known for 10 failed companies but 1 good one. But those 10 got me to the last one that worked."

—Craig Rabin,
Founder of the Airhook

O ur culture today often expects conformity, especially for young people, but each of you needs to have the courage and confidence to do what's right for *you*. If you truly find something that excites you, it will energize you to excel, and, in most cases, the money will follow. Here are 10 ideas to help you find your passion.

1. LEARN ABOUT YOURSELF

I was born in Chicago, the manufacturing mecca of the U.S., during the late 1950s. My parents ended up getting divorced, and my sister Kelly and I moved to Jacksonville, Florida—a great city but not (yet) exactly a manufacturing hub. I excelled in math and science.

I started in public school; however, my parents thought private school was a better match for me. I took the entrance exam for The Bolles School. Somehow, I got in! Bolles was previously an all-boys military academy that became co-ed in 1972, the year I was accepted (I was glad for that!). Bolles set me up for success at a young age. I was able to balance academic expectations with social, athletic, and other priorities such as work. Overall, I came out with a great high school experience because I learned so much about myself. I hope the same for all young people.

Even today, I feel attending Bolles was the biggest break for me, both personally and professionally. The environment I was in was the most challenging I had ever been in—and I knew that I loved a good challenge! At Bolles, I learned the art of over-achievement—performing over your natural abilities through persistence and hard work.

The time you take to learn about how you approach problems, your strengths, and your true passions will inform your career decisions.

HARRY MOSER: ABOUT ALIGNMENT

For example, years later, one of the people who inspired me to get into the education path is the same person who founded the Reshoring Initiative®. I became inspired by Harry Moser, in particular by how he influenced many in the boardroom and C-suite offices to turn the spreadsheets inside out and consider the full cost of ownership when making decisions on where to manufacture your goods.

Here's what Harry has to say about choosing a career and balancing this with your passion:

> **Harry Moser's thoughts:**
> As a country, we need to give young people encouragement and permission to find their passion. Explore how young people can do this effectively. Take a look at skills assessments, the high schools who are doing this well, why some guidance counselors are doing this well and some aren't, and other supporting information. How do you know if you are a good fit for manufacturing? How about listing the traits manufacturers look for in people (respect, curiosity, hunger to learn, diligence, problem-solving, etc.) and the strengths one should sharpen (goal setting, listening).

Around 2010, after retiring from the machine tool industry, Harry founded a movement that became known as Reshoring. Both Harry's passion for informing students about manufacturing careers and his reshoring efforts inspired me more than anyone else I had come to know. Harry Moser is someone I respect and admire. According to Harry, the future is all yours. As he says,

"Get a career that will pay for you and your family. Develop a passion for that career. Pursue your other passions using the time and money generated by your career. Work entitles you to what you earn and desire."

DANA WARD: BE AN INDIVIDUAL

I came across Dana Ward while reading up online on one of the Chicago Bears draft picks. Dana was on an online TV show that covered upcoming college football games. I called out to my wife, Kathy, "Hey, I think I see Dana online. Come here and watch." From there, Dana went into ClevverTV, where she was on the red carpet interviewing Hollywood stars. Just like some of the others I am writing about, she then crossed over to the entrepreneur and manufacturing side when she developed a new product called PreHeels, created to prevent women from getting blisters from new shoes. Dana shares how looking inward can direct your compass in life.

> **Dana Ward's thoughts:**
> It can be difficult to embrace all of the characteristics that make you unique. I know that growing up, there was so much homogeny to fit in, be cool, etc., and I really tried hard to always be true to myself. I think it's a good thing that individualism is much more celebrated today than it was when I was young (almost to a fault, actually, but let's focus on the good right now). Think about it this way: If you're so used to trying to fit in, passively going along for the ride or even just pursuing the path that someone said you're supposed to take without thinking for yourself for a moment, you might be missing out on

a class that's more interesting, an internship that's more inspiring, a project that's more lucrative or a career that's more personalized to you.

And it's OK to not know what you want to study or what you want to do for a living (hey, I'm still evolving!), but make sure that you actually take a few moments to think about it before you set off on some path because society tells you it's a good one. Think about your strengths and passions and consider future employment trends. Consider YOU. Be an individual. Think for yourself. And if you're trying to help someone else find their career path in this wacky world—whether a parent, counselor, writer, mentor or friend—perhaps you see something in that person that they don't see themselves, so share it. Remember that the re-education process from individuals and parents to mentors and teachers to society and media takes way too long and is on an extreme delay, so think for yourself. Do your own research and find the best strategy for you.

2. CONSIDER THE THINGS YOU'VE ALWAYS LOVED TO DO

One young man I got to know from our daughter's class is Craig Rabin, a modern-day inventor and entrepreneur who took a chance, followed his passion, and successfully brought a product called the Airhook to market. The Airhook is a product you take on a plane so you can hang up your coat, mount your electronic device for viewing, or hold a drink—all while your tray is in the upright position.

Craig was a techy geek early on. He is a very gentle soul and genuine to the core. During the early days of internet and web design, he was very entrepreneur-driven, and I used to pay him hourly to work on my iversonandco.com website. We would huddle around my laptop while Craig did HTML code to develop the website that would expand Iverson & Company's presence on the web. Craig helped me on my second revision of the site around 1999-2000. Eventually, Craig was hired at Microsoft and moved out to Washington. Like a lot of young people who I try to keep in touch with, we kept in touch on Facebook.

CRAIG RABIN: THE UNEXPECTED INVENTOR

Craig was one of the very first contestants on Steve Harvey's show "Funderdome," a business reality competition. On the show, entrepreneurs compete head-to-head for money to advance their products to the next level. The audience then votes on which of the two should get the money. Craig won the first round and the $20,000 prize, making him also the very first winner on the show. I think part of what drove Craig to succeed is that he realized what he loved to do in life.

> **Craig Rabin's thoughts:**
> From a young age, my dream was to be an entrepreneur. The real goal was to be an inventor. But I wasn't a super book-smart person. To be honest, my brother, who is five years older than me, is a frickin' genius. So, coming up after him, it was a lot of pressure to be smart. That forced me to be street-smart, always coming up with different things to fill that void. I was in the library for hours.

Years went by. I was 30; I was single and experiencing a third-of-a-life crisis. I had a great corporate job at Microsoft. *Do I try my hand at being an entrepreneur?* I decided I wanted to take one more chance. I had this notebook of ideas for different products and concepts. My pivot in the road was 3D printing, so I could get a machine in my house that could do the prototyping. So I bought one, and for a year, taught myself how to use it. I thought of Airhook when I was sitting on an airplane and had no idea where to hang my sport coat. Inventing it was amazing. I had to relearn geometry.

The only piece that didn't air on 'Funderdome' was the cancer ribbon that I wear. That was because we do a donation on every Airhook in honor of my mother, who passed away from cancer in 2016. We want to be that leader. Even the smallest brands and companies can help change the world. Cancer is something we all have to fight together. I want to continue to fight for other people. It's been a really rewarding part of this journey. Every sale represents one step closer to a cure for cancer. It boils down to that. It gives me and my team a push forward. Every day, we're accomplishing something for the greater good.

It was hard for me to figure out what I wanted to be. All I knew was I liked the idea of owning a business in developing markets. My guidance counselor had absolutely no clue what to tell me! For me, what has worked when there is an unknown is to ask for help. I remember thinking how hard it was to figure out what I wanted to be. I didn't fit that norm. I didn't need a guidance counselor telling me—especially one who didn't know—what

it was that I was talking about. It wasn't until I started asking people I looked up to, how they got there and what advice they had for me.

In some stories, such as Craig's, the young people are quick to admit that they are not the smartest sibling in their family. These young people are bright and talented but, equally as important, they are dedicated, motivated, and driven. Toss away your inhibitions about what you might consider limitations. This holds you back. Instead, focus on your strengths, and get the most out of them. Knowing your limitations and understanding how to compensate for them is important, but they are not your sole focus. Your confidence and persona going forward depends on you knowing who you are and what your passion is. This gives you the recipe for success. I was so very fortunate to have people mentor me. Not only my dad and uncles, but coaches, teachers, and my mom's friends.

3. COMMIT TO YOUR DREAMS–AND PERSEVERE

Outside of school, I worked most of my junior and senior years. I played football and soccer and excelled in the latter, as the leading scorer on the team. Most nights that I worked, I got home about 1:00 a.m. and had to be up at 6:30 a.m. for school. My AP Physics teacher (nicknamed Boo Boo) told me one day that I would be academically ineligible for Friday's soccer match, as I had scored a wonderful "50" on my test. (Needless to say, I had worked a lot that week before.) Now, he had my attention!

I would not and could not let my soccer teammates down. I asked my teacher when our next test was, and he said, "Thursday."

"What would I have to make on the test to be eligible?" I asked. I added, "Would you grade it that afternoon to see if I could play?"

He agreed and said I would have to make a 95 in order to play. "OK, then. Deal."

Boo Boo was stunned at my confidence and matter-of-fact statement. "You really think you can do that?" he asked.

"I know I can. It's all about priorities. I will have to take some shifts off at work, but I *will* get the grade."

That Friday, Boo Boo gave me my test back—on the top of the test was a 97. He shook his head in disbelief.

Friday's game, I started at center forward—disaster averted. Boo Boo challenged me. Even if he didn't understand his role, he made it real for me. He was awesome. He cared.

As for me, I was committed to my dream of playing soccer. It taught me that if I believed in what I was doing, that I would somehow always come out on top. This also taught me the value of making sure not to disappoint my teammates, those who are depending on you.

Be tenacious when it counts. Never give up. Perseverance will serve you all your life. (Thank you, Boo Boo, for teaching me this.)

4. CHOOSE OPTIMISM

Remember Dana Ward, inventor of PreHeels? I believe optimism is one of her strongest qualities. Life is not always great, but choosing an optimistic mindset can make things a lot easier and less stressful. Dana's energy and optimism were key to her success–and they can be yours, too, as you think about what you want to do in your life. Here's what she has to say about it.

Dana Ward's thoughts:

I'm a pretty optimistic person, and I think that's important—at least to me—in entrepreneurship. Sometimes it feels that if it can go wrong, it will go wrong. So you need to be able to keep your head down and keep working through the storm in hopes that the sun eventually comes out to shine. Now I don't want to scare people away from entrepreneurship, but I think it's important to understand why you're choosing to launch something. Don't do it just because it is trendy or the cool thing to do. Entrepreneurship is not for everyone. It can be extremely difficult on your mind, your body, and your soul. It requires sacrifice, self-motivation, and calculated risks. Just be honest with yourself about the reason you're building a product or business, and ask yourself how it is new or better from what already exists in the market.

I'm very happy that you're writing this book. I think we all need a refresher on this topic and seeing the entire picture and multiple examples is always helpful; there's so much noise out there with digital media, so it's too easy for us to be moved by a thought or action-item for a split-second but then unconsciously move on, swipe up, double-tap something else in the social media feed, and the inspiration is gone. Let's keep the stories and framework in a single place for easy access and promising follow-through.

5. MAKE YOUR OWN PATH

Carrie Kurczynski is Technical Project Manager/Operations for GE Power. She grew up in our church, which her parents attended. Learn how she made her way into engineering and manufacturing—with hands-on learning making the biggest difference.

Carrie Kurczynski's thoughts:

I was lucky to have hands-on teachers who taught us to 'see' the theory, not just memorize it. In high school, I remember my physics teacher laid on a table with a board across her stomach and challenged students to hit the board with a bat to teach the dispersion of energy.

When I was in college, our physics teacher dropped a stuffed gorilla and marble from the ceiling of the lecture hall at the same time to demonstrate terminal velocity.

GE saw my experience working in the machine shop at Purdue. They saw that my senior project was being a part of the Mini Baja team and my hobbies included working on motorcycles. They directed me to apply for a field engineering position, where I ended up spending the first five years at customer sites leading teams in tearing down and inspecting steam turbines.

6. TRUST YOUR GUT

In college, I was naïve as to what I wanted to do as a career and what I wanted to study. I had a newfound interest in photography after my mom gave me a nice camera for high school graduation.

Upon entering general studies at Florida State University, I thought both photography and psychology held promise as far as potential choices for a major and subsequent career.

After careful thought, I realized that even though sports photography was an awesome dream job, how many photographers would be on the sidelines for any variety of sports? Not only is there a limited number of opportunities for this position, but the pay was probably somewhat limiting, too.

When I thought about psychology as a major, I realized that in order to succeed in that field, most people went on to grad school. Despite thinking it was a fascinating subject matter, the thought of sitting and listening to people's problems all day long quickly deterred me from pursuing that major.

And then came my strong suit—math and science. I decided that if I was to go into engineering, Florida State University was probably not the strongest choice at the time for that subject. I then decided to transfer to UW Madison in Wisconsin. I still enjoyed taking photos of sporting events and continued this well into my education at the University of Wisconsin Madison. There, I became a staff photographer for the school newspaper. I was now at a strong engineering school but determined that I could still satisfy my interest in photography as a hobby.

My college career took many turns. I transferred several more times as I struggled to find the right match for me. This was more complicated by the fact that my girlfriend at the time was still in Florida. Long-distance relationships are very difficult to manage—to put it mildly. Pursuing our relationship led me to transfer back to the University of Florida Gainesville, get engaged, and move back north to Wisconsin. There I took a job with my uncle's machine shop and went to Marquette University for engineering classes in the evening.

By this time, I had decided that my goals for earning expectations and my strong math and science capabilities were a great match for one of the family businesses in manufacturing. Even though I did not finish mechanical engineering school, the background that I accumulated along the way was more than satisfactory for the machining or machine tool business that I ultimately ended up entering into.

I trusted my gut. I've never looked back.

FRANK FRANGIE: FOLLOW YOUR HEART

I met my future wife-to-be in my junior year in high school while working at a movie theater. One of my co-workers came to a movie with one of her good friends. As we became serious and close to engagement, Kathy indicated there was one person I had to meet to get "his approval"—her best friend in high school, Frank Frangie. Frank was someone that was like a big brother to her. Fortunately, he approved, and 42 years later, we are fortunate to have a very blessed marriage and life together. I could not have found a better partner, supporter, and spouse. As the following remarks by Frank reveal, following your heart applies to your career paths in much the same way it does to finding a life partner. In both cases, you need to trust your gut instinct, risk your heart fearlessly, and commit 100 percent.

> **Frank Frangie's thoughts:**
> I grew up wanting to be a sportswriter. That's all I ever wanted to do. I graduated from college in 1980. There weren't a lot of sports writing jobs open. For family reasons, I took a job at a bank. I was in the personnel and human resources department. I learned a lot about

how to lead, manage people, teach leaders to lead, and how to develop young people, all of the stuff that I had no idea that I didn't know. Sometimes you don't know what you don't know, right?

I knew very early on, at that bank, that that wasn't me. I was going to be a sportswriter, and it wasn't ever about the money. That was never the plan. Hell, I grew up without any money. We lived in a 900-square-foot home. I just realized that the banking thing wasn't for me. I got out of that pretty quickly. The most interesting career change was the one from sports writing to broadcasting. That was the one I never saw coming.

I tell young people: Find your passion. If you find something you love doing, you'll never work a day in your life. Wake up in the morning passionate. Go to bed at night passionate. Drive around during the day passionate. Think about it at lunch passionately. Make yourself not think about it at church, you're so passionate about it. Find something you're *that* passionate about.

I wondered to myself what would have happened if he had stayed at the bank. He might never have had the stories he shared with me, his eyes on fire thinking about the exciting experiences he had. Looking in my rearview mirror, I can honestly say that I followed my passion, too. So much so that it led me to sharing my passion for youth and manufacturing with readers like you who care about these things as well.

7. BE TENACIOUS AND FIND YOUR PASSION

When people talk to me about helping young people, they inevitably settle on the word "passionate" as a trait of mine. Some things are hard to define in words. When you invest much more time and effort into something than can ever be justified, this is where passion resides.

I have run a company for over 35 years and realized early on that results matter. At the end of the day, the bills must be paid. You cannot miss payroll and filling commitments matters. It would be easier to not put in the extra hours or to not miss a personal commitment. Over my 42 years, I have outworked many of my competitors by caring about the customers' value proposition more than mine. At the end of the day, tenacity has to prevail. Don't make excuses, put your head down, and grind ahead. You cannot tell yourself you should have done enough to succeed. "Overdo" to ensure that you succeed. This is one reason I have had so many at my company dedicate their careers to my company. I have their back and they have mine.

One of my beliefs is that this largely came from my participation in sports. At 5'7", I was commonly one of the shorter competitors on any field I played. Hard work and tenacity allowed me to compete at a very high level, something I could not have done otherwise. Compete at a high level, wherever that is. Be tenacious and overachieve—because you can.

8. ASK FOR HELP

Airhook inventor Craig Rabin makes the point that asking for help is important. He's right. Asking for help can be hard and even seem embarrassing sometimes. The truth is that we all need

help sometimes. And if you don't ask, you don't get, and that's a fact.

> **Craig Rabin's thoughts:**
> Craig says that "when you find that thing you love and you don't look at the clock, it's fantastic." Given that, isn't it worth looking for answers outside of yourself? He goes on to say, "It's always harder to ask for help than it is to give help. Failure is good as long as you learn from it. If you can turn your failure into learning, you can turn it into success. I've had eleven companies. Why did the eleventh one work? Well, I learned from those 10. I don't want to be known for 10 failed companies, but one good one. But those 10 got me to the last one that worked."

9. OVER-PREPARE AND THEN GO WITH THE FLOW—TONY SCHUMACHER

In Chapter 2, Tony Schumacher talks about making products in America and the choice we make by purchasing products made outside this country. Here Tony talks about how each young person should make a conscious decision about how to advance their young lives to the next level as they near graduation.

> **Tony Schumacher's thoughts:**
> I think my favorite expression that I use is just to over-prepare and then go with the flow. Too many people show up and just wing it. If you showed up for a test, just winging it, you wouldn't be very good at it. I think what that entails is, number one, choose your job. Don't let it choose you. Choose it, figure out what you want to

do. If you won the lottery, what would make you wake up and be happy every day? Then, learn it. Don't learn it like you're trying to get an 'A,' learn it like you've got two brakes on a car with two car seats in the back seat, and it has to work. Learn it that well. It has to be done right. If you can do your job like that, you'll be proud. Everyone around you will be proud, and let me tell you something, man, when you do a good job, your friends want to do a good job, and so does everyone around you. It starts the world in a better place. I just think we're in a little bit opposite position right now. We need to fix it.

10. STRIVE FOR BALANCE

In my first book (and the parent edition), I went back to Cathy Hurst because of the profound work she, her husband, and son Hayden have done around mental health. During our interview, Cathy mentioned a person they have worked with on the concept of social and emotional intelligence. This was a concept that I kept hearing, and I realized I was unaware of what it was. I reached out to Tom McSheehy from the Teaching Heart Institute and learned a great deal. His thoughts challenged my definition and perception of what "intelligent" is. What a difference it would be to many young people who feel they are not intelligent enough to be successful. Maybe they just need a better understanding of what their intelligence actually is.

TOM McSHEEHY: SMARTER THAN YOU THINK

A lot of people don't think they are smart. Part of the reason is that they only look at one aspect of themselves: IQ, which is

based on linguistic intelligence and mathematical or logical intelligence. According to Tom McSheehy, however, "there are at least six other ways to display intelligence that IQ testing doesn't measure." We need to broaden our definition of intelligence in line with the theory of Howard Gardner of Harvard about multiple intelligences. According to Gardner, there are eight areas of intelligence:

- Linguistic, or your ability to read and write
- Math and logic
- Movement intelligence or kinesthetic
- Spatial or visual intelligence
- Interpersonal, or the ability to get along and work with others
- Intrapersonal, or the ability to self-reflect, go inward, and set goals
- Naturalist, or the ability to understand nature and the connections within nature
- Musical ability

McSheehy continues:

Tom McSheehy's thoughts:
We really need to broaden our definition of intelligence. There are so many people walking around like me who think they are not smart. I thought that the only reason that I got good grades was that I worked very hard. It wasn't until I was 38 years old that I realized that I *was* intelligent when I was young, just not in reading or writing. I struggled a lot in those areas. It pains me to listen to people say, 'He's smart' or 'She's smart,' as if

other children and teenagers aren't smart. All people are smart, but in different ways.

Encouraging young people to explore their different intelligences—and then pursue those that interest them most—also gives them room to breathe. Helping students find their areas of intelligence is so connected to mental health. Because when we are seen and valued for our strengths and areas of intelligence in classrooms, we feel valued and a part of the classroom team and belong. When we focus on kids' strengths, they naturally want to work on their weaknesses. When you focus on their weaknesses and what they can't do, they get discouraged and shut down and go away or get very angry. We need to change the way we see students in terms of their intelligence. We don't spend time in schools talking about purpose with middle or high school students. Sometimes our purpose is connected to areas of intelligence, and sometimes, it is connected to areas where we struggle or encounter pain. It is very important for students to explore their purpose on this earth.

DON'T WAIT
TO BE INVITED

"St. Louis city is 85 percent Black and I don't see 10 Black people (on the shop floor), or if I do see 10 Black people, they are the janitors."

—Andrew Crowe,
Founder of the New American Manufacturing Renaissance

One story that I need to share is the day that I realized that there were terms that African Americans were not OK with. In the South, the term "colored" was used for decades. Keep in mind I was born in 1959, and this story probably took place around the late 1960s when I was 10 years old.

When I started playing baseball, I usually played shortstop or left field. While I could not hit worth a lick, I could usually field and throw fairly well, and those positions suited my skill set. Our third baseman that year was named Bruce, and he played next to me when I played short. We would sit on the bench together, waiting for both of our turns to go up to the plate to bat. One game, we were sitting in the first base side dugout, and Bruce started a conversation.

"A friend of mine hit a home run here last week over the wall," he said while pointing to the right-field outfield wall. (Keep in mind we were 10 or 11 years old at this point, so hitting a baseball that far is reason to take notice.)

"Oh, was he colored?" I responded.

Bruce, very matter-of-factly, responded to me, "No, he was Black."

That moment in my life was all-changing. I am not even sure what I said to Bruce after that. I do know that was the last moment that I referred to any black person as colored. That was over 50 years ago. I cannot tell you Bruce's last name. I cannot tell you where life took Bruce beyond our time on the Knights of Columbus baseball team. I do know that I owe Bruce a word of gratitude and thanks. Bruce taught me a valuable lesson that I did not even know that I needed. So, if you are out there, Bruce, thank you for this life lesson. Five decades have passed, and I have met many people since then. Here I sit thinking of the time we spent on that bench having a casual conversation. Little did I know!

You might be thinking, *Sure, you can say that I shouldn't wait for an invitation, Terry, but you're a middle-aged white guy.*

You're right, I am, but I also know what I'm talking about here. Manufacturing is a great career for people of all kinds of cultural backgrounds for one simple reason. We need *you*—the best and the brightest.

In Chapter 6, you read about some fascinating people. Each of them has an interesting story about how they discovered and nurtured the Greatest Champion inside each of them. But what about the plethora of young people who may not have the support or intuitiveness to find their way—especially in the field of manufacturing?

In the days since I wrote my initial book, a lot has occurred. In 2020, this country underwent a racial awakening. I find it insane that this movement did not transfer to the ranks of manufacturers in our country, where there are too few people of color. While I made a significant push to highlight the need for more women in our companies in my first book, I failed to highlight the need to include more people of color and from diverse backgrounds. In this book, I am committed to doing a better job by showing that to give those who are people of color can also have good-paying careers that are there for the taking, providing a path to success.

According to the book *Made in Illinois: A Modern Playbook for Manufacturers to Compete and Win*, the state of Illinois only has 64 companies that are black-owned out of the 13,000 manufacturers in the state.[1] If this is not a shocking statistic, I am not sure what is. Something needs to change in order to bring the manufacturing dream to this sector of our population!

I grew up in the South, after having been born in the North. I was taught never to see black vs. white. Instead, I just saw people.

That being said, I often ponder why there are not more people of color in manufacturing, a career path that has so much to offer. Yet those who might need these careers the most do not know of the opportunities that wait for them.

DAUGHTERS, STEP INTO THE LIGHT!

Why are there so few women in manufacturing? It is a rarity that I talk to a woman involved in the manufacturing or engineering part of the business. I married the smartest (and prettiest) woman I ever dated. I just could not think of spending any significant amount of time with a woman who did not challenge me intellectually. I never claimed to be a rocket scientist; however, I did engross myself in a lot of engineering coursework, AP Calculus, AP Physics, and the like. I really enjoyed seeing parts being made, math equations that gave solid answers, and the science of physics and how things work and why. Many men are linear thinkers. Not all the answers come from a linear process. Many women think much differently. There is a tremendous amount of good that could come from looking at things differently—not to mention that we have a void of talent in the labor pool. Why not draw from areas of the workforce where we have not done so in the past?

Our family has been blessed with strong women—from my mom, my wife, both my younger sisters, my cousins, my daughter, and daughters-in-law. I don't understand why there aren't more women in our industry. I do know that when you meet a woman in manufacturing, she is commonly strong and very determined and driven to succeed. There aren't enough stories to tell; however, I will do my best to share those that have inspired me!

Going back a few years, I went to visit a machine shop closing that was a GE division where they machined turbine blades. We had sold them a very high-end CNC surface grinder that I was interested in.

When I arrived, a young woman answered at the window. "I didn't know you were going to be here!" At first, I thought someone was behind me... until I realized the lobby was too small for someone to have walked in behind me. "Oh, OK," I said, in a confused manner. We exchanged small talk until she escorted me to the shop. She asked someone else to take me to the machine. On the way back, I asked my chaperone, "Help me out; what is her name?! I know that I know her, but I cannot place her name."

"Carrie," he said.

"How about her married or maiden name?" I inquired. "Kurczynski, I think," he said. That must have been her married name, but I still could not figure it how I knew her.

As I was taking my photos and videos of the machine, she walked back to check on me. "Help me out here," I said. "I know that we know one another, but how? What is your maiden name?"

"Johnson," she said.

"Ken and Muff are your parents!" I proclaimed. At the same time, we said, "Kingswood!" That is the church that Kathy and I attend. We have known Carrie and her parents for her entire life.

CARRIE J. KURCZYNSKI: YES, YOU CAN

I knew Carrie went into engineering, but I rarely had a chance to talk to her about her interests, her education, or her career. Shortly after our impromptu meeting, I called and asked to interview her for my book. I asked her how she made her way into engineering, then ultimately manufacturing.

Carrie J. Kurczynski's thoughts:

At a young age, I was taught what you did and how you did it had nothing to do with what was under the hood.

It's hugely related to my parents. When I was 12, we rebuilt my dad's motorcycle. It wasn't our first project; he was always tinkering with something, but it was the deciding project when my dad kindly insisted I should consider engineering—telling me that I would love it. When I reached high school, my mom helped point out all the tech classes so I could better understand the school side of engineering. Since math and the sciences had always come easy to me, she didn't want me to think it would all be easy.

When I finally got my driver's license, my dad wouldn't let me take the car out until I could prove I could change the oil and change a tire. Ironically, the only time I have ever needed to change a tire was on my way to a wedding as the maid of honor. I was already dressed for the ceremony when I heard the tire blow. Lucky for me, it was right in front of a mechanic shop, and they offered to change it before I could assess what was going on. I knew I needed to let them, as my heels and dress were not going to survive me doing it myself. But I called my dad and vented my frustrations at needing to accept help when I could have handled it.

While I liked all the hands-on projects, enjoyed my technical classes, and found that math and science came easy, I was diagnosed with ADD and a slight form of dyslexia, mostly with numbers, at a young age. In high

school, I was able to control or work around it with minimal accommodations. Sometimes I would lose points on tests or homework because I switched a number here or there but nothing that affected my overall semester grades. But I was worried about getting in over my head in college. With the help of my parents, we were able to look into what accommodations were available at a college level. It turned out that Purdue had many more resources available than I even ended up needing, but they were always there if I asked.

Our (high school) graduating class had 1,065 students. If I had to guess, maybe, easily 10 percent of the women had the ability to do it (go into engineering). I can only remember three or four who did—there could have been more. After college, a lot of companies tried to get me to go in the direction of technical sales. It would have been twice the salary, but I couldn't imagine not getting dirty on the shop floor or sitting in some office eight to ten hours a day. It almost felt like they thought I enjoyed getting dressed up in the suit and heels and putting on makeup. No, thank you!

I had spent the last year of my college career on campus 12 to 13 hours a day, bouncing between classes, labs, and the machine shop. Sitting still just was not for me, and heels weren't for me (well, not boring black ones and certainly not every day). When I started learning what a field engineering was, I was hooked. There was no other option for me, and not once in any of the conversations did anyone care that I was a girl. All they cared about was that the long hours, hard work, and technical issues wouldn't stop me from pushing forward.

I would tell young women to drop the notion that being female has anything to do with what makes you happy or what you want to do in life. Don't compare yourself to the guy down the street or another girl or your siblings. Do the best you can do and do what makes you happy. Ask questions! Just because no one else has asked something doesn't mean they aren't wondering also. You would be surprised how many people just don't want to talk. I don't know if I never cared what other people thought or if, at some point, I just stopped worrying about it, but I've always sort of ended up doing my own thing (for better or worse). You can come with me or not.

I was lucky. I was brought up to believe that what you did and how you did it had nothing to do with what was under the hood. Maybe that is a little blunt, but my work and work ethic was what counted. I wasn't always the best, but I worked my butt off. In school, it was the same way. I didn't always have the best grades, but I worked hard. And now, I work for a great company and they support me, not only as an engineer but also as a mom and a wife—no need to pick one over the other.

CARRIE MEET MOLLY!
A GENERAL ELECTRIC COMMERCIAL

Right around the same time of our meeting, I saw the GE commercial about a young woman inventor named "Molly." As I watched it, I could not help but make the correlation between "Molly" in the GE commercial, with the nonfictional real-life "Carrie" working for GE. I texted Carrie and told her about the commercial and the uncanny connection of her working for GE

making turbine blades. Wow, some coincidences are just too timely to be anything short of "a sign." GE has shown up as a leader in trying to make a statement on the role of women in the manufacturing workforce.

Hopefully, there will be more women entering the ranks of STEM (Science, Technology, Engineering and Math) or STEAM (Science, Technology, Engineering, Arts, and Math) fields going  forward. Dana Ward, the awesome inventor of PreHeels you met earlier, tells about her parents' influence on her path to success.

Dana Ward's thoughts:

I think it is key to understand that failure is just a normal part of life because, as an entrepreneur, you're going to experience failures of varying degrees through-out the journey. You need to be okay with it or work towards accepting it. I try to consciously address an issue quickly, learn from it, and move on. You cannot allow failure, or even fear of failure, to paralyze you. No one has time for that!

Something that you should always try to make time for—and this is just me preaching, but for others who are motivated by value, it can be helpful too—is to support others in their endeavors. At some point, you'll need help from your network, friends, family and even strangers, so put out what you'd like to receive. If you support some-one for who they are, ask how you can support… or if you like an idea or product, then buy it and review it.

I give a lot of credit to my parents for helping struc-ture a healthy mindset; they really were responsible for

teaching me at a young age that I could do anything that I wanted to do. I mean, I'm pretty sure that if I decided that I wanted to become an astronaut and go to space tomorrow, I would find a way to make it happen (even if logically and logistically that means buying a ticket for when a public flight is available!). Find that confidence and hold on to it tightly. Inevitably, you'll need it.

STEPPING UP TO ENCOURAGE GIRLS AND MINORITIES TO GO INTO STEM

How can we, as a culture, ignore the talents and energy that the female gender offer? The highest percentage of the working population in manufacturing that I have found is 29 percent. We are still missing out on 10-20 percent of highly talented workers. We need to empower women to have the courage and confidence to enter into STEM-related fields. According to the Bureau of Labor Statistics data, women account for 47 percent of total employment, but just 27 percent of manufacturing employment.

Colorado certainly seems to keep surfacing as a state that is doing all the right things when it comes to STEM and getting more young people involved in coursework and activities. Monte Whaley writes about various contributions that are making a difference in their state.

Monte Whaley's thoughts:

In Denver Public Schools (DPS), $10 million in bond funds are supplying laptops for 9,000 students (in 2017) this school year. The effort encouraging girls and minorities to pursue careers in STEM (Science, Technology, Engineering, and Math) fields, DPS officials said. Many

businesses, nonprofits, and individuals are stepping up to help cash-strapped families meet their back-to-school needs. More than 400 volunteers donated their time to help run the Action Center school supply giveaway in Jefferson County. They sorted supplies and stuffed backpacks and then formed a well-oiled machine to check IDs and match students with the appropriate school gear during the week-long event. One of the biggest donors to the Jeffco effort is local home builder Cardel Homes, which began donating as many as 3,000 backpacks a year to the Action Center in 2014.[2]

One of the best movies that I have ever seen speaks to the impact of a group of black women in the 1960s on the NASA space program. The movie *Hidden Figures* is nothing short of amazing and inspiring. It speaks to the ways that biases against women and people of color have prevailed for too long and need to be eradicated from our culture. I think of the multiple correlations between the young women and their messages included in this book and the women featured in the movie. They are today's best versions of the role models of Katherine Johnson (played by Taraji P. Henson), Mary W. Jackson (played by Janelle Monáe), and Dorothy Vaughn (played by Octavia Spencer). Even though this movie took place decades ago, the situation of these skilled women reflects a problem that is still ongoing: the lack of representation of women, and Black women in particular, in technical fields.

A COLLEGE FOR TRADESPEOPLE?—MIKE ROUNDS

I interviewed Ryan Pohl for this book, and through our conversations, Ryan introduced me to someone who runs a school in

Pennsylvania that brings dreams to young men in the way of a technical education for good-paying careers. One reason manufacturing has a place for you is because it has so many opportunities for success. Mike Rounds, president of Williamson College of the Trades, tells it best. Williamson College of the Trades in Philadelphia gives free tuition and schooling in 6 different trades for 100 young men each year. This program gives these students a pathway to earn a great wage, regardless of their background. Rounds says:

Mike Rounds's thoughts:

It's just really rewarding to see the young men who come in, who have very little confidence a lot of times in their own abilities and their own situation. And then to see their confidence in their skills and their abilities dramatically increase over the three years so that when they leave, they are confident in their ability to go out and be a great citizen and a great worker, and a great opportunity to be very successful—probably more successful than they ever thought they were capable of before.

Another amazing thing about the demographic of our students—which is young men near the poverty level—is the ability to complete any further education after high school. The national numbers are very, very small, but we graduate, on average, 75 percent of our young men in three years. And the best part of the whole thing is that not only are they graduating with an associate degree and no debt, but they usually have four, five, or six job offers.

MANUFACTURING WELCOMES ALL—VONDALE SINGLETON

It does not matter what neighborhood you come from, the color of your skin, your gender, or any other facet of your background. You are America's Greatest Champion, and there is a place for you in manufacturing. Several years ago, I reached out to someone making a difference in the lives of young men on the south side of Chicago. His mentoring program goes under the name of CHAMPS. Of course, the parallel in name and focus with my 501(c)3 were too obvious not to make an introduction. His name is Vondale Singleton, and he gives hope on the south side of Chicago, where that concept sometimes is not often found.

Vondale Singleton hails from the inner city of Chicago and grew up in the "housing projects," as he calls them.

Vondale Singleton's thoughts:
We talk about it as if it's some mythical place. But that was a real place for me. It was a frightening place for me. To watch my mom get hooked on drugs at an early age, or at least succumbing to that warfare of drugs that ended her life in 1994. When I was 14, she was only 29. Imagine a 14-year-old burying his mom, and she's 29. She didn't even get a chance to experience life. Yet I had to navigate that and still navigate it, and now I'm almost 40 years old. I'm blessed and I'm fortunate because I would have been another statistic had it not been for my mentor. They eventually came into my life in '97 and really did a very powerful thing by modeling for me a high level of consistency. Many of my peers didn't have

a father. But then, many of my peers had real struggles. Mentorship was my lifeline.

I heard a lot about manufacturing in the '80s and '90s. And as the technology boom, I think, has arrived, it has kind of lessened the conversation around manufacturing. I don't know why that is but in our educational field, I think the contents of the fields of study that most of our teachers are pushing these days are more in line with the wave of the future, if you will, right? There are many aspects of manufacturing that touch technology, math, health care, so on and so forth, right? So, I think, to a degree, our educators are at fault for not having the education behind it to be able to share information around it.

JOSSIMAR MENDEZ: THE SKY IS THE LIMIT

During the time that I spent with Leah Coglianese McConnell, I asked her for the names of people who went through the TMA program who could be an inspiration to other young people. Leah spoke highly about Jossimar Mendez. Do you see yourself in his words?

Jossimar Mendez's thoughts:
I graduated from East Leyden H.S. in 2009, which is located in Franklin Park, IL. One of my favorite classes was auto class, where we learned how to fix basic car issues and do maintenance. Senior year was definitely tough because I had no clue what I wanted to do after high school. Growing up, I was huge on sports, specifically soccer, and really never put much emphasis on what

career I wanted to pursue. I really liked working with my hands; I was mechanically inclined.

I then started working for a car dealership as a car fleet attendant. I was in charge of cleaning the cars, making sure they were filled up with gas, and organizing them in the car lot. I worked there for about six months, before I was laid off due to a drop in sales. I then filed for unemployment and decided to freeload off the system. While on unemployment, I received the news that my girlfriend was pregnant! I was about to be a dad with no financial stability, no motivation, zero guidance, and I was completely terrified.

I remember telling my parents at the dinner table. My dad looked up at me with major disappointment and said, 'Son, I will not financially support you. This is your doing. You need to grow up and take care of business.' He also advised me to pursue a career in manufacturing as he stated, 'You don't need much schooling, and most jobs are hands-on experience.'

I found a job as a CNC operator through an ad and decided to apply. After two interviews, I got the job working as a CNC operator with wood/plastic components. I learned how to operate, set up, and even program on a CNC lathe. After several months there was a major drop in orders, and me being the newest guy, I was let go. The news felt like I got hit by a semi going 80 mph! I was scared, and honestly lost. The one job I was starting to enjoy just ended. After this, I started applying at all sorts of different places in manufacturing.

Two weeks later, I got a call from a friend explaining that this manufacturing shop was hiring. He also

explained the duties, which entailed janitorial work, sorting, and shipping & receiving. Even though I wouldn't be working on machines, it was a good way to get my foot in the door, so I took the job. I was working 10-hour days plus Saturdays, so the money wasn't bad. They also saw a great work ethic from me. I was always on time, didn't miss work, was organized, and my goals were always completed.

A couple of months after, one of the supervisors offered me a position as a machine operator. The machine I would be running was pretty basic. It would just grind a sharp edge on an angle onto a shear. I got the hang of it pretty quick, but months later, they decided to have the ground angle as part of another operation and no longer needed that machine. I thought I was losing my job again.

My supervisor offered another spot as an operator, but now running 150-ton stamping presses, which was a whole different world. I was ecstatic and agreed to the offer.

Running stamping machines reminded me a lot of CNC work with very similar processes within quality and engineering checks. After months of working on presses, it all was kind of natural to me. Working with my hands was always my strength, and I was really good at it. After proving myself to the team, I became the floater. I was basically training/running machines in different departments every month depending on demand. This was extremely beneficial to my growth as I became

versed in different departments and had added value to the company.

I have always been an open-minded individual, and so what I did was to combine the knowledge from everyone that trained me into my own recipe, which resulted in major success. To me, knowledge is power, and growth was not an option but a *must* since I had a family depending on me now. I was able to set up/run almost every job on that shop floor from point A-Z, my bosses saw the motivation/drive I had, and how contagious it was with others.

My persistence led me to enroll in TMA (Technology & Manufacturing Association) school. School wasn't easy, and between work, family, and school, my schedule soon became completely booked. After my first year of TMA, and showing my supervisor my good grades, they decided to start giving me some time in the Tool Room.

I would spend half of the morning in the tool room and the afternoons in production setting up dies. The tool room was a blast. My training consisted of hands-on training with all the tool room equipment (surface grinders, lathes, jig-bores/grinders, mills, I.D./O.D. grinders, honing machines, EDM sinkers, etc.) first. My favorite was the mills; I would machine punch plates, die blocks, and other die components. They had a cutting oil used on the mills that would end up giving you a hint of honey whiskey with the heat from the end mills. I worked in the tool room for about a year before the next opportunity presented itself.

I was in the process of buying a house now with two kids and the wife; the one-bedroom condo we lived in was extremely small. I remember being scared about being a homeowner since, at the time, I was the only one working and not making enough money to buy a property without some extra income. I also knew that my little family needed more room, and I did not give up on our dream. I decided to move 45 minutes away from our parents because it was a more affordable area with good school districts.

The day of the closing of the house, I was not happy, but terrified. I knew it was going to be extremely difficult to pay my mortgage, but I was already looking into a second job during the weekends. Three days after the closing of the house, I was given an opportunity that would change my life forever.

One of the pros about me is my personality. I love working with people and always see the positive in the individual or situation. I was always looking at better ways to do my job and the benefits for my company. This was a trait that my bosses clearly saw in me, and soon enough, I was given the opportunity to become the supervisor. There were several things that popped into to mind before my decision. *Why me? I'm the youngest buck in the whole shop. Will I fail? Am I qualified?* All these questions obviously made me scared and uncertain, but my Human Resources (HR) department reassured me that I would have the leaders' support throughout the process. I knew that if I took this job, I would be able to pay my mortgage without working a second job and would get to spend that time with my kids. I also know

that knowledge is power; I had already thought of how I would be able to contribute to the business. I decided to take the job and was promoted to the new Production/ Tool Room supervisor.

My goal as a leader was to build an environment where people loved their job and had excitement about accomplishments for themselves and the business. After two years of being a supervisor, I was then again faced with another decision.

On August 30, 2019, my HR gave me the opportunity to become the Plant Manager, and my answer was quick and loud: 'YES!' I remember taking a walk through the shop that afternoon after everyone was gone and just reminiscing on all the hardships/great moments shared on that floor. That brought tears to my eyes. I went from a janitor to a plant manager in the course of nine years. This was all thanks to an amazing HR, staff, amazing company, and God. Now, at 29 years of age, my plan is to pursue an education in business and continue to grow with my team/company.

One of my favorite lines is 'the sky is the limit.' I truly believe that you do not need a four-year degree to become successful. There are a ton of technical careers that will give you the life you want as long as you show honesty, reliability, respect, and hard work. I'm currently the plant manager for a manufacturing facility located in Broadview, IL. I have been working in this shop now for nine years. Within the nine years, I have taken on several roles from janitorial work, shipping and receiving, press

operator, set-up man, tool and die maker, shop supervisor, and plant manager. Manufacturing has been part of my family for many years, and a lot of my relatives have had successful careers in manufacturing.

The lessons from Jossimar are too many to count, but they include his attitude, his drive and determination, and his willingness to be mentored by others in the company. In Chapter 8, I lay out many points about how to take charge of your career, and Jossimar's actions emulate many of them.

PALATINE HIGH SCHOOL—A MODEL FOR OTHER SCHOOLS

While working with Palatine High School, I wanted to figure out a way to encourage young people to enter Project Lead the Way classes. I met with Mark Hibner, their instructor, and let him pick the top 10 students to be ambassadors around the school. I came up with a poster program that would be the marketing campaign for the class. The poster would feature photos of young people in their high school activities, as well as photos of them in potential future manufacturing-related activities. The tagline on the posters was "They were Champions THEN and they are **CHAMPIONs Now!**" I also designed **CHAMPION Now!** shirts with fabric pens provided. Each of the students was given the task of getting peers to sign the shirt. The front of the shirt said **CHAMPION Now!**, while the back coined my Manufacturing Create$ slogan. Wouldn't you know that two of the young ladies took the challenge and ran with it! They got so many signatures that it was obvious they *really* got engaged in the task. This is the type of program that

could revolutionize Project Lead the Way programs throughout the country.

YOUR TURN

Now, it's your turn to create your path of action. You don't have to have all the answers. You just need the desire to figure things out, the space to talk to your parents and other mentors in your life, the awareness to consider what makes you happy, and the belief in yourself that the best of life is just up ahead. You CAN control your own destiny!

CREATE
YOUR PATH
OF ACTION

*"I tell young people: Arrive early,
leave late, and tell the truth."*

*–Finding America's Greatest Champion:
Building Prosperity Through Manufacturing,
Mentoring and the Awesome Responsibility of Parenting*

By now, you already know I started an organization named **CHAMPION Now!** to change how manufacturing is perceived. Well, this chapter is the call to action for you, a young person ready to take on the world.

Why? Because you're not in this alone. We all need to step up.

Companies need to quit thinking about next quarter's results and think more altruistically about our country's future, by way of their future. Adults need to look beyond their own desires for their children and consider their children's strengths and interests.

Positive influences like guidance counselors, internship programs, job shadowing, and sports teams make a difference, especially when negative influences like drugs, gangs, and overdependence on technology come into play. Please know this: There are many people working hard not to fail you. We all need to encourage and empower the positives and educate and empower against the negatives. We all need to give our young people the best we have.

KATHLEEN BURLEY: FIND YOUR CRAFT

When Gary Skoog retired from the organization formerly known as Golden Corridor, a group dedicated to young people in manufacturing, there was a void that needed to be filled. This group of visionaries needed a leader, someone who was passionate about the industry—and about young people in our great country. Kathleen Burley is a great example of this. She is the former executive director of the Greater Chicago Advanced Manufacturing Partnership (as of the time of this writing, GCAMP is led by Dawn Curran). Kathleen has long championed young people and has become a strong voice for young girls entering manufacturing.

You will love her backstory because, like many in manufacturing, she has walked in your shoes.

Kathleen Burley's thoughts:

The Greater Chicago Advanced Manufacturing Partnership, or GCAMP, was started in 2010 (formerly the 'Golden Corridor Advanced Manufacturing Partnership') with a handful of northwest suburban manufacturers and Gary Skoog, the director of economic development for Hoffman Estates.

The first event that GCAMP took part in was IMTS 2010 (International Manufacturing and Technology Show) by funding buses for local high school students to attend at McCormick Place. Loaded with automation, robotics, and more, IMTS hosts the Smartforce Student Summit, which is the perfect place to introduce students to the amazing, high-tech careers in manufacturing. GCAMP hosts a booth at the IMTS Student Summit, which is held every two years.

GCAMP is a bridge between manufacturing companies and their future workforce. Our work previously focused on the 'Golden Corridor,' an area which runs along I-90 from O'Hare to Rockford. We originally worked primarily in the Northwest suburbs of Elk Grove Village, Schaumburg, and Hoffman Estates with local manufacturing companies, Harper College, and High School districts 211 and 214, the two largest high school districts in Illinois. GCAMP was instrumental in assisting high school District 211 and high school District 214 in getting manufacturing programs back into the schools. (Note: Both Mark Hibner & Dr. Laz Lopez, who were

interviewed in this book, were a big part of the CTE curriculum and programs in each district.) We have helped to place countless students into internships, apprenticeships, and employment positions.

In 2021, GCAMP joined forces with and became a part of the VIA (Valley Industrial Association) and changed their name to The Greater Chicago Advanced Manufacturing Partnership. In large part, this was done to expand GCAMP's reach so that we could help schools in a much larger area and connect with industrial and manufacturing companies to continue finding work-based learning opportunities such as paid internships, student apprenticeships, and employment after graduation for many more students and companies.

When I was 19 and had just finished up my freshman year of college, I had no direction and no idea what I wanted to do. I was told, 'Your mom didn't have the opportunity you have to go to college, so you need to go.'

There was no talk about what I wanted to do and what interests I may have had. No high school counselor spoke to me about college pathways or potential careers. I went to college anyway because that was what was expected of me to have a career, to support myself.

My freshman year was not very successful, and I was on academic probation. I decided that I would get a full-time job and I was going to let life be my education. I found a job working for a cutting tool distributor, thinking, *This is going to be the most boring job ever.* Now,

I cannot believe I am a girl working in the tooling industry. It became interesting to me. I started in shipping
& receiving but quickly moved into inside sales. I was
good with customers and I really liked learning, so with
that, I became knowledgeable about the tools. It was
just cool to learn how things were made. Fast forward
three years later, I ended up buying into a cutting tool
company and became VP and managing partner at 22.
I never saw manufacturing or knew what it was until I
got that first job, and I said, 'This is cool. This is really
cool.' And I love the fact that, I mean, well, there were
not very many women. And I thought, well, *I could blaze
a pathway here. I can be* that *girl,* that *woman.*

My mother never went to college. She studied to be
a hairdresser, like many women. Back in the '50s and
'60s, they got married and had kids. She did not have an
opportunity to go to college, and so the expectation was
for me to go because many of my female classmates were
going to college; it was expected I would as well. I was
not the best student back then, with a lack of direction
or motivation (later learning that I had ADHD). There
were never conversations as to 'what are your interests?'
or 'what do you think you would be good at?' It was
always 'You're going to college.' I signed up for our local
college and said, 'Okay, accounting,' which later became,
'Okay, so I will be an English major, something.' I just
picked something.

I think at that age, you just do not know what direction you want to go. You are 18, 19 years old. Bottom
line was that without direction or interests, I was not
ready, nor did I want to go the college route.

When I talk to companies and they say, 'We want to take this student on and put them through a six-year apprenticeship,' I say, 'So you're going to have to explain this to them. You cannot just tell them that they should do this. You must explain the path better and explain what they're doing.'

Part of the reason that work-based learning experiences and internships as a junior or senior in high school are so important is because we must let them see what manufacturing is all about.

Almost every young person in our culture experiences what Kathleen recounts. You might be that same person too. This book is intended to give you the tools to break the mold, to use a manufacturing metaphor!

YOUR ACTION PLAN

MINDSET. Attitude is everything! I will take a great attitude over superior talent any day of the week. This one personality trait speaks volumes as to who you are. So many people in my company would run through a wall for me if asked. That is the ultimate compliment. The fact is, I feel the same way and I try on a daily basis to support my co-workers.

LEARN EVERY DAY. Customer service in this country as a whole is declining in quality dramatically. Much of this can be attributed to lack of training, being new to the task or job at hand, and attitude. Speaking to someone who is naïve and unfamiliar is much more palatable when someone has a great attitude. Learn

all you can—above and beyond what is expected. Be curious, ask questions, do research, and even take on jobs that others don't want for the sheer purpose of learning more. My words "arrive early, leave late" are all about the attitude to learn and absorb any and all information your mentor can offer.

EXPAND YOUR NETWORK. One of the reasons I wrote this book is to make a difference in the workforce, in the parenting world, and for you, young people. One of the biggest reasons I was able to write this book is my network. So many talented people have agreed to give me input and feedback. I consider many of these contributors to be some of the best at what they do in their given field. Each of them has a story. Each story speaks to someone. By allowing them to share their stories and their opinions, I am able to reach more people and make more of a difference in this world. Without my network, the outreach and range of this book would not be nearly as impactful.

People do not realize how critical the base of people you know is. Utilize your network and other people's networks. Of course, there is a correct and incorrect way to do these things. Start by reaching out to help someone else with your network. That is always the best start. From there, people will be more willing to do the same for you!

WORK ETHIC. Having a hard work ethic is one of the most undervalued traits. From what I have witnessed, the work ethic in the Midwest is one of the best in the U.S. I theorize it is because of the number of farm families in the area, and it carries over into the culture. Each part of the country has what I think of as representative traits. For example, you have always heard of Southern hospitality, mentioned down in the southern part of

the U.S. Effort is everything. By trying our best, we learn how to be great.

PASSION. As a young person, I think that I was always trying to find what I was passionate about. I was a great student up until a time that I remember making the decision to be well-rounded. That meant not just being a good student and making good grades. I wanted to be a hard worker, a good athlete, a good friend, and be more social. By making this decision early in my life, I found I made choices and then lived with the consequences thereafter. I remember my dad telling me, "Terry, I do not care if you are out late having a good time. You can come in at whatever time you want, but you better not let it show the next morning when you are at work. You give me your best and nothing less."

Passion led me to write this book. It is what gives me the drive to give back hundreds of hours a year and thousands of dollars a year through the **CHAMPION Now!** organization. I want you to be so passionate that you feel *obligated* to give back. Making a long-lasting impact is the best feeling in the world. In my opinion, this is the definition of success, not how much you own or the amount of money in your account. This is what we all should strive for in our country.

BE DRUG-FREE. So many employers are shocked by the fact that applicants cannot pass a drug test. Even in my small company, in two of the most recent hiring opportunities, once I got to the final candidate, I told them that we have a drug testing requirement. Of course, we pay for the test. Both of these applicants said that they would take the test, accepted the information on where to take it, and neither of them showed up. Neither

called back. This is a terrible problem in this country, and somehow we need to solve it. As a young person, make a commitment to yourself not to let this happen. You deserve better. Your family deserves better, and your employer wants all of their employees to be happy and drug-free.

During the pandemic, people endured very difficult times. Staying home for extended periods of time was not the norm until March 2020, when all of that changed. If you have a problem as a result, reach out for help. Get into a program, whether it be for substance abuse or the vast array of mental health issues we're facing. Chances are, many people have struggled as well, and many have found solutions and can share their stories to help you reach similar success and independence.

MENTOR YOUNGER PEOPLE AS YOU GET INTO YOUR PATH. Ideally, young people mentor younger people. The response and end result are so much more effective that way. When someone older, who has been in the field for decades, mentors a young person, the relationship never gets past a certain point. The generational differences are so significant that this impedes effective progress in any mentoring program. Students mentoring students is a missed opportunity for everyone. Employers are going to be impressed with a new employee's leadership skills as evidenced by some sort of mentoring program. It is a win for the system and a win for you individually.

One little-mentioned concept is also reverse mentoring. When you get into a circumstance to be mentored by someone older, more experienced, and wiser than yourself, look for the reverse opportunity. Mentor them back! You probably have more technology skills from growing up during the technology boom. There is a good chance you have something to offer back. This

offers a great opportunity for a deeper, more meaningful experience for both people involved. Don't assume it has to be just a one-way street. You might be surprised by the value that you can also bring!

EXECUTE. What do they say? "The path to failure is lined with good intentions." Don't let excuses define you. Let execution and results define you. Be tenacious to get the results you expect. This is not easy. Complacency and procrastination abound. I am a big advocate of being responsible for bringing yourself to a successful path in whatever you choose. If you are able to execute, then you will become the best you can be.

IT'S TIME: GO MANUFACTURE YOUR FUTURE

I recently watched a 1997 video of the late Steve Jobs from Apple talking about rebranding Apple products. He spoke of many concepts and ideas, but there was one thing that resonated greatly for me: "People with passion can change the world for the better, and those crazy enough to think that they can, actually do."[1]

One additional thing that Jobs says is that Nike became one of the best brands in the world by honoring great athletes (not, in his words, by talking about "speeds and feeds," a manufacturing metaphor). **CHAMPION Now!** is well-suited to honoring great manufacturers and great manufacturing—those who elevate the image of manufacturing and promote great careers and emphasize the importance of it in our culture and our lives. In this, we will be "Finding America's Greatest Champion!"

Job's words challenge us all to think differently.

You, as a young person, should take the initiative. After you are done with your half of this book, give it to your parents

to read their half. Ask their opinions, then tell them what you want to accomplish. Tell them what you enjoy and what you are truly passionate about. In the center of this book are questions to start a conversation. Have a sit-down after you have read your half and they have read theirs. This is where some powerful and life-changing conversations can occur. Your path to success can be a great deal quicker, more effective, and more efficient. Who knows where it can lead?

This much I know: You are in control of your future. After running my company for so many years, I have found that people want answers from me, without having the diligence or patience to dig for the facts required to make a good decision. I defer an answer until I feel I have enough of the facts to decide. This practice has served me well. By doing this, you have a tendency to feel good about your chosen direction. This also ties into the advice one of my life mentors, John Comparini, gave me. His words have resounded long after he retired and recently passed. Here's what he told me: "Terry, I never made a decision that I thought was wrong at the time that I made it."

No one who picks up this book was unaffected by the COVID-19 pandemic. I vividly remember March 13, 2020, when Illinois went on lockdown. I drove back from a customer visit and started new protocols in our company to safely work as an essential worker, continuing to make both medical products and national defense products. No one knew that a year later, almost to the day, we would still be contending with the changes in our personal and corporate daily routines. I think all of us have learned that relying on countries like China to produce and provide so many of our products leaves all of us vulnerable and at risk. The silver lining is that I hope we have a reawakening of the importance of making things in the U.S. This prospect

should bring hope and many manufacturing jobs to be filled by people like you!

My words in closing: Do your research. Get all the facts. Make your decision and feel confident you made the best decision at the time. Good luck. Go manufacture your future and be a **CHAMPION Now!**

CONVERSATION STARTERS

T ime to meet in the middle (literally, starting with the questions in this book). Below are questions for parents and their children to ask each other.

The earlier you have candid conversations on life after high school, the better. Parents, explore your child's passions, talents, and vision for life beyond high school. Kids, ask your parents about their life—you might have a lot more in common than you might think.

KIDS, ASK YOUR PARENT:

1. What were your dreams as a young person?
2. What was your favorite class in high school?
3. What would you do for a career if you were me?
4. Do you have any regrets or positive thoughts about your career path?
5. How did you decide what to do after high school?
6. What can I afford as far as an education?
7. Is it critical to you that I go attend a college or university?
8. How do you feel about me attending a technical college or applying for an apprenticeship?
9. If you could start your career over, what advice would you give your younger self?
10. What is your view of manufacturing now that you've read the book? Has your view changed?

INTERVIEWS SHARED WITH BOTH EDITIONS:

- Tony Schumacher — Eight-time NHRA Top Fuel Drag Racing Champion
- Rand Haas — MCIP Program Manager Business and Career Services, Inc.
- Titan Gilroy — CEO of TITANS of CNC Inc., creator of the TV series "TITANS of CNC" and TITANS of CNC Academy
- Mark Hibner — Applied Technology Teacher at Palatine-Ill. High School
- Andrew Crowe — Founder of the New American Manufacturing Renaissance
- Dr. Laz Lopez — Associate Superintendent Township High School District 214
- Sheyenne Kreamer — Triangle Solutions Alliance
- Leigh Coglianese McConnell — TMA Director of Training and Workforce Development
- Harry Moser — Founder of the Reshoring Initiative®
- Craig Rabin — Entrepreneur and Inventor of the Airhook
- Dana Ward — Inventor of PreHeels, Founder and President of Barefoot Scientist
- Frank Frangie — Radio play-by-play voice of the Jacksonville Jaguars
- Tom McSheehy — Teaching Heart Institute (Social Emotional Learning)
- Carrie J. Kurczynski — Technical Project Manager/ Operations for GE Power

- Mike Rounds   President of Williamson College of the Trades
- Vondale Singleton   Founder of CHAMPS Male Mentoring Program
- Kathleen Burley   Executive Director, Greater Chicago Advanced

INTERVIEWS UNIQUE TO STUDENT EDITION:

- Tim Fara   Sr. Executive Vice President, Sales & Marketing at Accutek Inc.
- Jossimar Mendez   Plant Manager for ITW Shakeproof Industrial

INTERVIEWS UNIQUE TO PARENT EDITION:

- Gary Skoog   Makerspace Advocate
- Tim Tumanic   CEO of JR Machine
- Virginia Rounds   German American Chamber of Commerce
- Ryan Pohl   Founder of Praeco Skills
- Nicole Wolter   President and CEO of HM Manufacturing
- Cathy Hurst   Vice President of Hayden Hurst Family Foundation
- Ed Dernulc   Director of the Foundation at the Fabricators and Manufacturers

ENDNOTES

CHAPTER ONE

1. Henrico Workforce & Career Development, "Letter of Intent Signing Day, 2022," https://henricocte.com/about/letter-of-intent-signing-day/.

2. National Coalition of Community Colleges (NC3), "National Signing Day," July 2019, https://www.nc3.net/wp-content/uploads/2019/07/Signing-Day-2020-Flyer-Save-the-Date.pdf.

3. SkillsUSA, "National Signing Day, 2022," https://www.skillsusa.org.

CHAPTER TWO

1. Richard Frye, "Baby Boomers Are Staying in the Labor Force at Rates Not Seen in Generations for People Their Age," PEW Research, July 24, 2019, https://www.pewresearch.org/fact-tank/2019/07/24/baby-boomers-us-labor-force.

2. The Manufacturing Institute/Deloitte, *Creating Pathways for Tomorrow's Workforce Today: Beyond Reskilling in Manufacturing*, (Deloitte/The Manufacturing Institute, 2021). https://www.themanufacturinginstitute.org/research/creating-pathways-for-tomorrows-workforce-today-beyond-reskilling-in-manufacturing/.

3. US Bureau of Labor Statistics, "News Release: Bureau of Labor and Statistics," August 2022, US Department of Labor, https://www.bls.gov/news.release/pdf/empsit.pdf.

4. US Bureau of Labor Statistics, News Release Bureau of Labor and Statistics, August 2022 News Release, US Department of Labor, https://www.bls.gov/news.release/pdf/empsit.pdf

ly-industry-crib-sheet-boeing-forecasts-double-demand-in-20-years/

5. Jim Peltz, "Tony Schumacher Wraps up His Eighth NHRA Season Title in Top Fuel," *LA Times*, November 16, 2014, https://www.latimes.com/sports/la-sp-nhra-finals-20141116-story.html.

6. Associated Press, "Tony Schumacher breaks NHRA Top Fuel Speed Record," *USA Today*, February 23, 2018, https://www.usatoday.com/story/sports/motor/nhra/2018/02/23/schumacher-breaks-nhra-top-fuel-speed-record-force-returns/110766914.

7. Chuck Wilson, "The Great Resignation and How LPA Software Can Help," Ease.com, March 16, 2022, https://www.ease.io/the-great-resignation-and-how-lpa-software-can-help/.

8. US Bureau of Labor Statistics, "Employed Persons by Detailed Industry and Age," US Department of Labor, 2022, https://www.bls.gov/cps/cpsaat18b.htm.

9. Richard Frye, "Baby Boomers Are Staying in the Labor Force at Rates Not Seen in Generations for People Their Age," PEW Research, July 24, 2019, https://www.pewresearch.org/fact-tank/2019/07/24/baby-boomers-us-labor-force/.

CHAPTER THREE

1. NAM News Room, "2.1 Million Manufacturing Jobs Could Go Unfilled by 2030," National Association of Manufacturers, May 4, 2021, https://www.nam.org/2-1-million-manufacturing-jobs-could-go-unfilled-by-2030-13743/?stream=workforce.

2. National Association of Manufacturers, "Facts About Manufacturing: The Top 18 Facts You Need to Know," The Manufacturing Institute/NAM, 2022, https://www.nam.org/facts-about-manufacturing/.

3. Marketing for Manufacturers, https://marketing4manufacturers.com.

4. US Bureau of Labor Statistics, "Employed Persons by Detailed Industry and Age," US Department of Labor, 2022, https://www.bls.gov/cps/cpsaat18b.htm.

CHAPTER FOUR

1. Victor Yanev, "Video Game Demographics - Who Plays Games in 2022?," January 26, 2022, https://techjury.net/blog/video-game-demographics.

2. Indeed Editorial Staff, "Are Game Developers in Demand? A Look at Video Game Jobs," January 10, 2017, https://www.indeed.com/lead/video-game-labor-snapshot.

3. Statista Research Department, "Percentage of People Aged 65 Years and Older among Total Population in Japan from 1960 to 2020," Statista, February 15, 2023, https://www.statista.com/statistics/1149301/japan-share-of-population-aged-65-and-above.

4. International Federation of Robotics, "Robot Density Nearly Doubled Globally," December 21, 2021, https://robotics.ee/2021/12/21/robot-density-nearly-doubled-globally/.

5. Rick Romell, "Automation Will Prompt More Employers to Add Jobs Than to Cut, Manpower Says," *Milwaukee Journal*, January 19, 2018, https://www.jsonline.com/story/money/business/2018/01/19/automation-prompt-more-employers-add-jobs-than-cut-manpower-says/1048467001/.

CHAPTER FIVE

1. Charles Sykes, *Fail U: The False Promise of Higher Education* (New York: St. Martin's Press, 2016).

2. Richard Vedder And Christopher Denhart, "How the College Bubble Will Pop," *Wall Street Journal*, January 8, 2014, https://www.wsj.com/articles/SB10001424052702303933104579302951214561682.

3. Advisor Magazine, "The Burden of Debt - A Student Debt Snapshot," Lifehealth.com, February 23, 2018, https://www.lifehealth.com/student-debt-snapshot/.

4. Thomas Snyder, *The Community College Career Track: How to Achieve the American Dream Without a Mountain of Debt* (Hoboken, NJ: John Wiley & Sons, 2012).

CHAPTER SEVEN

1. Illinois Manufacturing Excellence Center, *Made in Illinois: A Modern Playbook for Manufacturers to Compete and Win*, ed. David Boulay (Fig Factor Media Publishing, 2021).

2. Monte Whaley, "Colorado Families Struggle to Pay Skyrocketing Back-to-school Costs," *The Denver Post*, August 14, 2017, https://www .denverpost.com/2017/08/14/back-to-school-costs-colorado.

CHAPTER EIGHT

1. Steve Jobs, About Apple's Core Value (1997), YouTube, https:// www.youtube.com/watch?v=dR-ZT8mhfJ4